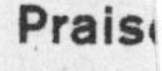

Praise

"A fabulous look into the wor... ...enly celebrate our success but rarely discuss fail... ...sions will benefit from the authors' perspectives...

—...Fasano, chief information officer of Kaiser Permanente

"This engaging book demonstrates how even very smart businesspeople can make very bad mistakes—and how we can learn from them and so avoid their fate."

—**Dr. Michael Hammer,** author of *Reengineering the Corporation*

"*Billion-Dollar Lessons* is an MBA degree in one read. The lessons to be learned from the parade of failed mergers and acquisitions the authors have studied are simple yet engaging and powerful. From creating devil's advocates to empowering more voices inside of companies, this book offers serious doses of explanation and hope."

—**Larry Kramer,** founder, chairman, and CEO of Marketwatch.com and former president of digital media for CBS

"Carroll and Mui have provided an opportunity to learn from the major mistakes of others, and in doing so they make an important contribution to protecting shareholder value. It is a must-read."

—**Jack M. Greenberg,** chairman of Western Union and former CEO of McDonald's

"Baseball is a game of failure . . . but so is business. In baseball, go three for ten over a career and you're going to the Hall of Fame. In business, a 70 percent failure rate will get you into Paul and Chunka's sequel. This is a book about failures that can and should be avoided. Read, learn, win!"

—**Vice Admiral John G. Morgan, Jr.,** chief strategist of the U.S. Navy (August 2004–July 2008)

"This book identifies the seven strategies that sound safe, but have tripped up some of the smartest leaders of otherwise successful companies. Learn from their expensive mistakes."

—**L. Gordon Crovitz,** former publisher of *The Wall Street Journal*

"It is a lot easier to talk about our successes than our failures. Carroll and Mui have written a book that helps us get serious about learning from our failures, as painful as it may be. And they give us some good ideas to help avoid future failures."

—**Michael Moskow,** vice chairman and senior fellow for the Global Economy, The Chicago Council on Global Affairs

"*Billion-Dollar Lessons* is a must-read for any manager contemplating a game-changing investment. It will help ensure winners, not losers. It will help create, rather than destroy value."

—**Adam Gutstein,** CEO of Diamond Management and Technology Consultants

"*Billion-Dollar Lessons* provides a set of tough questions and ideas to help us avoid making big strategic mistakes. Perhaps the biggest question is whether we choose to learn from others' mistakes." —**Daniel Roesch**, director of General Motors Strategic Initiatives

"Mui and Carroll have developed a methodology to keep your business healthy. Through extensive research on real world companies, the authors have identified seven strategies that will likely make your business sick. Then they tell you, in a compelling and accessible way, how to avoid them like the plague."

—**Martin Nisenholtz**, senior vice president of digital operations, The New York Times Company

"This book draws you in with engaging stories of smart experienced leaders delivering spectacular failures. The insights and learning are essential for every modern manager and leader who wants to win in the twenty-first century."

—**Toby Eduardo Redshaw**, global CIO of Aviva

"Paul Carroll and Chunka Mui show how to avoid the catastrophic strategic failures that have laid low so many companies over the past few decades. More important, they point the way for making decisions that will help you confront the reality of your future business. Reading this book is like having a wise strategy consultant at your side every step of the way."

—**B. Joseph Pine II** and **James H. Gilmore**, coauthors of *The Experience Economy* and *Authenticity: What Consumers Really Want*

"A fascinating compendium of well researched corporate screw-ups and how to avoid, learn from, and mitigate against them."

—**Gordon Bell**, principal researcher, Microsoft Research

"Replete with thoroughly researched, well known and not so well known, entertaining but sometimes horrifying stories and anecdotes, *Billion-Dollar Lessons* should be mandatory reading for every senior manager and public company director."

—**Mel Bergstein**, chairman of Diamond Management and Technology Consultants

"Read and learn about the costly mistakes of others; it could save you tremendous time and money. In fact, *Billion-Dollar Lessons* might yield the best return on any time investment you will ever make."

—**Vince Barabba**, general manager (retired) of corporate strategy and knowledge development, General Motors Corporation

"As someone who has had many failures and learned some of my most significant business lessons from them, I gained business insights from the 'billion dollar lessons' Paul and Chunka detail in their book." —**Robert Pasin**, CEO of Radio Flyer

"A lot of huge business mistakes have been made over the years, and it sure makes sense to try not to reproduce the mistakes of others. Why not cash in on the tuition others have paid to be educated? There is a huge amount we can learn from these stories."
—**David S. Pottruck**, chairman of Red Eagle Ventures

"You'll want to read this book more than once in order to assimilate both the insight into human behavior and the wisdom it offers to avoid costly mistakes of your own."
—**Kim Volk**, president and CEO of Delta Dental Plans Association

"Carroll and Mui have trumped conventional wisdom with two new ideas: to increase our odds of success, we need to study failure, and even the most intense focus on execution doesn't deliver if you have a failed strategy. A must-read for executives who intend to aggressively build their companies." —**Glen Tullman**, CEO of Allscripts

"An engaging guide to improve the quality of both 'bet the company' decisions and everyday ones. Drawing insights from notable flawed decisions, Carroll and Mui identify practical steps to counter the forces of human nature, which are powerfully arrayed against rational analysis."
—**M. Carl Johnson, III**, senior vice president and chief strategy officer of Campbell Soup Company

"Chunka and Paul expose the lack of critical analysis and thinking that sits behind many of the strategic clichés we use to justify big deals. If you are considering a big strategic move, read this book first." —**Rick Leander**, chief strategy officer of The Clearing House

"*Billion-Dollar Lessons* rigorously analyzes the biggest failures of the past decades and delivers not only practical advice on what to avoid, but also invents the 'devil's advocate' process—which you can implement to stop your own organization from happily going off a cliff." —**John Sviokla**, vice chairman of Diamond Management and Technology Consultants

"*Billion-Dollar Lessons* provides an outstanding framework for creating positive dissent and asking the best questions. All leaders want to do great things; hopefully this book will help smart leaders to cast a critical eye on some of our great ideas and avoid hubris."
—**Jennifer F. Scanlon**, vice president and CIO of USG Corporation

"If you believe that those who do not study history are doomed to repeat it, *Billion-Dollar Lessons* will help you learn from the strategic mistakes made by well-respected business leaders in the past. Time and time again, world-class companies execute flawed strategies. Remember the definition of insanity: Doing the same thing again and again but expecting different results." —**Eric Sigurdson**, leader, CIO Practice, Russell Reynolds Associates

"Without question, many M&A deals are driven by haste, ignorance, and hubris, others by real insight and intelligence. *Billion-Dollar Lessons* gives wise counsel to those who can create or destroy hundreds of millions of dollars of net worth with the stroke of a pen."

—**Michael Boyle**, senior vice president, CIO AF Technology, Allstate Financial

"A thoughtful account of how egos have obscured good business judgment. The business world could better use history and facts as a guidepost."

—**John Chu**, senior vice president of Hartford Financial Services Group, Inc.

"Growing and managing successful companies is an exercise that is grounded in pattern recognition. *Billion-Dollar Lessons* is an amazing collection of case studies—patterns—demonstrating the many ways in which executives and their companies have derailed."

—**Doug Collom**, partner, Wilson, Sonsini, Goodrich & Rosati

"Having been involved in many transactions during my career, I found the analysis and conclusions to be very accurate, and a must-read for any person continuing to do transactions." —**Morgan Davis**, CEO (retired), White Mountain Insurance Company

"An important contribution to understanding the causes of major corporate strategic failures of the last few decades, complete with a pragmatic approach to avoid these strategic mistakes."

—**Bernie Hengesbaugh**, chairman and CEO (retired), CNA Financial Corporation

PORTFOLIO

BILLION-DOLLAR LESSONS

Paul B. Carroll wrote for *The Wall Street Journal* for seventeen years. The author of *Big Blues*, he founded *Context*, the first "new economy" magazine, in 1997. He lives outside Sacramento, California.

Chunka Mui is the coauthor of the major business bestseller *Unleashing the Killer App*. He lectures and consults widely on strategy and innovation and lives in Chicago, Illinois.

BILLION-DOLLAR LESSONS

What You Can Learn from the Most Inexcusable Business Failures of the Last 25 Years

PAUL B. CARROLL

AND

CHUNKA MUI

PORTFOLIO

PORTFOLIO
Published by the Penguin Group
Penguin Group (USA) Inc., 375 Hudson Street, New York, New York 10014, U.S.A.
Penguin Group (Canada), 90 Eglinton Avenue East, Suite 700, Toronto, Ontario, Canada M4P 2Y3 (a division of Pearson Penguin Canada Inc.)
Penguin Books Ltd, 80 Strand, London WC2R 0RL, England
Penguin Ireland, 25 St Stephen's Green, Dublin 2, Ireland (a division of Penguin Books Ltd)
Penguin Group (Australia), 250 Camberwell Road, Camberwell, Victoria 3124, Australia (a division of Pearson Australia Group Pty Ltd)
Penguin Books India Pvt Ltd, 11 Community Centre, Panchsheel Park, New Delhi – 110 017, India
Penguin Group (NZ), 67 Apollo Drive, Rosedale, North Shore 0632, New Zealand (a division of Pearson New Zealand Ltd)
Penguin Books (South Africa) (Pty) Ltd, 24 Sturdee Avenue, Rosebank, Johannesburg 2196, South Africa

Penguin Books Ltd, Registered Offices: 80 Strand, London WC2R 0RL, England

First published in the United States of America by Portfolio, a member of Penguin Group (USA) Inc. 2008
This paperback edition with a new foreword and revised chapter 11 published 2009

3 5 7 9 10 8 6 4 2

ISBN 978-1-59184-219-4 (hc.)
ISBN 978-1-59184-289-7 (pbk.)
CIP data available

Printed in the United States of America

From Paul:

To my wife, Kim; my daughters, Shannon and Clare;
and my parents, Charlie and Yvonne

From Chunka:

To Beth, Kai, and Zoë, with love

Contents

Preface to the Paperback Edition

Make that "Trillion-Dollar Lessons"

When the economy fell off a cliff just as our book was coming out in the fall of 2008, any number of friends, colleagues, and reviewers suggested we should quickly update it to incorporate the lessons from the mistakes that caused the crisis. So what are those new lessons?

The short answer is: There aren't any.

At least, there aren't any new strategy mistakes that led to the latest crop of staggering failures. However, our experience in working with clients to leverage the lessons to be learned from failures *has* provided new insight into how companies can avoid making the same old mistakes and, as a result, can increase their odds of success. So, we'll use the foreword for the paperback to explain what those insights are and to suggest ways that executives can dig themselves out of the current mess—and maybe even to profit from it.

No New Mistakes

The mistakes that precipitated the economic crisis are certainly bigger in magnitude than the 2,500 failures that we and a team of twenty researchers investigated for some two years as the basis for *Billion-Dollar Lessons.* The write-offs we studied totaled hundreds of billions of dollars, which we thought was a staggering number, yet Wall Street firms alone have written off more than $1 trillion of assets since the financial crisis began.

We seem to have aimed low. Maybe we should have called the book "Trillion-Dollar Lessons."

But the lessons from the current crisis aren't any different from the earlier lessons. In fact, the story of Green Tree Financial, which we tell in detail in chapter 2, is exactly analogous to what happened more recently. In the 1990s, Green Tree devised a new mortgage product that took the market by storm. It booked enormous profits. It assured investors that all its financial assumptions were hopelessly conservative. But the mortgages were fatally flawed, eventually resulting in an avalanche of defaults. Green Tree's blinders about the mortgages' problems even occurred for the same reason that subprime lenders didn't see the problems with their financial innovation. Green Tree booked all its profit up front, so the whole game was to generate as many loans as possible, then exceed that number the following quarter, and the quarter after that, and the quarter after that. No one was accountable for the profitability of the loans five or ten years down the road, so potential problems were glossed over until it was too late.

The analogies don't stop with Green Tree. Conseco bought Green Tree in 1998, making the same mistake that Bear Stearns, Lehman Brothers, Merrill Lynch, AIG, and many others made when they bought investments based on subprime loans. Conseco reasoned that buying Green Tree was a simple move into an adjacent market. After all, Conseco was a major insurance company, and mortgages looked like just another form of financial service. When the problems with Green Tree's mortgages became apparent, Conseco wrote off all the profits that Green Tree ever booked on its mortgages and filed for bankruptcy. The bankruptcy was the third largest in U.S. history at the time. True, the Conseco bankruptcy is dwarfed by the recent crisis. Conseco is just one company, not a whole industry, and the bankruptcy filing didn't precipitate a recession that has analysts drawing analogies to the Great Depression. Still, Conseco made the same errors of omission a decade ago that others made this time around.

At the *Wall Street Journal,* there is a saying, "There are no new stories, just new reporters." It seems the same is true of businesses. There are no new mistakes, just new executives and new companies.

You'd think that with the lessons of the crisis now in full view, companies might learn some of the lessons that failures have to offer. Instead, the same old mistakes continue to be made.

Bank of America made what it thought was a great move into an adjacent market when it agreed to buy Merrill Lynch in September 2008 for $50 billion. Bank of America had long coveted Merrill and decided that the collapse in Merrill's stock price made it a bargain that couldn't be passed up. In the process, Bank of America made many of the mistakes that show up in our chapters on adjacency moves (chapter 5) and on industry consolidation (chapter 7). Bank of America focused so much on what it was going to gain that it underestimated potential problems. Bank of America didn't take the time to understand the full extent of Merrill's toxic mortgage assets. Bank of America also underestimated the cultural conflicts that would arise when it tried to combine its brokerage arm, which aimed at the middle-class market, with Merrill's white-shoes types. Finally, Bank of America assumed it would gain by taking over Merrill's investment banking business even though it isn't a clear fit with Bank of America's retail banking—and even though Bank of America had tried on its own to get into investment banking and had run, kicking and screaming, from the market.

Bay Harbour Management, an investment firm, likewise made a mistake when it agreed to buy clothing retailer Steve & Barry's out of bankruptcy proceedings for $168 million in August 2008. Steve & Barry's turned out to have a business model based on faulty financial engineering. The company only made money from the up-front payments that mall operators gave the company to open stores, a model that clearly wasn't sustainable. Three months after the purchase, Bay Harbour announced it was liquidating Steve & Barry's nearly three hundred stores.

We're not just saying in hindsight that Bank of America and Bay Harbour made mistakes. We said so at the time in our blog, www.billiondollarlessons.com, that both Bank of America and Bay Harbour were making grand errors. We started the blog in 2006, during our research phase, as a way of testing our hypotheses. We wanted to be sure that the lessons we were deriving from failure could be applied in real time to spot bad ideas. And it turns out that identifying flaws isn't that hard—our record has been nearly flawless, even though we're operating only with information available to the general public, not the nitty gritty that the companies involved possess.

The problem isn't identifying bad ideas, at least if a thorough review of past failures is done. The problem is doing so early enough and in a constructive fashion, so that flawed plans can be fixed or killed before the momentum is so great that almost nothing can stop them.

Being Careful Is Not Enough

Marshall McLuhan famously said, "I'm not sure who discovered water, but I'm pretty sure it wasn't a fish." The same notion applies to business: It's not likely that people swimming around in an environment that creates a bad idea are going to be able to spot that bad idea, much less do something about it. Even after the financial crisis began, when companies were being especially careful, they still made the same old mistakes.

This fact underscores the point we make in part 2 of the book, that it isn't enough to just try to be more aware of potential pitfalls. Some outside mechanism needs to be applied as a safeguard to head off bad deals and bad strategies.

Look at what has happened with risk management. Following the collapse of Long Term Capital Management in the late 1990s, a problem that almost caused the kind of meltdown of the financial system that occurred this time around, some companies ginned up new models and new procedures to manage risk more closely. The models and procedures almost universally made sense on paper. Almost universally they failed.

The problems with the models can be myriad:

- They may rely too heavily on historical data, even though new situations can render history meaningless. The models at Fannie Mae, for instance, didn't even allow for the possibility of a decline in housing prices, because there had never been one.
- Models often don't reflect the full dynamism of markets. In the case of subprime mortgages, for instance, no model that we're aware of allowed for the possibility that liquidity would dry up

in markets instantly. Everyone seemed to assume that they'd be able to sell securities, albeit at a lower price.

- Models are hard to challenge. They tend to be cooked up by small armies of people with PhDs in exotic specialties, so it's difficult for an executive to dig into the details and objectively question the predictions.
- Even when models work perfectly, they create a false sense of security. Tools that were developed by financial firms typically said that losses could be capped at a certain level 99 percent of the time. Well, 99 percent sounds an awful lot like 100 percent, especially after a long stretch has passed during which no major losses occurred. Yet that final 1 percent can be awfully dangerous, as we've learned. AIG, for one, thought it was collecting free money by selling insurance on securities that were based on subprime mortgages. AIG's models had convinced the company that there was virtually no chance the securities would go bad. And yet they did.

New procedures, such as those referred to as Enterprise Risk Management, suffered from the human factor. Citigroup, for instance, instituted elaborate procedures for evaluating risk. These were done at the direction of Robert Rubin, who knew just what world-class risk management looked like because of his decades at Goldman Sachs, where he was CEO before leaving to become Treasury Secretary, then special counselor to Citigroup. But the person who was in charge of evaluating risks was a friend of the two executives who were in charge of building new businesses for Citigroup by taking on risks. The three became such close pals that the risk management executive often waited outside the office of one of the risk-taking executives for forty-five minutes so they could drive home together. It's no wonder, then, that the person in charge of saying no didn't, in fact, utter the dreaded word very often. Even when friendship wasn't involved, the financial crisis shows that it's awfully hard to kill dangerous ideas when the need for earnings (and bonuses) is very real and short-term while the potential problems are ephemeral or long-term.

An outside perspective could have spotted many of the problems with the models and procedures that were adopted to manage risk. Indeed, there were many outsiders who said for years that the mortgage industry's models were flawed. For instance, Edward M. Gramlich, a governor of the Federal Reserve Board, published a book in mid-2007 called *Subprime Mortgages: America's Latest Boom and Bust.* As for procedures, it didn't take a genius to figure out that the person determining the propriety of a risk shouldn't carpool with the person who wants to take the risk.

The trick is to not only get the outside perspective that was missing at Fannie Mae and Citigroup, among many others, but to make sure people act on it.

We'll say that a different way: It isn't enough to know that an idea is probably flawed. There has to be a method, agreed on ahead of time, for discussing possible problems and making sure they are given due weight. Otherwise, once a strategy starts to build momentum it will steamroll any possible objections.

Our research shows that this is a perennial problem. But it is particularly pertinent in the face of the economic meltdown, which brings with it myriad opportunities and pitfalls.

Beyond Fear and Greed

Even more than most economic downturns, the withering recession that we're undergoing seems likely to fundamentally change the business landscape over the next two years. Many companies, long venerated, will fall by the wayside. Many others, perhaps not currently thought of as leaders, will emerge dominant when the recovery comes. Where companies end up will depend on their strategic choices in response to the current crisis.

History is replete with success stories about those who made the most of recessions. Several of the robber barons, including Andrew Carnegie and John D. Rockefeller, took advantage of the Panic of 1873, which occurred after the bursting of the post–Civil War railroad bubble. They bought competitors at fire-sale prices and built empires. Southwest Airlines expanded rapidly in the recession in the early 1980s. Although it was a small upstart at the time, Southwest became a major force by the end of the decade, and CEO Herb Kelleher soon became a household name. After 9/11, while other airlines cut back, Southwest lowered fares and stepped up advertising to gain market share. It is now the most successful in the industry. Similarly, in the early 1980s, Intel was skating on the edge of bankruptcy. Yet it responded to horrible problems in the memory-chip market by making a bold move into microprocessors, where the company soon won a near monopoly in the personal computer market. Since then, Intel has consistently invested in additional capacity during downturns. In the process, it has outdistanced IBM, Sun, Motorola, Advanced Micro Devices, and many other formidable competitors, making heroes out of Gordon Moore, Andy Grove, and other Intel CEOs.

As Grove has said, "Bad companies are destroyed by crisis. Good companies survive them. Great companies are improved by them."

To be numbered among the great companies, it makes sense to follow Warren Buffett's guiding principle: to "be fearful when others are greedy and greedy when others are fearful." There's certainly plenty of fear out there, and thus plenty of opportunities to get greedy. As Buffett well understands, greed does not necessarily translate into wealth. It might well send overzealous executives down the wrong path. So, it's important to be both greedy and prudent at the same time.

A Note about Mergers and Acquisitions

Acquisitions are tempting for a CEO. While many issues such as organizational change get filtered through level after level of a business, the CEO can, almost alone, transform a company by making the right, strategic purchase. Besides, CEOs typically don't want to just occupy the chair for a few years. They're usually bold people and want to attempt something that will leave a mark on their companies and their industries. Acquisitions can accomplish that goal.

The environment in which CEOs operate practically demands acquisitions. Securities analysts often argue for them. Investment bankers and consultants offer a steady stream of targets, along with assurances that buying them would be guaranteed successes. If earnings ever falter, investors insist on having a story—ready by the next earnings report—about how the company will soon return to prosperity. Boards may share investors' impatience. Often, M&A offers the only quick fix.

If history is any guide, some time in the next few years there will be a burst of M&A activity. That's because lulls, such as the recession has caused, are almost always followed by a stretch of heavy deal making.

Yet acquisitions usually fail, partly because decisions have to be made fast when an opportunity arises. Something is for sale. Do you want it? Well, do you? The clock is ticking. (Bank of America CEO Ken Lewis spent less than an hour negotiating the Merrill deal because he was so sure someone else might snatch up this once-in-a-lifetime opportunity.)

The other main problem is that the evaluation of deals can happen in an echo chamber. If the senior executive team perceives that the CEO wants something to happen, they often censor objections and gloss over potential problems. Even the best investment bankers and consultants become too optimistic about the chances for success. (Studies have shown that, try as they might, their judgment is influenced by the prospect of getting big deal fees or additional work following a merger.) Boards can spot problems, but directors are sometimes reluctant to speak up because they don't have as much information as the CEO and seldom have as much background in the industry. In addition, vetoing a deal or demanding major changes to a strategy is usually a bring-on-the-next-guy decision, so, when in doubt, boards tend to acquiesce in silence. Even Warren Buffett says in *Snowball,* the recent biography of him, that, while on the board of Coca-Cola, he failed to challenge the CEO about an issue even though he was quite sure the CEO was making a serious mistake. He was right.

Given the tough environment, CEOs should utilize independent devil's advocate reviews as a way to get a fast, objective read on the potential problems with deals, perhaps as a warning that a deal should be avoided at all costs but more often to shape negotiations and to warn ahead of time about where problems with post-merger integration will occur. We cover the devil's advocate process in detail in chapters 10 and 11.

While it might seem at first that installing an additional check into a process that necessitates speed and daring is counterproductive, such a check provides four key benefits. First, it helps get to the best answer. No plan is perfect; the devil's advocate helps get to the strongest option as quickly as possible. Second, the process identifies key risks up front. It helps the CEO be clear-eyed about the implementation challenges, rather than let the process of selling the strategy paper over potential issues. Third, the process helps to build real consensus. The best way to achieve consensus is to have a constructive yet contentious deliberation, so that key issues are considered. Doing so helps avoid self-censorship, which makes problems fester. Fourth, the process preserves a graceful exit. Too often, the political capital expended to launch an initiative commits leaders to see it through, even to a bitter end. By installing a formal review, even as he drives the acquisition process forward, the CEO preserves a politically tenable exit.

While the temptation might be to wait until a deal is on the table before deciding whether to conduct a devil's advocate review, that would be a mistake. Those advocating the deal will want to dispense with any reviews, lest they kill the potential acquisition. The result will be emotional arguments about how, "Well, we have to do something."

Our colleague Dan Ariely, author of the engaging bestseller *Predictably Irrational,* has conducted research that shows that people act very differently when they're in what he calls a hot state than when they're in a cold state. A potential deal creates a hot state in which thinking is clouded. So, it's important to take advantage of the current lack of deals to consider, coldly and rationally, what the best possible process is for heading off mistakes. That way, when deals become possible—as they surely will, in droves—the advocates for those deals can't argue for dispensing with a devil's advocate review. They'll have already agreed that it's necessary.

The Role of the Board of Directors

If the blame game goes as it usually does, criticism about the mistakes that led to the current recession and to poor performance at so many companies won't stop with the CEO. Aspersions will be tossed at boards, too. To see how this might look, read the withering complaints about the Lehman Brothers board that failed to stop the CEO from running the company out of existence.

While it's obviously not possible to reset the clock and avoid mistakes that have already been made, it's possible to learn from errors and protect yourself from future attacks. This is true even for companies and boards that aren't having problems: You can learn from others' mistakes.

Interestingly, directors often saw problems coming but failed to prevent them. In those cases, the board's interaction with the CEO took one of three forms:

- Because outside directors have less information than management does and generally have less experience in the industry in which the company operates, board members may censor themselves. Why take the chance of looking silly? At Samsung, as discussed on page 221, directors had doubts about moving from electronics into car manufacturing in 1997 but deferred to the chairman, even though there was already too much capacity in the Korean auto market and Samsung had no particular strength in cars. Samsung spent $5 billion on the venture, which went into receivership and was sold three years later for some $700 million.
- Even when board members speak up, the CEO may outmaneuver them. At Ames Department Stores, a case we discuss on page 171, two directors objected to the purchase of another discount department store chain in 1988, in a misguided attempt to match Wal-Mart's scale. The CEO cut them out of conversations on the topic and had them go last in any voting so their opinions wouldn't influence others. Ames bought the chain—and soon filed for bankruptcy protection.
- Directors sometimes objected so strongly to a bad idea that they went public and still failed to head off disaster. At Oglebay Norton, a case discussed on page 118, directors concurred with a decision to move away from the iron ore business and into limestone, but two objected strenuously when the CEO went on a buying spree and paid inflated prices for limestone operations. The two resigned in protest, but the CEO cowed the rest of the board, arguing that he hadn't been hired to be a custodian. Oglebay Norton filed for bankruptcy protection in 2004, then was sold.

In looking for approaches to head off embarrassing strategic errors, we found that the key lies in the board's ability to change the dialogue with management. Boards and management agreed ahead of time that major decisions would be discussed openly, with numerous alternatives on the table, before management committed to a strategy.

Although there are numerous ways to change the dialogue, we have found the devil's advocate process to be useful for boards as well. We've used the process to head off any number of bad strategies, and many successful companies do something similar. At Intel, the board discusses possible strategies with management before they get so far along that rejecting an idea becomes a bring-in-the-next-CEO proposition. It's hard to argue with Intel's results.

If you, too, will embrace the devil's advocate process, you'll greatly increase the odds you'll be viewed more like Intel, not like Samsung, Ames, Oglebay Norton, and the other failures we describe in the pages that follow.

Introduction

Can Fatal Strategic Flaws Only Be Recognized in Hindsight?

International Business Machines Corporation lore says that, in the early 1960s, CEO Tom Watson Jr. summoned to headquarters an executive who was responsible for a venture that lost $10 million. Watson, whose fierce temper was legendary, asked the man if he knew why he'd been called in. The man said he assumed he was being fired. Watson responded: "Fired? Hell, I spent $10 million educating you. I just want to be sure you learned the right lessons."

Corporate America has spent hundreds of billions of dollars producing educational failures in recent decades. But executives shudder at the very word "failure," so people rarely try to learn any lessons from them—unless that lesson is how to make sure someone else catches the blame. As we've seen with the subprime mortgage crisis in 2007 and 2008, which mimics earlier financial crises, businesses keep making similar mistakes, over and over again.

We propose to help executives and investors learn the lessons to be had from failure. Organizations involved in life-and-death situations—such as hospitals, airlines, and the military—routinely do after-action analyses that help them keep from repeating catastrophic errors. We think it's time managers did likewise. And executives need to learn not just from their own experiences, but from the lessons financed by others, as well. Why spend $500 million, and a decade of your life, repeating someone else's mistake when you could learn to avoid it by spending a few hours with a $26 book (less on Amazon)?

Business books routinely look at successes and suggest how readers can emulate them. But no one looks at failures and lays out methods for how *not* to emulate them. Imagine a sports team that decides it will only play offense and not play defense. It's time executives focused some of their attention on defense.

To glean the lessons from failure, we undertook an extensive research effort to examine the most significant business failures of the past quarter century. We defined failure as writing off major investments, shuttering unprofitable lines of business, or filing for bankruptcy. Working with leading information vendors, we built a comprehensive database of more than 2,500 such failures suffered by publicly traded companies in the United States. We did a literature search to look for failures that didn't show up in the vendors' databases—for instance, companies that sold themselves before having to account for a major problem. Then, using various screens, we narrowed the list to the 750 most meaningful. Aided by a team of researchers, we spent more than a year poring over the data.

The extent of the failures was stunning. Since 1981, 423 U.S. companies with assets of more than $500 million filed for bankruptcy. Their combined assets at the time of their bankruptcy filings totaled more than $1.5 trillion. Yes, that's *trillion,* with a *t.* Their combined annual revenue was almost $830 billion. Some of these companies went into bankruptcy multiple times; in other words, they couldn't even learn from their own mistakes.

Over those twenty-five years, 258 publicly traded U.S. companies combined for more than $380 billion in write-offs. Sixty-seven companies had combined losses from discontinued operations that totaled almost $30 billion.

What caused all those flameouts? The current emphasis in business literature suggests that everything boils down to execution. Generals say a battle plan never survives the first contact with the enemy, and business executives have much the same attitude. They reason that they can only do so much planning. After that, they have to plunge ahead, hoping to execute better than the other guy and maybe catch a bit of luck. Yet, despite all the books written about how to improve performance by making individuals and companies more effective, we found that failures often don't stem from lack of execution. Nor are they due to timing or luck. What we found, instead, is that many of the really big failures stemmed from bad strategies. Once launched, the strategies were doomed to fail, and these failures probably could not have been prevented by even spotless execution—unless the implementers were licensed to kill the strategy itself.

The situation is rather like the Charge of the Light Brigade. Faulty intelligence and vague orders contributed to the disastrous decision of the British to charge overwhelming Russian artillery in the Crimean War. Once the charge was set in motion, disaster was inevitable—"Into the valley of Death / Rode the six hundred," as Alfred, Lord Tennyson put it.

With strategy often to blame, the next question is: Are doomed strategies avoidable? Or are the fatal flaws only recognizable in hindsight?

To answer this, we sifted through the database to eliminate cases where failure stemmed from poor execution or from environmental factors beyond management control. For instance, we didn't ding airlines for the plunge in traffic following the terrorist attacks on 9/11. Still, we found hundreds of cases where a strategy led directly to a major failure. We then did a root-cause analysis into those cases. We reviewed financial filings, business and popular press reports, and assessments from industry analysts to understand the failures. We used numerous techniques to avoid giving ourselves the benefits of hindsight—looking at what was written at the time, seeing whether everyone in an industry was making the same mistake or whether our failure case stood out, and so forth.

What we have found is that as many as 46 percent of the failures could have been avoided if companies had been more aware of the potential pitfalls. A significant percentage of the other failures, the ones that we didn't classify as avoidable, could have been mitigated if companies had seen warning signs and had proceeded more cautiously.

Looking at the avoidable failures, we identified repeating patterns, where failures across multiple industries were variations on a theme. We then drilled into the repeating patterns, or failure modes, to draw the lessons about the common problems and ways that those problems might be averted.

What we found is that failures tended to be associated with one of seven types of strategy. Failures could certainly happen for other reasons, but if a company followed one of these seven strategies it was far more likely to flop. Those seven strategies are:

- ***Synergy.*** This "whole is greater than the sum of the parts" approach often led companies to overestimate the benefits from a merger. Synergy fades in and out of vogue, even though studies have found that companies have only about a one-in-three chance of reaching their goals for revenue gains driven by synergy. We found dozens of major examples—from the granddaddy of them all, AOL Time Warner, on down—that let us identify the warning signs that a given synergy strategy is based on smoke and mirrors.

- ***Financial engineering.*** We don't mean fraud. We're talking about legitimate, albeit aggressive, ways of using accounting or financing mechanisms. The aggressive approaches did sometimes lead to fraud because they were addictive. Once companies started, they couldn't stop. They had to keep increasing the aggressiveness until they crossed the line into illegality. But even companies that thought they were merely being aggressive sometimes found they were constructing a fairy tale—such as the major lender that generated a huge amount of business by offering thirty-year loans on assets with a useful life of only ten to fifteen years.

- ***Rollups.*** Much to our surprise, we didn't just find tons of examples of companies that had run into problems while trying to "roll up" an industry, buying dozens or even hundreds or thousands of local businesses and turning them into a regional or national behemoth. We found that many of these failed attempts ended in fraud. We also found it hard to uncover successful rollups. Even companies that are sometimes cited as successes, such as Waste Management Incorporated or AutoNation Incorporated, went through horrific problems along the way and had to back off much of their initial rollup strategies.

- ***Staying the course.*** This may seem like inertia, not a strategy. But, in the face of a clear threat to the heart of a business, staying the course was often a conscious, strategic decision—and a bad one. Eastman Kodak Company, for instance, was aware as far back as 1981 of the significant threat that digital photography posed to its century-old film, paper, and chemicals business. Yet Kodak never reoriented itself to allow for the fact that the world would go as thoroughly digital as it has—and we have a long way to go. Kodak thought it could use digital technology to "enhance" its traditional business and kept investing heavily in that business. The result was a betwixt-and-between strategy that, among other things, produced a digital camera that required film. Not a big seller.

- ***Adjacencies.*** While moving into an adjacent market could be a great way for a company to stretch itself, adjacency moves also turned out to be perilous. Some of these strategies would have been amusing if they hadn't cost investors so much money. In some cases, the "adjacencies" were only semantic, not real. For instance, a big cement company went into bankruptcy proceedings after moving into a series of new markets, including lawn mowers. The company's rationale was that its cement was used in homes, and homes have lawns, so it should start selling lawn mowers. Nope.

- ***Riding technology.*** This can be great, as eBay Incorporated and others have shown. But managers sometimes trick themselves into riding the wrong technology. We're not talking Betamax, which had a legit chance of beating out VHS as the standard for videocassette recorders. We're talking Zapmail, which cost FedEx Corporation hundreds of millions of dollars in write-downs in the mid-1980s because FedEx executives didn't allow for the fact that faxes would keep getting cheaper while improving in quality.

- ***Consolidation.*** As an industry matures, and the number of companies in it is shrinking because of a diminishing pool of profits, executives sometimes make mistakes. They may buy up competing companies that have more problems than they think. Or they may make an even more basic mistake: deciding to be the consolidator when they should actually sell out and let someone else deal with the pressures of consolidation. An example: the paging companies that were buying up other paging companies to consolidate that industry in the late 1990s, right before cell phones wiped out a vast chunk of that business.

To be clear: We aren't saying that these seven strategies are doomed to failure. Far from it. In the right circumstances, all of these strategies can succeed splendidly. All we're saying is that these strategies are danger zones. If you're pursuing one of these strategies, you need to be extremely alert to what can go wrong, and ready to react before your business is flirting with disaster.

To help you be more careful, we begin part 1 of the book with a chapter on each of these failures. We draw on dozens of examples, plus others' research, to tease out of each strategy the three or four reasons it may fail. We end each chapter with a list of tough questions that you can ask yourself before proceeding with the type of strategy covered in that chapter, to minimize the chance that you'll fall victim to one of the common problems.

We conclude part 1 with a coda that lays out some broad principles about failure. The coda summarizes the problems we've listed in the first seven chapters and lays out general mistakes that companies make. For instance, looking at problems with several strategies, we found that companies that fail often do so because they overestimate the loyalty of customers. We may care deeply about our customers, but the feeling often isn't reciprocal. We're an afterthought to them. They may not even know that a particular utility supplies their electricity. They certainly aren't going to buy insurance from that utility because they're so enamored of the brand name—as more than one utility learned the hard way.

While the temptation might be to read just one chapter on a specific strategy or to head straight to the coda, we think it's important to read through at least a significant part of part 1 because it runs counter to what business executives typically think about failure. They tend to assume that failures are due to circumstances beyond management control, that failures are unique in some way that limits generalization, that failures generally happen to companies out of the mainstream, or that the principals were (to put it mildly) idiots. Executives convince themselves that a catastrophic failure couldn't possibly happen to them. After all, they're brilliant, they've gone to the best schools, they've had nothing but success their whole careers, they're . . . You get the idea. Our research shows, however, that many of those who fail were brilliant, went to the best schools, had never had anything but success their whole careers, and all the rest. Similarly, many failures occur at companies that were long established. Many were considered to be well managed, didn't seem to be taking excessive risks, and weren't undone by widespread fraud.

Our findings should be, as a result, all the scarier. They can't be dismissed as anachronistic or as extraneous data points. As Alfred Hitchcock said, the scariest villains aren't the ones who arrive on camera wearing black hats and accompanied by eerie music; the scariest are those who seem like normal, even nice, people and only gradually reveal themselves to be evil at the core.

We hope the scariness in part 1 will be enough to provoke study and raise awareness.

In part 2, however, we argue that awareness isn't sufficient. Based on what we saw in our research, it isn't enough to just know where the pitfalls lie. We found plenty of companies where senior people knew that a strategy was flawed yet still failed to head it off. People have known in general terms about certain pitfalls for years—for instance, in synergy strategies—yet still fall into them. Companies have paid investment bankers and consulting firms billions of dollars to help them be more careful. Yet companies continue to have an iffy record with the strategies we investigated.

So we begin part 2 with a chapter that looks at individual psychological issues that make it likely that businesses will, from time to time, come up with strategies that are clunkers. We cite research such as Stanley Milgram's work that shows just how much people are inclined to conform, rather than stand up, even when they know something is wildly wrong. Milgram is the person in the 1960s who got numerous subjects to "teach" others by administering electric shocks when they gave a wrong answer, gradually increasing the shocks until they went beyond what those running the experiment had told subjects might be a lethal dose. (There were, of course, no shocks being administered, but the subjects of the experiment didn't know that.) We supplement the discussion of psychological impediments with a quick review of an anthropological study that shows that these impediments are universal to all cultures. The point is to underscore that the issues are so deep that we can't avoid them just by trying a little harder.

The second chapter in part 2 extends the argument that awareness isn't enough. This chapter looks at organizational issues that hurt corporate decision making—along the lines of Friedrich Nietzsche's statement that "madness is rare in individuals, but in groups . . . it is the rule."

While business seems to outsiders to be rational, it is, in fact, very emotional and, as a result, subject to irrational behavior. Strategy formulation in particular is as much a social process as it is an analytical one. Armies of bright young people go to business school so they can learn strategic frameworks, regression analysis, and other arcana. Yet most analysis goes to support a decision that's already been made, rather than to see whether it's really a good idea in the first place. A CEO sees that all his major competitors are pursuing a certain idea and decides over his morning newspaper that he can't be left behind. Maybe he decides he has to have a story to tell when he confronts securities analysts on the quarterly earnings call. Maybe he reads the latest *Harvard Business Review* and falls for some surefire template for success. Maybe he falls in love with a tale told by his investment bankers (who get their fees anytime a company completes a transaction, regardless of whether it succeeds—and who get paid again when they're hired to unwind transactions they proposed in the first place). Maybe he believes that he needs to set a potentially unattainable goal to rouse the organization out of its inertia. Whatever the reason for the CEO's initiative, most managers in the organization understand that it's death to get in the way. The reality is, unfortunately, often not unlike this cartoon:

"All those in favor say 'Aye.'"
"Aye." *"Aye."* *"Aye."* *"Aye."* *"Aye."*

This chapter also looks at more subtle issues, such as the fact that risk is often poorly understood within companies and that commonly used analytical tools, such as net present value, can lead companies to misunderstand their situations and come up with bad strategies.

The final two chapters in part 2 are the book's real payoff. Based on what we've seen in our research and in our work over the past two decades, the only way to avoid the kinds of bad strategies we chronicle is to add one or more processes that will build disagreement into the formulation of strategies. We explain how to do that in these final two chapters, 10 and 11.

Chapter 10 introduces the concept of devil's advocacy as a powerful tool for deliberating strategy, and it offers several relatively low-key, everyday ways to increase contention. For instance, we explain how to set up alarm systems so you know when your competitive environment has changed enough that assumptions that are crucial for your strategy are in danger of becoming untrue.

Chapter 11 lays out the formal process that we call the devil's advocate review, which we feel any company should use whenever it is about to embark on a major strategy. We borrow the name from the Catholic Church, which for centuries appointed a "devil's advocate" to challenge the credentials of anyone being seriously considered for canonization as a saint.

In business situations, the devil's advocate would "argue the 'no' side," to use the phrasing of one CEO, who lost his job after he failed to have someone do just that.

That doesn't mean kicking the strategy back to the group that produced it and asking them to list everything that might go wrong. Finding a devil's advocate doesn't mean asking for an analysis by your investment banker, who will put up a nice façade but has no incentive to talk you out of a deal that will generate millions of dollars in fees for his bank. It may mean turning to an independent board member. It may mean assigning a trusted senior executive. It may mean hiring an outsider.

The process is simply designed to bring all possible objections to the surface, given that strategy-setting processes often smooth over objections. Note that the devil's advocate process isn't designed to override the top executives of a business. We'll say that again: The devil's advocate process isn't designed to override the top executives of a business. Despite the profusion of failures that we detail in this book, we aren't saying that every venture is doomed to fail. This isn't *Hamlet* we're writing here. Not everybody needs to die in the end. So we have no interest in helping those who would, for whatever reason, stand in the way of good ideas.

The process is designed to prompt executives to think about certain things, but decision making still rests with them. They're the ones in the best position to evaluate what strategy is best. Note also that the process doesn't present alternatives to a strategy that is being evaluated. That gets too messy and introduces too much ego into the process. This can't become a game of "I'm smarter than you are." Considering alternatives would also slow the process too much. We're not trying to stifle innovation—much of our work for the past decade has been about encouraging innovation. We're just trying to stop the bad ideas before it's too late. The good strategies will still sail on through.

We think about it this way: The process isn't designed to produce the best answers; it's designed to produce the best questions. After all, business isn't physics. Business isn't about finding the exact right answer, but rather is about avoiding the wrong answers and then executing as hard and as well as possible the answers that might be right.

In general, we think of the book as offering failure insurance. Though we aren't providing insurance in the strict sense of the word, anytime you have a major discussion about strategy you will be able to see if you're taking the same approach that tripped up others. If so, you'll need to ask yourself how your effort differs from the failures identified in our research. This extra round of well-informed due diligence will at least let you mitigate your risks; you might still lose money, but at least you'll lose a lot less. Better yet, you may kill doomed efforts before they get started, saving yourself and your investors a ton of money.

The book is, obviously, written primarily for business practitioners, but we mean that in the broadest sense. If you're a middle manager, you clearly don't have to decide whether to make a multibillion-dollar acquisition in the name of synergy, but you do produce more limited strategies and can benefit from the methods we lay out to bring possible problems to the surface and to use disagreement in a constructive way. You can use this book to gather information you wouldn't otherwise see. You can do a limited devil's advocate review, either relying on an outspoken subordinate or, perhaps, a peer.

We also hope you can use this book as a sort of career coach, maneuvering your way into projects that have a better chance of being winners by dodging projects that have a good chance of being doomed. As careers play out, there's nothing sadder than watching talented people paint themselves into a corner by being associated with a string of corporate failures. So, in a world where powerful senior executives aren't omniscient, we hope to help managers in the trenches figure out how to do the independent thinking that can help prevent them from burning up years on a project headed nowhere.

In many ways, this book is more about human nature than strategy—how we humans are flawed, how those flaws show up in the business world, and how to keep those flaws from leading to bad decisions. Those lessons apply at every level of a business.

Beyond what it tells day-to-day practitioners, the book holds a lot of value for independent board members and for savvy investors.

Outside board members are often outgunned when it comes to assessing a complex strategy advocated by management. The directors aren't immersed in the industry or the operational details of the company in the same way that management is. Outside directors can ask a few questions, but anything more requires, in essence, a vote of no-confidence in management. Our research gives you outside directors good reason to call for thorough, open-minded, and independent due diligence. The book also provides a template for conducting that due diligence, in an unobtrusive way that can improve the governance of a business while not interfering with its management.

Serious investors have, perhaps, the most to gain from our book because, while lacking the inside information that executives have, investors still must constantly size up which corporate strategies will succeed and which will fail. If you can analyze a corporate announcement and see one of our failure patterns, you can avoid a stock or identify a short-sale candidate and reap the appropriate rewards.

As you'll see, there have been many situations, especially with rollups, where what we classify as a failure actually were spectacularly successful projects for those who got in on the ground floor, then sold before the problems became apparent. Those sorts of "failures" will surely continue until investors learn to shun them.

Now, we're not saying that we're going to be able to identify and head off every mistake. Business is a contact sport. Companies win. Companies lose. That won't change. We cannot guarantee success. Our goal, instead, is to help avoid failure. Because, at the least, executives need to find new mistakes to make; there's no excuse for making the same ones that people have been making for decades.

PART ONE

Failure Patterns

ONE

Illusions of Synergy

Succumbing to the Eighth Deadly Syn(ergy)

One Saturday morning, Groucho Marx was walking by St. Patrick's Cathedral in New York when he saw a bride stepping out of a limousine, her train floating gently behind her in the wind. As he strode past her in that chickenlike lope of his, he twitched his cigar for emphasis and said, "Doan do it. I tried it tree times. It dudn't woik."[1]

Executives might say the same thing when told that a strategic acquisition will produce gobs of synergies. It dudn't woik. But executives can be like Elizabeth Taylor, who has said that, with each of her eight marriages, she was convinced that somehow, some way, this marriage would work.

A Bain study of 250 executives with responsibility for mergers and acquisitions found that 90 percent accepted historical data showing that two-thirds or more of takeovers reduce the value of the acquiring company. In fact, the vast majority of respondents had personally seen problems with mergers and acquisitions. Half the respondents said their due-diligence processes had failed to head off bad takeovers. Half said companies they acquired had been dressed up to hide problems. Two-thirds said they routinely failed to achieve all the synergies that had been identified before the takeover. Yet almost none were deterred. Almost all said they'd proceed with their M&A activity. They had learned from their prior mistakes. Next time would be different.[2]

Numerous studies show, though, that next time wasn't different. A McKinsey study of 124 mergers found that only 30 percent generated synergies on the revenue side that were even close to what the acquirer had predicted. Results were better on the cost side. Some 60 percent of the cases met the forecasts on cost synergies. Still, that means two out of five didn't deliver the cost synergies, and forecasts were sometimes way off—in a quarter of the cases, cost synergies were overestimated by at least 25 percent. The McKinsey study concluded that it takes only a small error in synergy estimates to make a merger stumble, so having companies miss their goals so often and so badly bodes ill for synergy strategies.[3]

A second McKinsey study, of more than 160 acquisitions, found that only 12 percent of the acquirers managed to significantly accelerate their growth over the next three years. Despite hopes for synergies, most poor performers remained poor performers, while most solid performers slowed down. Over all, the acquirers in the study produced organic growth rates that were four percentage points lower than peers in their industries.[4]

A study by BCG helps explain why synergy goals aren't met. The study found that more than 80 percent of companies don't do detailed work in advance of an acquisition to make sure that the synergies that seem theoretically possible can, in fact, be produced. The BCG study found that the companies that do the advance work learn quickly that many synergies aren't possible, because of environmental factors and because of how competitors will respond to the takeover.[5]

Another study by Diamond helps explain why critical planning is not done. The study found that as companies are becoming ever more dependent on technology, achieving synergy targets is heavily dependent on the combined entity's ability to integrate their business platforms and operate as one. Yet the research found that awareness of business platform integration issues is typically missing at all stages of planning—the predeal, deal, and postdeal merger teams typically fail to understand both the value and the risk that business platforms bring.[6]

"So many mergers fail to deliver what they promise that there should be a presumption of failure," says Warren Hellman, former president of Lehman Brothers. "The burden of proof should be on showing that anything really good is likely to come out of one."[7] (Hellman, a billionaire who now runs a private-equity fund, reminds his partners of their failures by putting the names of bad deals on the stalls in the bathrooms.)

Yet synergies are seductive. They promise something for nothing. They fill the need for CEOs to make some bold move that will redefine an industry and establish their legacy. It's hard for a CEO to make his mark just by blocking and tackling. There is something emotionally appealing about trying the long bomb.

Besides, some synergies seem so obvious. Of course you can cut costs by combining similar companies. Of course you can increase a product's sales by pushing it through a powerful sales force. Some synergy strategies seem as easy as having the cashier at McDonald's ask, "Do you want fries with that?"

Are there successful synergy strategies? Certainly. Banks have consistently found cost synergies by merging and closing branches that duplicate another's customer base. Cisco Systems Incorporated has consistently produced revenue synergies by buying small companies and adding their products to the portfolio of Cisco's sales force. General Electric Company has consistently managed to improve the companies it acquires by introducing its management disciplines.

Still, our research found dozens and dozens of companies where attempts at synergy didn't just fail to produce gains. The attempts led to disaster.

One of those cases, the saga of Unum's takeover of Provident, shows just how seductive a synergy strategy can be—and how dangerous.

UnumProvident: Giving "Disability" New Meaning

When Unum Corporation and Provident Companies completed their $5 billion merger in 1999, the logic was generally treated as impeccable. Unum was the largest provider of disability insurance in the United States for groups. Provident was the largest provider of disability insurance for individuals. Combining them would produce one large, efficient company that would span the whole range of types of disability insurance.

Spokesmen for the companies touted all sorts of potential synergies. Unum could sell Provident products as extra insurance to individuals already covered under Unum group policies. Unum could also sell its life insurance to the individuals who bought Provident's disability policies. Together, the Unum and Provident sales forces would combine to reach people not covered by any sort of disability policy. The companies would innovate, coming up with types of disability insurance that combined features of group and individual policies. The companies would become more efficient, saving on costs. The benefits would appear so quickly that earnings per share would increase in the first year of the merger over what they would have been if the companies had stayed independent.

Unum and Provident insisted customers would see major benefits. Customers would be dealing with a bigger, more solid company that would provide better service and lower prices.

The merger "creates a real dominant company in the disability market," said Gloria Vogel, an equities analyst. "It will be a terrific balance."[8]

The two top executives at the combined company could have come from Central Casting.

James F. Orr III, who was the first CEO at what became known as UnumProvident, had been CEO at Unum for twelve years. He had aggressively pruned away numerous businesses, including annuities and pensions, and repositioned Unum for growth as the major player in group disability. Along the way, Orr earned a reputation as an intelligent and frank operator. A former track star at Villanova, where he majored in science, Orr had an MBA from Boston University and sat on an impressive array of boards. A seasoned fifty-six years old at the time of the merger, he was a director at American International Group. He was a trustee at Villanova and at Bates College. He was an overseer at the Harvard School of Public Health.

J. Harold Chandler, who became president of UnumProvident, had a résumé that read almost like Orr's. Chandler had been CEO of Provident for six years at the time of the merger and had taken much the same tack as Orr: Chandler got out of businesses such as group health insurance so that Provident could focus on a single market—in his case, the market for individual disability insurance. In the process, Chandler was credited with a major turnaround at Provident. Chandler even had two major acquisitions under his belt: Paul Revere Life Insurance Company, another big provider of disability insurance, and an insurance services business called Genex Services Incorporated. Chandler, fifty at the time of the merger, was on the boards of AmSouth Bancorporation and Herman Miller Incorporated and of numerous educational, civic, and industry organizations. An athlete like Orr, Chandler had been quarterback of the football team at Wofford College, where he graduated Phi Beta Kappa and was valedictorian of his class. He earned an MBA from the University of South Carolina and an advanced management degree from Harvard Business School.

The venerable companies—Unum was founded in 1848, Provident in 1887—approached the merger with great care. They assembled every imaginable integration team, as though they were "operating from some consultant's textbook," according to an executive who worked on the process.[9] The companies focused so much on benefits for customers that they decreed a particular day within a month of the merger as "Customer Day One."

But none of the plans worked. They didn't even come close to working. Everything started to fall apart almost from the moment the merger was completed.

Within four months of the merger, Orr was gone. Reporting on the first quarter of combined operations, UnumProvident announced a surprise $623.7 million charge in the fall of 1999. The charge mostly related to problems with group disability policies and with a reinsurance business that was being sold. The charge also included $42.5 million of unexpected expenses related to the merger. Orr's credibility was shot. He left.

Chandler stepped into the CEO job, but he didn't find the going any easier than Orr had. Chandler said he thought of the merger as a threefold combination—"threefold" because, apparently, Paul Revere hadn't really been integrated into Provident in the two years that preceded the merger with Unum, so Chandler was having to find a way to truly combine three large companies. But Chandler said at the time that the merger was actually much more complicated. He noted that something like a claim for lower-back pain might be handled at Unum by its group disability department or by either of its two other main divisions. The same held true for Provident and for Paul Revere; a claim for lower-back pain could be handled by any of three divisions. Yet, the plan for the Unum-Provident merger was to have all lower-back-pain claims handled by one hyperefficient department.

"We had to do a lot of reorientation behind the scenes," he said. "There were a lot of moving parts. Each of those companies had three major divisions, so it was really like three times three."[10]

Over the next few years, Chandler tried to integrate the businesses and find the expected synergies, but he never could.

Unum and Provident talked before the merger about back-office efficiencies. But they began as a combined company with thirty-four separate information systems that didn't talk to each other. As of 2005, six years after the merger, UnumProvident had managed to eliminate just four of those thirty-four systems.[11]

The sales forces didn't cooperate; they didn't want to sell each other's products. In fact, it would have been hard for them to cooperate even if they'd tried. Individual disability insurance tends to be sold by specialists, because of the complexity that the personalization of the policies requires. Group disability insurance, by contrast, tends to be sold by generalists; it's usually just a small part of a broad sale of health insurance to corporations. The agents who bored in on the details of individuals' policies couldn't have been more different from those who schmoozed HR executives at major corporations.

Customers behaved pretty much as they always had. In other words, those who hadn't bought disability insurance continued to avoid it. Those who had some insurance through their employers continued to resist attempts to get them to buy more on their own.

A meaningful hybrid between group and individual disability insurance never materialized.

In addition, just because both Unum and Provident issued disability policies didn't mean the businesses had much in common beyond the word "disability." Group policies operate based on demographics and actuarial tables. Deal with a big enough organization, and you can assume that its members pretty much match the characteristics of the population as a whole. With policies for individuals, however, the whole equation changes. Individuals buying policies have some particular reason to think they need it. A cat-and-mouse game ensues, in which the insurer needs to investigate the health and other circumstances of the person applying for insurance to make sure a profitable policy can be written.

As it happens, Unum knew very well the problems that could crop up with individual disability policies. It had tried to move into the market on its own just a few years before and had failed miserably.

The problem with the market was that many companies had simultaneously decided they could do lucrative business by insuring professionals such as doctors against the possibility they'd be too injured to work. As a result, according to a memo by a senior vice president at Provident in 1994, "the policies sold during the period were poorly written and underpriced."[12]

Unum lost $61.7 million just in the third quarter of 1994 on such policies. It laid off 350 employees and announced that it wouldn't write new policies, which at the time had accounted for 15 percent of its business.

Yet, by 1999, Unum decided to make a far bigger bet on individual disability.

Despite all the talk about how the merger would benefit customers, UnumProvident had other plans. The company intended to take advantage of its newfound size, which gave it a 30 percent share of the U.S. market for disability insurance. UnumProvident planned to raise prices 14 percent in 2000 and a similar amount in 2001. But customers resisted, and competitors used the transition to woo customers away. UnumProvident managed to increase prices just 7 percent in 2000, and prices were flat in 2001.

The company sought synergies by applying across the board Provident's techniques for reducing payments and getting claimants back to work as soon as possible. Instead of boosting profits, though, the attempt at synergy dumped UnumProvident in the midst of lawsuits that clobbered the company's reputation and imperiled its finances.

By 2001, juries had begun awarding judgments in the tens of millions of dollars to individuals who had sued UnumProvident for unfairly disallowing disability claims. The situation got so bad that major media, including *60 Minutes*, did pieces on UnumProvident's practices. *60 Minutes* found an eye surgeon with Parkinson's disease whose disability claim had been disallowed. "I knew that if I tried to operate on someone I might blind them," said the surgeon, John Tedesco, as the broadcast showed his shaking right hand. "There's not a person on this earth who would say that a person with Parkinson's disease could do eye surgery."

Although appellate judges drastically lowered the initial verdicts, UnumProvident still had to pay many individuals more than $10 million each for unfairly disallowed claims, and the sheer number of lawsuits was daunting. More than three thousand people sued UnumProvident, eventually resulting in class actions. The suits claimed that the unfair actions were systematic, that UnumProvident set monthly targets for disallowing claims and even convened "roundtables" after hours or on weekends to compile "hit lists" at meetings where notes weren't taken so there'd be no paper trail.[13] Those on the hit lists were targeted because they represented high costs for UnumProvident, not because of any problem with their claims, according to the suits. UnumProvident allegedly handed out a "Hungry Vulture" award to claims agents who were especially aggressive about denying claims, according to lawsuits; the award carried the slogan "Patience my foot, I'm gonna kill something."[14] Some doctors supported the suits, saying they had been hired by UnumProvident to rubber-stamp its attempts to disallow claims. Opinions issued by federal courts chastised UnumProvident for claim-processing practices "that defie[d] common sense" and "bordered on outright fraud."[15] State regulators intervened, getting UnumProvident to pay a $15 million fine and to agree to reexamine two hundred thousand cases in which disability claims were denied.[16]

UnumProvident denied setting targets for disallowing claims. The company said the percentage of claims it disallowed didn't increase during the stretch when those suing the company said it was stepping up pressure to deny claims. UnumProvident said Dr. Tedesco's Parkinson's developed after his claim had been disallowed; the initial claim related to a back injury, according to the company. UnumProvident said it didn't pressure doctors into incorrect judgments.

UnumProvident returned to profitability in 2000 and 2001, but investors had doubts. They could see the problems with integration following the merger and the serious threats related to the handling of individual disability claims. Investors also knew that interest rates had dropped, meaning UnumProvident would earn less from investments it made with the money from premiums. In addition, economic growth had softened, which tends to increase disability claims; people who are unemployed or underemployed are more likely to file for disability. At the end of 2001, UnumProvident's stock price was still down some 50 percent from its level at the time of the merger.

The investors turned out to be too optimistic. UnumProvident's individual disability business continued to deteriorate, and in 2002 Chandler made *Forbes* magazine's list of worst CEOs, which was based on comparing a business's performance with the compensation of the CEO. By March 2003, Moody's said it was considering cutting UnumProvident's bond rating to junk status. That would undercut UnumProvident's ability to raise money. The stock plunged, reaching levels 90 percent below where it was at the time of the merger. Chandler was out.

Chandler's number two, Tom Watjen, took over. Though he had been a disciple of Chandler's, reaching back years before the merger, Watjen quickly disavowed what he called the overemphasis on growth and the arrogance of the previous years. Under Chandler, he said, UnumProvident exhibited "very much a top-down, 'don't really care what the employees think' attitude."[17]

Watjen also basically dismantled the merger. He took a write-off of almost $1 billion to cover the problems with the individual disability policies that Provident had written before the merger. Watjen also greatly scaled back plans to write more individual policies in the future. Watjen even got rid of the "Provident" part of the company name, reverting to just Unum.

Watjen raised prices on many policies to try to return to profitability but found that Unum's size still didn't give it the pricing power that had been expected before the merger. Many customers simply went elsewhere rather than pay the higher fees. Competitors were using the turmoil at Unum as a way of aggressively attacking its customer base. Unum posted a $253 million loss for 2004.

As of this writing, Unum is again solidly profitable, but the stock price is still only about a third of what it was in 1999, even though the market as a whole has risen significantly. The company still must deal with class actions from claimants and from investors.

RED FLAGS

The UnumProvident story shows the three main reasons that synergy strategies fail:

- The synergy may exist only in the minds of strategists and not in the minds of customers.
- Excitement over the prospects for synergies can lead a company to vastly overpay for an acquisition.
- While the idea behind synergy strategies is that one plus one can equal three, clashes of culture, skills, or systems can mean that synergies that seem easy to achieve can be impossible to get.

Customers Don't Care About the Synergies

While press releases proclaim a strategic fit that will change customers' lives forever, many customers don't notice any change—and many customers find themselves being treated worse. One study found that customers thought they got better service or prices from only 29 percent of mergers. Another found that as many as 30 percent of a company's customers may leave during the postmerger phase. Of those who leave, two-thirds do so because of what they perceive as bad service.

Plenty of UnumProvident's customers certainly felt they were being treated worse. Who wants higher prices, plus the prospect of having legitimate claims denied? As for the supposed benefits that customers would get from cross-selling, well, those benefits were all for UnumProvident, not for the customers. Someone with an individual disability policy with Provident didn't need to buy life insurance from Unum. That customer already had access to plenty of life insurance in the market. Maybe a group-disability customer of Unum's would find it slightly more convenient to check a box on an HR form and buy supplemental insurance of the sort that Provident traditionally provided, rather than seeking it separately. Or maybe not.

The misunderstanding of the customer goes all the way back to one of the first synergy deals, when UAL Corporation, the holding company for United Airlines, bought Hertz Corporation and the Westin hotel chain in the 1970s. UAL thought customers would value being able to plan a whole trip—airline, hotel, and rental car—just by making one phone call. They were right. They were also wrong. UAL was right that customers valued convenience and, in that long dark age that was the pre-Internet era, they couldn't just hop on Expedia. But UAL was wrong in that it overestimated the value customers ascribed to convenience. Just because someone called United didn't mean he'd stay at a Westin hotel or rent a Hertz car. A customer might prefer Avis or be sensitive enough about price that he'd go with a lesser brand. Perhaps a Westin hotel wasn't as close to the traveler's destination as some other hotel. Besides, if a customer wanted to plan a trip in one fell swoop, he could always call a travel agent and give himself the whole gamut of hotel and car choices. Where United's strategists saw synergy, customers saw next to nothing. United sold Hertz and Westin in the 1980s.

Sears, Roebuck & Company made basically the same mistake when it bought the Dean Witter Reynolds Incorporated stock-brokerage business and the Coldwell Banker & Company real estate–services business in the early 1980s. Sears had hoped that it could deal with all its customers' home needs—that the customer who wanted Sears power tools would also want Sears financial tools. Sears probably had a little more justification than United did, because Sears had founded Allstate Insurance back in 1931 and had been successful selling insurance to its department-store customers. If insurance worked, then why not stocks and real estate? However, Allstate was formed in the relatively early days of the insurance business and succeeded as a stand-alone business, not because of its connection with Sears. A customer shopping for a hammer on a Saturday afternoon simply wasn't thinking about investments and wasn't going to chat with a bond salesman even if he stumbled across a Dean Witter office in the middle of the store. While Sears had a trusted name, customers also weren't going to hire a Coldwell Banker Realtor just because one was in the department store. Sears had convinced itself that it was going to serve the whole customer by adding financial services, but customers weren't buying. Sears paid a heavy opportunity cost. It should have been preparing for the onslaught named Wal-Mart Stores Incorporated and for the general malaise that hit department-store chains in the 1990s; instead, Sears wasted time and money on a synergy strategy.

Retailers, which are supposed to be so good at understanding their customers, seemed to be especially likely to see synergies where none existed. J. C. Penney Company for instance, felt there was synergy between department stores and pharmacies, so it bought five drugstore chains in 1996 and 1997 for $4.4 billion, in the process assuming $1.1 billion of debt. Penney figured it could steer customers to the drugstores by letting them use their Penney credit cards in Penney's pharmacies. Penney also felt it could beef up the product selection at its department stores by bringing in selected products from the drugstores, and vice versa. Finally, Penney felt it could generate catalog sales for its department store by putting Penney catalogs in the pharmacies. If that seems like a pretty weak array of possible synergies, well, it was. No synergies appeared, and focused competitors started taking business away from Penney's drugstores. In 2000, Penney took a $500 million write-off on its pharmacies.

In 2005, Penney sold the business, reporting a $1.3 billion loss on the sale.

Some retailers actually chased customers away in pursuit of synergy. Dillard's Incorporated had that problem after it bought Mercantile Stores Company in 1998 for $2.9 billion in cash and became the third-largest department-store chain in the United States. Mercantile offered heavy promotions to its credit-card customers and was known to all customers for its "Midnight Madness" sales. To make Mercantile conform to the Dillard's model, making cost synergies possible, Dillard's eliminated the discounts and sales in favor of an everyday-low-price strategy. Mercantile's customers balked so completely that the former Mercantile stores soon found themselves stuffed with inventory and had to resort to discounts after all to clear out the goods. Even after the transition to the Dillard's format, Mercantile customers continued to desert. Dillard's took almost $800 million in write-offs on the Mercantile acquisition and didn't have two consecutive profitable quarters again until 2006.

Overpaying

It's well documented that most acquisitions don't pay off, mostly because the company doing the buying overpays. It makes sense that the problem would be even more acute when synergies are in play. In any sort of auction, the acquirer is going to go absolutely as high on price as it thinks it reasonably can; if it sees synergies—whether real or imagined—it's going to be willing to pay for them. Even without a competitive situation, if the investment bankers representing the company on the block smell synergies, they're going to push for a higher price. Why let the acquirer get all the benefit? Why not capture some of that for the shareholders of the company being bought?

Unum certainly overpaid for Provident. (Although the companies describe the union as a merger, Unum shareholders received 58 percent of the equity in UnumProvident.) Given the problems that cropped up in Provident's policies, Unum should have paid a small fraction of the $2 billion in equity that Provident holders received.

Unum should have known better, and not just because of its painful personal experience in the individual disability market in the early 1990s. Arthur Andersen raised questions publicly in a report it prepared for the Maine Bureau of Insurance, which was reviewing the potential merger, as long as Unum was based in Portland, Maine. The report said there were indications that Provident was being unfairly aggressive in denying claims as a way of shoring up profits. That report suggested strongly that Provident's earnings weren't all they seemed and might not be sustainable.[18] Other testimony at the hearings was stunningly colorful in its complaints about Provident. A doctor wrote to the superintendent of the bureau that "a Provident claimant suffering from manic-depression, in desperation after several months of torment by Provident's claims handlers, sent Provident a letter written in her own blood. . . . This woman admitted to me that she feared being driven to suicide, and, if she was, she was going to do it on the steps of Provident's headquarters in Chattanooga. These are not the acts of satisfied customers!"[19]

Like Unum, Quaker Oats Company overpaid horribly when it purchased Snapple Beverage Corporation for $1.7 billion in 1994. Although analysts warned at the time that the price could be as much as $1 billion too high, Quaker saw synergies. Snapple's drinks would fill out the Quaker Oats product line and freshen up the dowdy Quaker brand. Quaker would improve Snapple's distribution system; after all, Quaker had made Gatorade into a hit and had much more muscle with distributors than Snapple did. Meanwhile, Snapple's distributors could help Quaker's Gatorade drinks win additional shelf space.

But Quaker never dug deep enough to understand Snapple's distribution system. Given the quirky appeal of Snapple, it was a cause as much as a product. Distributors were personally invested in seeing Snapple succeed and made all sorts of unusual side deals to get space for it on store shelves. These distributors didn't care at all for the sort of bureaucratic, corporate approach that Quaker took. They also had no financial incentive to help with Gatorade. Quaker told Snapple distributors to turn a certain percentage of Snapple's space over to Gatorade, but the distributors made four times as much per unit of shelf space on Snapple as they would on Gatorade. The distributors said, "Thanks, but no thanks," to Quaker. Although Quaker had convinced itself that Snapple would continue to own its market, other companies saw Snapple's success and began to compete aggressively with new drinks. The Snapple business began to deteriorate.

Quaker sold Snapple for $300 million just three years after buying it. William Smithburg, Quaker's longtime CEO, retired that year at age fifty-nine.

Sometimes, as with Unum, focusing on synergies blinds companies to the fact that they're acquiring problems as well as opportunities. When Federated Department Stores Incorporated (now known as Macy's Incorporated) bought Fingerhut Companies for $1.7 billion in 1999, it was excited about adding expertise in cataloging and e-commerce. Federated, which owns high-end retailers such as Macy's and Bloomingdale's, didn't see that Fingerhut's move into e-commerce was just a quick, opportunistic foray inspired by the high valuations afforded to Internet businesses at the time. In fact, Fingerhut's order-fulfillment software was faulty, its operations were sluggish, and its management was overwhelmed by the complexities of the Internet marketplace. In addition, Fingerhut had beefed up its numbers by aggressively acquiring customers by offering credit cards to riskier customers.[20] When Federated finally saw the problems, they were overwhelming. By early 2002, Federated had given up and said it would sell Fingerhut in pieces. Federated took write-downs and posted losses related to Fingerhut that totaled as much as $2 billion.

Sometimes, talk of synergy leads companies to overpay in a more subtle way, through excessive opportunity costs. In other words, companies focus so much management time and attention on a synergy strategy that they lose the ability to pursue other, more fruitful opportunities. For instance, when Safeco Corporation bought American States Financial Corporation for $2.8 billion in 1997, the goal was to combine Safeco's presence in the West with American States' presence in the Midwest and East to form the largest insurance agency sales force in the country. The goal was also to have Safeco's focus on personal insurance complement American States' focus on commercial insurance. While Safeco was integrating the two businesses, though, it missed that its underwriting methods had become outdated. It accepted lots of business that other companies had rejected and wound up with a $1.2 billion write-off.

One Plus One Doesn't Equal Three; One Plus One Equals One

While synergy strategies count on having different businesses help each other, sometimes they don't want to. Companies anticipate these problems and hire change-management experts to get everyone pulling together. But the use of those experts calls to mind Warren Buffett's warning: "Never ask a barber whether you need a haircut." No change-management expert worth his $10,000-a-day fee is going to tell you something can't be done. And yet there are times when the incentives not to cooperate are just so great, when habits are so ingrained, that change is prohibitively difficult.

At Unum, the sales reps who called on corporations to sell group policies weren't equipped to sell policies to individuals, and vice versa. The same goes for the underwriters: Unum's had their expertise, and Provident's had theirs. There wasn't any particular reason to collaborate.

The merger of America Online Incorporated and Time Warner Incorporated showed the problem on a much larger scale. At the time of the merger in 2000, when the company's market capitalization was $280 billion, AOL's Steve Case and Time Warner's Gerald Levin proclaimed that they had done nothing less than reinvent media by combining an old-line media company with a new-age one. They said AOL would feed customers to Time Warner's magazines and its cable, movie, music, and book businesses. Time Warner would provide new kinds of content that would help AOL sign up even more customers for its online subscription service. But, well, we all know how that one turned out. Case and Levin had made the conceptual leap about forming a new type of media company, combining old and new media, and they did everything they could think of to get all parts of the business to collaborate, including offering financial incentives for doing so. But the folks on the Time Warner side, in particular, didn't make the jump with them. *Time*, *Fortune*, *Sports Illustrated*, and scores of other magazines had prospered for decades. They had well-established practices for how they produced their stories and sold their ads. Why did they need the help of a ten-year-old company run by a guy who looked like he should still be in college? When the merged company tried, for instance, to get the magazines and other Time Warner properties to join together and sell ads with AOL, it just didn't happen.

In a quieter way, Safelite Glass Corporation had a similar fall from grace. It seemed to be in great shape when it bought its biggest rival, Vistar Incorporated, for $269 million in 1997. Safelite, which replaced glass in automobiles, had a management team that was widely admired and hoped to transfer some of its process improvements to Vistar. Among other things, Safelite had figured out that an insurance company's administrative costs might amount to $100 on a $300 repair job. So Safelite integrated its computer systems with insurers' and took on the administrative role. Insurers' administrative costs dropped to as little as 25¢ per repair job—and Safelite's business boomed. Safelite also boosted worker productivity by 20 percent by adopting a sophisticated form of piecework. But Safelite didn't fully understand the difficulties it would have transferring its practices to Vistar. For one thing, Vistar farmed out much of its work to independent shops, where costs for replacing a windshield were much higher than Safelite's and where Safelite had no leverage to push improvements. Safelite also underestimated the difficulty of integrating the two businesses. Sales efforts slowed, and productivity improvements stopped, while the two companies focused on combining. Customers felt ignored. Safelite lost a huge contract with Allstate, the second largest auto insurer. Safelite had taken on debt to finance the acquisition, and a mild downturn in the market for replacement glass was enough to push it into bankruptcy in 2000.

Even when "synergistic" businesses do want to work together, it can be hard to generate anything close to the expected benefits, as an IBM strategy from the 1980s shows. IBM had made the personal-computer market explode with the introduction of its PC in 1981, creating an environment where software start-ups such as Lotus were thriving. Yet IBM was nowhere in terms of a PC software business of its own. IBM decided on a synergy strategy. It bought pieces of numerous small software companies, then announced that it would sell the products through the IBM sales force. The idea was that the companies' stock would get a big boost from the IBM relationship, so IBM would immediately generate a large profit.

Meanwhile, the entrepreneurial spirit from these smaller companies would transfer to IBM and let it finally get its own PC software business going. Instead, IBM smothered the small companies. IBM ran scores of salespeople through the companies for training, meaning that these small outfits had to just about stop everything they were doing so they could deal with all the love IBM was pouring out on them. The companies soon began performing so badly that IBM's $100 million–plus of investments were rendered almost worthless. For good measure, the entrepreneurial spirit didn't transfer to IBM. It eventually took some $2 billion of losses on PC software before giving up on the business.

Information systems can be an especially large obstacle when it comes to getting businesses to integrate and cooperate; if the computers can't talk to each other, it's cumbersome for the individuals to share much information. When Union Pacific Corporation bought the Southern Pacific Rail Corporation in 1996, Union Pacific anticipated enormous cost synergies because the combined railroads would become the largest railroad network in the country. But the two railroads' information systems didn't work together, and all initial attempts to patch up the differences failed. The combined companies eventually had so many delays that the federal government declared an emergency and intervened.

Union Pacific had reason to be cautious, because it had already gone through a disaster in the search for synergies, based on unexpected difficulties in managing a business that sounded similar but that turned out to be quite different from a railroad. The problems arose after Union Pacific bought Overnite Transportation Company for $1.2 billion in 1986. The logic was simple. Rather than just transport freight on its railroad, Union Pacific would provide an end-to-end service for customers, picking up freight at their door and dropping it off at its destination. The problem was that running a trucking business, with its fiercely independent drivers and unlimited starting and ending points, wasn't at all like running a railroad. Union Pacific almost ran Overnite off the road. Union Pacific made an especially large blunder in 1995 when it mishandled a surge of business at the nonunion Overnite that occurred because of a Teamsters strike against unionized competitors. In 1998, Union Pacific took a $547 million write-off on Overnite. Union Pacific then tried off and on to get rid of Overnite, before finally spinning it off in 2003 in a transaction that valued the business at a bit more than a third of what Union Pacific paid seventeen years earlier.

Tough Questions

When consulting firms do studies like those cited at the beginning of this chapter, on how hard it is to achieve synergies, the suggestion usually is that there are ways to get those synergies if you just execute properly—by hiring that consulting firm. But some synergy strategies should simply be abandoned. No amount of consulting would have saved the Unum-Provident deal, for instance.

The way to figure out which should be pursued and which abandoned is to start with a thorough list of potential synergies, then subject them to a withering set of questions and challenges, informed by the historical fact that synergies typically fail to appear. If you think you're going to defy the odds, you need to have strong evidence.

Once the list of cost synergies has been assembled, you need to go back through them, with some issues in mind:

- Many costs you expect to eliminate will likely just be moved to a different budget. Perhaps people who are cut from one department just get moved elsewhere because they're good folks and the company really doesn't want to lose them.

- Likewise, many costs will stay because of the inevitable compromises that come with a merger. We all know how this goes. Perhaps someone doesn't want to move even though a function is being consolidated in a different city. You don't want to lose that person, so you acquiesce. You just need to account ahead of time for the fact that this sort of compromise will occur and that keeping that person where he is may mean additional costs for office space, travel, and so on.

- Many people have a vested interest in seeing that cost synergies aren't realized. After all, one person's inefficiency is another's job. So, salesmen protect their territory. Managers protect their turf. Everyone tries to keep doing things the way they always have, rather than switch to a unified approach. You need to make a list of who will resist and how, both so you can tackle the problems effectively and so you can discount your projected cost savings to allow for those that won't materialize.

These first issues are the sort that the change-management discipline is designed to overcome. But sometimes the hurdles are too high, as AOL and Time Warner learned in their disastrous combination. While you may eventually be able to achieve the expected synergies, following the sorts of regimens laid out in books on leadership and execution, you may have to spend money on information systems, on incentives to get people to change, on change-management teams, and more. You may also have to divert management attention away from other pressing issues. So you should try to quantify the costs and subtract that number from the expected benefits. Sometimes the costs are so high that the strategy simply isn't worth it.

What other efficiencies are suspect? The projected benefits from scale are one place to look. In our research, companies often overestimated the purchasing power that would come from increased size. Companies also frequently overestimated the amount that they'd be able to streamline processes after a takeover, much as UnumProvident intended to standardize on a computer system yet, after six years, had eliminated only four of the thirty-four computer systems that the two companies had at the time of the merger.

Once you've looked at the net benefits you might reap in the way of cost synergies, you need to ask yourself: How far off can I be and have the synergy strategy still work? Given that history suggests that you have a 40 percent chance of being off, and one-in-four chance of being off by at least 25 percent, you should rethink your synergy strategy if you don't have a large margin for error.

You need to run through the same exercise on the revenue side, listing, very specifically, all the ways that synergy could bring in more business, then testing them against reality. This questioning should be especially severe because claims of increased revenue have such a checkered past.

The most important question is: Do you need to buy a company to get the synergies, or can you just form a partnership? United, for instance, could have constructed a deal for its agents to steer people toward Hertz rental cars and Westin hotels without buying the companies. We realize that companies sometimes say the only way to get businesses to truly cooperate is to have them operate under one roof, but we'd say that's a danger sign. If the benefits to the businesses and to their employees are obvious, people will cooperate. If the benefits aren't obvious, people will resist. And they'll resist whether they're under one roof or several.

If you decide you truly need to buy a business to get synergies, ask yourself questions such as: How do you know that customers will flock to a new product, service, or sales channel? The only way to truly know, of course, is to test. If that isn't possible, it's crucial to look for any potential flaw, because our research found so many cases where companies were too optimistic—for example, United assuming that customers would rent cars and reserve hotel rooms from United subsidiaries simply because they were on the phone with a United operator. If you think you're going to improve customer service, then how exactly will that look from the customer's perspective? (Hint to Unum: Customers don't see higher prices as an improvement.) What could competitors do to hurt you, especially during the transition while you integrate the company you're taking over? Keep in mind that, in our failure cases, companies routinely overstated their advantage over competitors. As with cost synergies, who in the combined organization will resist the attempts for revenue synergies? The first place to look, of course, is at those whose compensation will be hurt, such as the ad sales forces at AOL Time Warner, which had long worked autonomously but were being asked to bundle TV, online, and magazine ads in ways that would lower prices for clients. But there are many, many other people who might have cultural or personal reasons to resist change.

Again, it's important to look at the costs that will come with the projected revenue benefits. These costs come in two forms. First are the formal costs. You may have to provide incentives to your sales force to get everyone on board. You may have to invest in research and development and marketing if you're going to generate some new product or service and take it to market. Second, and more subtle, are the ways that your attempts at synergy may alienate customers. You may be producing something that is a step forward, but customers may not see it that way. People generally don't like change, so some percentage of your customer base may go elsewhere. Many companies, such as Dillard's, found that customers had particular tastes and didn't go for the changes it wanted to make in the Mercantile stores it acquired.

Once you've tallied the likely benefits and subtracted the costs, you have to ask yourself one final question about the revenue synergies: What are the chances you're right?

The tendency is to look at the theoretical maximum for benefits and assume that, with the help of some outside experts, you'll be able to get there. But, unless you have a long and successful record of acquisitions, the odds are that you're going to run into problems you didn't anticipate. Because studies have shown that some 70 percent of hoped-for revenue synergies don't appear, you need to either somehow discount the synergies you're expecting or at least ask how far off you can be without jeopardizing your chances for success. If you don't have a very large margin for error, you should reconsider.

Even once you've evaluated your chances for cost and revenue synergies, you aren't out of the woods. You still have to list all the problems that you may be acquiring along with the opportunities—this is a theme that spans numerous failure categories. Unum, for one, should have seen that Provident's individual-disability business posed potential problems, given that Unum had tried and failed to build its own individual-disability business a few years before buying Provident.

If you're still intent on proceeding, you have to deal with the fact that many acquisitions made in the name of synergy carry too high a price tag. You need to do three calculations. First, figure out what the business you're buying would be worth on a stand-alone basis. Second, what would the business be worth if you achieved all the synergies you've mapped out? Third, what would the business be worth if you discounted the synergies, to account for the fact that few companies achieve all the synergies they expect?

After you've settled on a value based on a discounted estimate of synergies, you need to affirm that you won't go beyond that price. The tendency in any bidding war is to go just a bit higher, but that can be disastrous.

Remember, the people who tried synergy strategies before you and failed weren't idiots. A lot of very smart people have lost a lot of money because of the siren song of synergy. Just because a synergy play makes sense at first blush doesn't mean you won't join the list of failures.

TWO

Faulty Financial Engineering

Taking a Shortcut Through the Numbers

"The two most dangerous words in Wall Street vocabulary are 'financial engineering,'" said Wilbur Ross, the turnaround specialist.[1] Warren Buffett refers to derivatives as "financial weapons of mass destruction."[2]

It wasn't always so. Originally, the term "financial engineering" evoked images of Wall Street math wizards taming the vagaries of risk by conjuring up esoteric financial instruments, in the process creating liquidity and enabling markets to function well. From 1987 through 1996, the average worldwide growth rate in the face value of the major forms of derivatives was 40 percent a year, according to *CFO* magazine. Paul Kasriel, director of economic research at Northern Trust, says profits from the financial sector now account for 31 percent of total U.S. corporate earnings—up from 20 percent in 1990 and 8 percent back in 1950. Profits from this country's financial engineers now far exceed those generated by mechanical engineers.[3]

As the wizardry spread, however, nasty surprises occurred—even before the subprime mortgage disaster that shook the financial world beginning in 2007 and 2008. Barings Bank, once the oldest merchant bank in London, collapsed in 1995 because of $1.4 billion in losses by one rogue trader, Nick Leeson. ING, a Dutch rival, bought Baring for one British pound. Long Term Capital Management, a hedge fund founded by legendary bond trader John Meriwether and whose partners included Nobel Prize winners in economics, dazzled with 40 percent–plus annualized returns in its first few years before losing $4.6 billion in the course of a few months in 1998. (While LTCM claimed the market had become irrational, it's worth remembering John Maynard Keynes's observation that "the market can stay irrational longer than you can stay solvent.")[4] In general, it only takes a few bad bets in the trading business to lose billions, as happened in 2006 when the Amaranth hedge fund lost almost $6 billion and was liquidated because it, essentially, lost some highly leveraged bets on the weather.

The wizardry spread from Wall Street into the rest of corporate America, where companies increasingly used financial and accounting techniques to enable broad corporate initiatives, such as restructuring, increasing financing available to customers, funding new ventures, and hedging operational risk.

Problems have shown up in the non–Wall Street crowd, too. Companies get sucked into the idea that they'll indulge in some creative accounting, but only briefly, until the business clears some hurdle and earns its way out of the current difficulties. But the one or two quarters of aggressive accounting can become three or four, then become a way of life—until disaster strikes. That disaster can sometimes mean regulatory censure and fines. In extreme cases, à la Enron Corporation, the aggressive accounting can turn into fraud and jail terms. But even if the accounting stays just this side of the line, once investors learn about it they can still punish a company severely.

Every once in a while, you even see a company that manages to come out the other side after a period of creative accounting. AOL's profits for years came from financial chicanery. The company blanketed the world with free introductory CDs to get people to sign up for its service but didn't absorb the costs as expenses right away. AOL capitalized the expenses, spreading them out over several years. The theory was that AOL was attracting customers who would be with it for years, so it was fair to defer much of the expense of acquiring those customers. The problem was that the average person who signed up because of AOL's free discs didn't stay with the company for even a year. The SEC investigated, eventually fining AOL $300 million and issuing a stinging rebuke in 2005, but by that point AOL had become a legitimate business.

But there have been enough failures associated with financial engineering that it's worth distinguishing, in Warren Buffett's words, acceptably aggressive accounting from attempts at alchemy. In the end, as

Buffett once wrote his shareholders, alchemy fails. Financial alchemists may become rich, but gullible investors rather than business achievements will usually be the source of their wealth. We're interested in spotting the alchemists and helping both executives and investors head off inherently flawed financial engineering strategies *before* they wreak havoc.

We'll begin with a story that, had it been studied by subprime mortgage lenders, would have warned of how mortgage lending can become so addictive that financial institutions can stop paying much attention to whether borrowers will ever pay off their loans.

Green Tree: Long-Term Loans on Short-Term Assets

Green Tree Financial Corporation was a darling of both Main Street and Wall Street through most of the 1990s. Through a number of financial innovations, it made trailer-home ownership more accessible to low- and middle-income people. This fueled a boom in trailer-home sales, also known as manufactured housing. From 1991 to 1998, annual sales of trailer homes in the United States more than doubled, to 375,000. In 1992, Green Tree lent $1.2 billion. In 1996, Green Tree lent four times that amount. At its peak, Green Tree financed more than 40 percent of the trailer homes sold.[5]

Green Tree's efforts were rewarded. Between 1991 and 1997, Green Tree's profits jumped sixfold, to $301 million. Its stock jumped thirtyfold. Lawrence M. Coss, Green Tree's chairman and chief executive, took home $200 million in pay during the boom. In 1998, Conseco Incorporated agreed to buy Green Tree for $7.6 billion.

The problem was that Green Tree was a house of cards, built on financial engineering that could not withstand the test of time. Conseco eventually wrote down almost all the profits ever recorded by Green Tree. Conseco then declared bankruptcy in 2002, in large part because of the problems it bought from Green Tree. As of September 2004, Green Tree and Conseco had accounted for 20 percent of all defaults of S&P-rated residential mortgage–backed securities.[6]

Green Tree's first financial innovation was to offer thirty-year mortgages instead of the fifteen-year terms that had been standard, thus making the monthly cost of ownership comparable to renting. Buyers loved the new mortgages. By 1997, the average Green Tree loan had a term of about twenty-five years, up from thirteen years in 1987.[7] Green Tree was lauded for making ownership an option for so many.

The innovation had a fatal flaw, however—one that should have been obvious to all concerned. Unlike conventional homes, which generally appreciate in value, trailer homes lose their value over time. Trailer homes are more like cars, which start losing value as soon as they leave the showroom floor. Trailer homes have a life span of ten to fifteen years—not thirty.

The value of a trailer home drops rapidly, but on a thirty-year loan, the principal balance shrinks very slowly. On a typical $50,000 mortgage, after five years the borrower still owes $49,000 in principal. In other words, after a few years, the owners are "upside down" in their loans; they owe far more than their homes are worth.[8]

Additionally, while a thirty-year loan at 13 percent annual interest requires a monthly payment of just $553, versus $633 for a fifteen-year loan, a borrower will pay an extra $85,000 over the life of the thirty-year loan.[9] That is something that many buyers of trailer homes could ill afford, making loan defaults even more likely.

"A lot of times, those folks are better off just filing for bankruptcy, so they can just start fresh," said Mark Tesh, a credit counseling director for a nonprofit family counseling center in Greenville, South Carolina. Tesh said his clients were often financially unsophisticated and focused only on their monthly payment, not the risks of signing a thirty-year note on a wasting asset. "A lot of folks that get into the mobile-home scenario, they get into it initially because it's more affordable," he said. "They honestly don't realize that a mobile home is going to depreciate. Most of them learn the hard way."[10]

Like lenders in the more recent subprime mortgage crisis, Green Tree used securitization to drastically increase the funds available for lending. It bundled thousands of small loans into a pool worth hundreds of millions of dollars. It then divided this pool into a series of bonds and sold them, promising to pay interest on the bonds from the interest it collected on the loans. Unlike many other lenders, Green Tree didn't sell the loans themselves. Instead, it held on to them to maximize the profit on the spread between the mortgage interest and the bond interest rates. (Green Tree typically charged borrowers 12 percent to 13 percent and promised to pay its bondholders about 9 percent.[11]) In addition, holding on to the loans allowed Green Tree to reap the processing fees from servicing the loans.

It also meant, of course, that Green Tree held on to the risk associated with the mortgages. But as long as the bonds had ready buyers, Green Tree had ready access to financing for as many loans as it could generate.

Green Tree used the aggressive "gain-on-sale" accounting method to record profits. Most lenders record profits on loans as they are repaid, which means that they book actual profits after defaults, prepayments, and other transaction costs. Green Tree, instead, calculated how much money it expected to make as the loans were paid back in the future and, when it finished each round of securitization, booked that as profit. Profits, therefore, depended on its own forecast of defaults and prepayments rather than actual performance.

Even for the most sophisticated modeler, such forecasts are extremely difficult. They depend on deep understanding of the borrowers' credit risk. They also require accurate forecasts of interest rates and economic conditions during the long life of the loan. A large drop in interest rates would spark refinancing and prepayments. An economic slowdown would affect borrowers' ability to pay, leading to a rise in defaults.

The advantage is that gain-on-sale accounting allowed Green Tree to show explosive growth and to essentially decree its profits. The estimated profits would, of course, have to be reconciled with actual performance at some point. But that might not be for years down the road. In the short term, Green Tree would have almost unlimited wiggle room.

In a different context, Warren Buffett laid out the dangers of this sort of accounting, using his trademark homespun language. Buffett noted that accounting theory says that companies are supposed to "mark to market" their securities, such as those Green Tree issued. In other words, if something is carried on the books as being valued at $100 million, and it suddenly becomes worth $50 million, the owner needs to mark down the value of the asset and take a $50 million charge against earnings. If the value goes up by $50 million, then the company records a $50 million gain. Companies have leeway on when they have to recognize the gains and losses, but the really squishy stuff happens when it isn't clear what the value of the securities are. With sophisticated financial instruments such as those generated by Green Tree—or, more recently, the subprime lenders—companies may "mark to model" their securities. But Buffett said we might as well call the practice "mark to myth," because companies get to generate the models that determine the value of the securities. He said the difference between the amount of the asset carried on the books and the actual amount that could be realized in a sale, in specialized markets that can freeze almost instantly, is the "difference between what purports to be robust health and insolvency." He added: "I'm sympathetic to the institutional reluctance to face the music. I'd give a lot to mark my weight to 'model' rather than to 'market.'"[12]

Whatever the dangers down the road, gain-on-sale accounting meant that, as long as Green Tree could find more borrowers, it could record higher profits. "When you're running a gain-on-sale shop, it's based on volume," said Bruce Crittenden, who became president of the business after it was bought by Conseco and renamed Conseco Finance.[13]

When profits are based on loan origination rather than the long-term performance of the loan, the unfortunate consequences are predictable. Investment bankers even have an acronym for it: IBG YBG, which stands for "I'll be gone, you'll be gone." It means that even though there might be long-term problems with a deal, the folks putting it together will have reaped their profits and be long gone.

In the case of trailer homes, IBG YBG motivations applied to everyone except the hapless borrower and the long-term note holder. Dealers stood to make $10,000 or more on every $50,000 trailer-home sale. They therefore had every incentive to help even unqualified buyers purchase new trailer homes. "It was easy," one dealer said. "The lenders were as greedy as hell." Lenders made loans with as little as 5 percent down, or less. There were reports that if would-be borrowers could not come up with a down payment, the dealer might tell them to bring in a used gun worth $200 and buy it from them for $2,000, then let them use that for the down payment.[14]

Dealers felt that lenders cared more about quotas than the quality of the loan. That is because they did.

Loan agents, to meet targets, would accept loans that didn't meet the company's credit criteria, especially near the end of each month. "There was pressure," one loan processor said. "The whole office was pushed to the maximum."[15]

Meanwhile, company executives were compensated based on profit, so they had extra incentive to keep the pressure on and keep cranking out the loans. Much of the $200 million of compensation paid to Coss, the CEO, was tied to Green Tree's reported profits.

In 1997, Green Tree's intricate design began to unravel as it became clear that it had overestimated its gain-on-sale profits. Both factors that were key to its rosy calculations turned against it. First, long-term interest rates started dropping, leading to a rash of early loan payoffs as borrowers refinanced. Second, loan defaults started rising. This was predictable as well. Borrower defaults tended to rise in years three to five of the loan, as overstretched borrowers grappled with the fact that their loans were upside down. And huge numbers of loans created by Green Tree's aggressive lending policies were reaching that age. In November 1997, Green Tree took a $190 million pretax write-off. Two months later, it wrote off a further $200 million.

Green Tree's stock took a beating. Even more damaging, commercial rating agencies downgraded its short-term commercial paper. Green Tree sold short-term notes to finance mortgage loans until it gathered them into big enough pools to securitize and sell. The write-offs and downgrading scared off the buyers of these notes. Suddenly, with no way to roll over its short-term debt, Green Tree faced default.

Then something strange happened.

A white knight emerged in the form of Conseco, an Indiana-based life and health insurer. Steve Hilbert, Conseco's founding CEO, had built Conseco by absorbing more than forty insurers over the previous seventeen years. He successfully folded his acquisitions into a superefficient consolidated back office. From 1987 to 1997, Conseco finished with a higher return than any other Fortune 500 company, as its stock gained a remarkable 52 percent per year.

Hilbert had already been attracted to Green Tree for several reasons. Green Tree had a 30 percent growth rate, whereas Conseco had well-run insurance businesses with more modest growth. Both companies served middle-market customers. And Hilbert thought there was a good cultural fit. "I realized not only that their market was our market," he later recounted, "but that their culture was our culture."[16] Hilbert thought that acquiring Green Tree would allow the creation of a broader financial-services company—a financial-services Wal-Mart for middle America.

So, as Green Tree's fortunes sank and most others saw a distressed asset, Hilbert saw the key to his adjacency strategy become available and, in pursuit of that strategy, made just about every mistake that can turn an adjacency move into a disaster. (For more on the potential problems with adjacency strategies, see chapter 5.)

Given their relative bargaining positions, it is all the more amazing that Coss, a former used-car salesman, got the better of Hilbert, a legend in the insurance business and an accomplished acquirer of companies. The two CEOs met to discuss the potential acquisition for the first time on March 30, 1998, just weeks after Green Tree's second major write-down. Coss had made Hilbert ask three times before he agreed to a meeting. Once in negotiations, Coss convinced Hilbert that there were other suitors; that an imminent bond and stock offering would, in any event, preclude Green Tree from needing any deal; that Coss would not consider any offer that set a stock price that didn't begin with a "5"; and that Conseco had just seven days to come to a deal.[17]

Never mind that Green Tree's share price was hovering in the $20 to $30 range and had never closed above $50; that the imminent debt offering was at expensive junk-bond rates; and that there were no other serious suitors.

Eight days after the initial meeting, Conseco announced that it had agreed to buy Green Tree for $53 a share, or $7.6 billion. The stock's most recent trade had been at $29.

Many observers had a dim view of the prospects of the combination. The markets drove Conseco shares down 15 percent on the day of the announcement. The drop in Conseco shares knocked $1.1 billion off the deal price.

Conseco must have done some due diligence since the first meeting, as it announced along with the deal that it was lowering Green Tree's forecasts and that more write-downs were coming. But Hilbert insisted the market was wrong in taking a negative view of the deal. "Wall Street sometimes takes a day or two to be fully enlightened," he said.[18]

It turned out that the market was actually much too optimistic. Over the next several years, Conseco's share price plunged 90 percent. As evidence of how hard it is to change course, Conseco continued to use the Green Tree model and actually increased the number of loans it made after the acquisition. It financed $6.3 billion in new trailer homes in 1999, 41 percent of the national total. But the quality of these loans was even worse than before the acquisition, and defaults mounted. Conseco ultimately wrote off almost $3 billion related to Green Tree, which essentially erased all profits earned by the unit between 1994 and 2001.

Hilbert resigned in April 2000, with Conseco shares at $5.63, down from $57.74 on the day before it announced the Green Tree deal. (Hilbert received a $72 million severance package. In sum, his pay from 1993 to 2000 was $530 million.[19]) Conseco filed for bankruptcy in December 2002. Its bankruptcy was the third largest in U.S. history to that point.

RED FLAGS

The rise and fall of Green Tree Financial and its ensnarling of Conseco embody the key shortcomings of financial engineering failures that we found in our research:

- Financial engineering strategies can produce inherently flawed financing products that are attractive to customers in the short term but expose the seller (and often the customer) to an incommensurate risk of failure over time.
- The strategies can produce hopelessly optimistic levels of leverage, leaving the company unable to withstand normal changes in market conditions.
- The strategies can depend on aggressive and unsustainable financial reporting, which draw regulatory scrutiny and ultimately shatter market confidence. (The latter can be more devastating.)
- The strategies can result in positive feedback loops, motivating further engineering to continue the gains and, eventually, causing the system to implode.

Flawed Financing

The seeds of Green Tree's demise were built into the very fabric of its mortgage product. Regular home mortgages, even subprime mortgages, are backed by the home as collateral, and homes usually appreciate over time. Even if they don't, homes tend to keep much of their value. Mortgage holders therefore have every incentive to maintain the mortgage to hold on to their assets. In case of default, much of the loan value can be recouped through resale of the property. By contrast, while Green Tree's borrowers had some incentive to maintain their loan and keep their credit in good standing, any economic hardship tended to tip the balance and make it sensible, even necessary, to walk away from a loan that greatly exceeded the value of the trailer home. When they did so, the underlying collateral did not cover the cost of the loan.

Green Tree, of course, took some of this into account. Its forecasting models predicted a 25 percent default rate. But even this high default assumption was not enough to protect Green Tree from the upside-down economic realities of its lending model. By early 2002, Conseco said it expected a 37.6 percent default rate. Some analysts said the rate could be as high as 50 percent.

The retailer Spiegel Incorporated provides another example of flawed financing.

Spiegel was founded as a furniture store in downtown Chicago in 1865 by German immigrant Joseph Spiegel. The company issued its first catalog in 1905, offering credit services through the mail. Long focused on catalog sales, Spiegel grew into a diversified retailer offering men's and women's apparel through Spiegel, Eddie Bauer, and Newport News brands. By 2000, revenue topped $3 billion, with sales occurring through catalogs, the Internet, and retail stores.

In the late 1990s and early 2000s, though, the company faced declining market share and low profitability because of sustained pressure from specialty catalogs for decades and, more recently, the appearance of new competitors online. Worse, SG&A expenses (selling, general, and administrative expenses, an income statement item that is a rough estimate of the cost of sales) increased every year from 1996 to 2001 as a percentage of retailing revenue. The percentage peaked at 52 percent in 2001. In other words, greater levels of advertising, catalog distribution, and other types of marketing were required to achieve the same amount of sales.

Rather than take some fundamental step to, perhaps, change its merchandise to deal with the growing competition, Spiegel boosted sales by aggressively granting credit financing to its customers. In 2001, 75 percent of sales from the Spiegel catalog and Spiegel store locations were made on Spiegel cards. In addition to increasing retailing revenue, a lenient approach to credit generated financing revenue. Without the profit from its financing arm, Spiegel would have had operating losses from 1996 to 2001. In other words, all earnings came from the credit-card operations.

Spiegel was also aggressive about reporting those credit-card earnings. When companies extend credit, they set up a provision for potential bad debts. Visa cards, known to employ strict criteria, expected around 6.7 percent of balances to default during that period. Target maintained a provision of 6.4 percent. But, in 1999, Spiegel's provision was just 2.4 percent; in 2000, the provision was 1.3 percent.

When the true circumstances came to light, analysts estimated that Spiegel had an actual default rate of 17 percent to 20 percent. Spiegel's 2001 financial statements, filed a year late because so much of the accounting had to be revisited, showed $112 million in losses related to financing.[20]

An independent court-appointed examiner later found that Spiegel had withheld information about its deteriorating credit situation and may have manipulated its disclosures to keep from going bankrupt. The examiner also criticized KPMG, Spiegel's auditor, for standing by as Spiegel violated securities law.

"They basically jacked up their sales by lending more to people with bad credit," one industry analyst observed. "It's one of those retailing things that just gets repeated and repeated."[21]

Spiegel filed for bankruptcy in 2003. All shareholders, including the majority owner, who had a 90 percent stake in the company, lost their shares to debt holders during the bankruptcy.

A gradual slide toward ever more lenient credit also sank Heilig-Meyers *even though its home-furnishing market was booming at the time.*

Founded in 1913 in Goldsboro, North Carolina, Heilig-Meyers

Company grew to a chain of 1,249 stores with $2.4 billion in revenue at its peak in 1998. Throughout most of its history, the company followed a consistent, winning strategy. It opened or acquired stores in small towns and rural markets at least twenty-five miles from large cities. Competition in these markets largely came from locally owned stores that generally lacked the financial strength to compete against the much larger Heilig-Meyers. It would then attract customers by granting easy credit through an in-store installment payment plan. "We used to call Heilig-Meyers a bank disguised as a furniture retailer," one analyst said.

For a long time, Heilig-Meyers's credit-based model was not only a source of profit but also of company pride. The company saw itself as being part of the fabric of local communities, serving customers who might not otherwise be able to afford the furnishings it sold. Store managers usually came from the community, were extensively trained, and, if they met incentive targets, were often among the highest paid in the community.

Much of those targets revolved around Heilig-Meyers's installment credit programs, which were administered at the store level. Local managers were responsible for extending credit, and company guidelines gave them latitude to tailor terms according to individual customers' ability to pay. Collections were also managed at the store level, with many customers coming to the store to make payments once or twice a month.

It was a winning strategy. In its first seventy-two years of existence, as the chain grew to become the largest publicly traded home-furnishings retailer in the United States, Heilig-Meyers never closed a store for nonperformance. Almost 90 percent of the company's three hundred thousand customers were using its credit plans to make purchases, paying annual financing charges of as much as 24 percent. Income from credit came to 16 percent of total revenue.

Problems arose in the early 1990s as Heilig-Meyers mismanaged both opportunities and threats. After an aggressive round of acquisitions and expansion, the chain was reaching a saturation point in its core geographical markets in Mid-Atlantic and Southeast states. At the same time, credit-card companies began aggressively issuing cards to Heilig-Meyers's traditional customer segments, giving potential customers more financing options beyond the company's installment plan.

Heilig-Meyers responded in two ways, both of which were disastrous.

Taking advantage of its strong balance sheet and superior access to capital as a public company, Heilig-Meyers expanded further, this time moving into unfamiliar geographies and, despite its long-standing rural focus, into metropolitan markets. Encountering the sorts of problems with an adjacency strategy that we explore in chapter 5, Heilig-Meyers expanded into and retreated from numerous markets, including California, Chicago, and Puerto Rico. It bought and divested several upscale brands. In the process, it piled on a mountain of debt. Having acquired hundreds of home-furnishing stores, it found that many customers didn't like the changes it made to fit the companies into the Heilig-Meyers family. For instance, in 1996, Heilig-Meyers bought Rhodes Furniture, the fourth-largest furniture chain in the country, with $430 million in annual revenue, and made the Rhodes stores more upscale. Customers hated the changes and deserted. Heilig-Meyers sold Rhodes in 1999. Rhodes went bankrupt in 2004.

Heilig-Meyers also extended financing to more marginal customers, that is, customers who still did not qualify for major credit cards. This was at the same time that personal-bankruptcy laws were being relaxed. Customer-financing defaults surged. The company's president estimated that one out of every nine Americans who went bankrupt in 1997 owed money to Heilig-Meyers. The company reported that losses on credit extended to customers ran at 6.5 percent of the total extended that year, some 45 percent higher than long-standing historical averages.[22] In August 2000, facing insurmountable debt payments, the company filed for bankruptcy. It soon took a $575 million charge, wiping out almost all remaining shareholder equity. Of that amount, $303 million was attributed to cleaning up and discontinuing the in-house credit program.

Ironically, Heilig-Meyers's demise came at a time when U.S. home sales were booming and homeowners were spending record amounts for repairs and refurbishing. The company should have been thriving. As one industry analyst observed, "The great pity is that they did not know how to take advantage of their advantages."[23] Another commented, "We've seen this kind of thing before, when the sale takes precedence over the credit concerns. It's highly conducive to bad underwriting."

Hopelessly Optimistic Leverage

Leverage, the practice of borrowing to finance further investment, acts as an amplifier. Used properly, it provides working capital that boosts the returns on good strategies. But, of course, leverage cuts both ways. It amplifies weaknesses and, in bad times, limits flexibility and accelerates the onset of failure.

Green Tree's model shows just how vulnerable companies can be when the tide turns. The model was both elegant and preposterous. Elegant because, in good times, Green Tree could borrow funds in the market for short-term commercial paper and pay 3 percent to 5 percent in annual interest, then turn around and lend those funds as mortgages and charge 13 percent annual interest. Green Tree would bundle the mortgages and sell securities based on them, book its profit, then start all over, this time at greater scale. It was a well-oiled moneymaking machine as long as there was confidence in the underlying assets. But the model was also preposterous because the machine seized up almost as soon as the flaws in the underlying mortgage product appeared and Green Tree's write-downs began. Being so highly leveraged almost immediately threatened Green Tree with default, closing off options and shortening the time it had to respond to adversity.

Stripped to its essential elements, whether or not some amount of leverage is appropriate comes down to a straightforward question: Will future cash flows be sufficient to cover the debt schedule, after factoring in reasonable and necessary costs for operating the business? Addressing this question, however, opens up boundless room for creative financial engineering and no lack of opportunity for alchemy and the manifestation of IBG YBG behavior.

The 1989 bankruptcy of Revco Drug Stores Incorporated illustrates the point. Revco was taken private in 1986 in a $1.4 billion leveraged buyout that was one of the largest LBOs to that point. Even though the company had been on a two-year slide, the price was a 48 percent premium over the average share price of the prior twelve months and a 71 percent premium over the price at which Revco bought out significant inside shareholders just eighteen months earlier. To justify the price, the deal engineers at

Salomon, Revco's adviser, and Wells Fargo, the lead agent, made optimistic assumptions about Revco's future earnings. These advisers—who stood to get paid only if a deal happened—assumed a base case of an 8 percent profit margin, before interest and taxes. That assumption, however, was almost double Revco's average margin of 4.2 percent over the previous two years. It was also a level of earnings that Revco had achieved just once in the previous dozen years and was 35 percent higher than the industry average margin over the previous twelve years. Deal engineers also forecast that Revco would grow 12 percent annually, even though the company had forecast just 9 percent. The "worst-case" scenario used Revco's historical growth rate of 8 percent, thus not allowing for even the remotest chance that there would be a continued decline in company performance or a recession (both of which happened).[24] Another investment bank, Goldman Sachs, advised Revco's outside directors that the deal's assumptions were "a bit aggressive" but were "realistically attainable."[25]

Grim reality set in almost as soon as the deal closed on December 29, 1986. Revco missed the forecasts for *that* quarter by almost 50 percent. In March, Sidney Dworkin, the Revco CEO who had led the deal, stepped down. Revco met $132.5 million in scheduled debt payments in that first year, but at the expense of needed working capital. It was unable to stock up for the December 1987 Christmas season. Many items were out of stock, and estimates are that as much as 20 percent of appropriate inventory was not available in stores. In June 1988, Revco missed its first interest payment. It filed for bankruptcy in July 1989, just nineteen months after the LBO.

The failure of the Revco LBO exemplifies the problems with how leverage is typically engineered. The obvious problem is IBG YBG, which means advisers, bankers, and other third parties may be more interested in seeing the deal done than done right.

Another, usually hidden, problem is that the case-based scenario analysis, even if it had contained more realistic assumptions, didn't offer any recognition of the deal's sensitivity to changes in the assumptions. In other words, having best-case, base-case, and worst-case scenarios didn't shed any light on how changes in key variables such as margin, growth, and asset sales would affect the timing, probability, and severity of a default. A similar problem holds true for standard measures of debt tolerance, such as debt-to-equity ratios. Ratios are point-in-time measures, whereas the real issue is the payment schedule over months and years, as mortgage holders with balloon-payment schedules well know.

Had the deal engineers been more honest about the problems facing Revco, the deal—and the bankruptcy—never would have happened. In a study using historical data and forecasts available for Revco and its peers at the time of the deal, Robert Bruner concluded that Revco had between a 5 percent and a 30 percent chance of meeting its debt schedule. Bruner derived this probability by using Monte Carlo simulation to map the entire range of cash-flow scenarios for Revco. He then measured the probability of its surviving its deal structure for the three years after the LBO. Even when using the deal engineers' optimistic assumptions about growth and earnings, he estimated that Revco's survival probability only approached 50 percent.[26]

Too-Clever Accounting

At some level, creative accounting is understandable, even if not justifiable. Cutting just a few corners can lead to higher share prices, lower volatility in the stock price, increased value for options, greater bonuses, and higher debt ratings, among other things. Managers are acting rationally by meeting the quarter-by-quarter demands of the markets. Investors can share in the benefits, as well, because stock prices stay high.

Not surprisingly, then, there is evidence that creative accounting is rampant. In one survey of financial professionals, 31 percent admitted observing manipulated timing of operating expenses, 18 percent observed manipulations of revenue recognition, 17 percent observed the use of overly large charges designed to make future earnings look good, and 8 percent observed creative inventory accounting.[27] In a survey of 743 U.S., European, and Asian senior financial officers, a third responded that if their companies were going to miss analyst expectations, they would use "discretion" to buff the numbers; 46 percent of the U.S. executives said they could influence earnings by at least 3 percent.[28]

Creative accounting lies on the slippery slope between aggressive, but legal, management of earnings and outright fraud. It often takes a squad of forensic accountants armed with subpoenas to prove that a company has crossed from legal to fraudulent. But disaster can strike even when the creativity stops short of fraud.

Green Tree's use of gain-on-sale accounting, where it booked future profits on its securitized mortgages upon sale, was perfectly legal. It was a practice used by some other lenders at the time. But it was a very problematic practice given the business in which Green Tree was operating. Gain-on-sale accounting makes sense when the returns are steady and easy to estimate. But, in Green Tree's business, future earnings would have been enormously difficult to get right even with the best of intentions.

Green Tree was actually praised by some analysts as being conservative in its forecasts. But Green Tree's forecasts were only conservative in a narrow window. It couldn't withstand the modest decline in interest rates that led to higher-than-predicted prepayments (and therefore less profitable loans than predicted). Green Tree also couldn't withstand the deeper flaw in the underlying mortgage product, in which a spike in "upside-down" mortgage holders led to a much larger than predicted number of defaults. This spike in defaults flooded the market with used trailers, which, in turn, depressed sales of new trailers and led to a lower-than-predicted value for repossessed trailers. The inevitable miscalculations led to significant write-downs, which shook investor confidence and quickly led Green Tree into Conseco's unfortunate arms.

Sometimes companies get outside auditors to pass muster on a creative technique, only to find the technique is still too good to be true. Amerco, the holding-company parent of U-Haul, the truck-rental company, found out the hard way that experts may not always catch problems.

Amerco faced numerous strategic struggles in the early 1990s. Competition was rising, and the full-service gas stations that were U-Haul's traditional rental locations were quickly disappearing. In response, the company bought self-storage facilities, correctly seeing them as ideal truck-rental locations and a natural adjacency business. Amerco worried, though, that investors wouldn't like the debt it took on to acquire the self-storage facilities. So, on the advice of its auditor, PricewaterhouseCoopers (PwC), Amerco created off-balance-sheet special-purpose entities, known as SPEs and later made famous by Enron because of their role in its collapse. The SPEs passed PwC's audits sixty times over a number of years. In early February 2002, however, as the collapse of Enron heightened scrutiny of all special-purpose entities, PwC told Amerco that its SPEs didn't pass key tests. The debt that had been hidden needed to be reported on Amerco's balance sheet. Uh-oh.

Creditors almost immediately cut Amerco's $400 million line of credit by half and forced much less favorable terms. By October 2002, Amerco had defaulted on more than $100 million in bond payments. Its stock, which was trading at around $17 a share before the disclosures, sank by more than 90 percent. In June 2003, Amerco filed for bankruptcy even though, as its CFO pointed out at the time, "our revenue continued to grow at a 5 percent annual rate."

Amerco sued PwC for $2.5 billion. Amerco claimed that PwC admitted that it had given Amerco the wrong advice seven years earlier when its national partner who specialized in off-balance-sheet entities had reviewed the accounting and said the approach was "fine." The suit said that the partner, a man who had since retired, admitted lacking technical knowledge about SPEs. "I wasn't aware of that component of the rules, and, you're absolutely right, I gave them wrong advice," the suit claimed he told his former partners.[29]

Amerco also hired Douglas Carmichael, who later became the chief auditor of the U.S. Securities and Exchange Commission's Public Company Accounting Oversight Board, to deliver an expert-opinion analysis of its claims. Carmichael was withering in his findings. PwC made "inexcusable and incomprehensible" errors in its work, he said. It "violated each and every duty owed to Amerco, its lenders, governmental agencies and the public," and it "improperly placed its own interests ahead of its clients' in violation of the industry's ethical and professional principles."[30]

PwC's response? "We're surprised . . . that the company has decided to bring this action," said Steven Silber, a PwC spokesman. Pointedly noting that primary responsibility for the accuracy of financial statements lies with the company, Silber added that "This action appears to be an attempt by company management to shift the blame away from themselves. We're confident that attempt will fail."[31]

PwC, admitting no wrongdoing, later settled by paying Amerco $51 million plus an additional undisclosed amount.

(We're not saying that Amerco was not complicit in its own downfall.

The company's history reads like *King Lear*, adapted for the modern corporation. Founded by Leonard S. Shoen in 1945 on a $5,000 investment, U-Haul grew into the country's largest provider of move-it-yourself rental equipment. By the early 1980s, Shoen had gradually transferred 95 percent of the company's shares outstanding to his seven sons and five daughters. Then, for almost twenty years, the father and various factions of the family fought for control of the company. Soap opera–like episodes included brawls at shareholder meetings, endless litigation, and even allegations of murder. The litigation resulted in almost $500 million in damages awarded to Shoen and his supporters but left control of the company to an opposing faction of his sons. The debt from the damages judgment loomed large on Amerco's books at the time of the PwC debacle and contributed to Amerco's default and bankruptcy. Shoen, however, did not live to see that outcome. He died in 1999 at the age of eighty-three, apparently from suicide.)[32]

For those—whether executives or investors—trying to recognize when too-clever accounting might be in the works, the SEC has identified five common creative accounting practices: taking "big bath" charges, where massive restructuring is done to clean up balance sheets or where one-time charges are overestimated to enable larger subsequent earnings; using acquisitions as a way of fiddling with the numbers; setting up "cookie jar" reserves, which are kept to smooth income; making self-serving decisions about what errors should be reported and what gains or charges are large enough to be made public; and recognizing revenue that smooths earnings. Some of the signs (though not proof) that creativity is being applied: Small reported losses are rare, but small reported profits are common. Small declines in profit are rare, but small increases in profits are common. Consensus forecasts are rarely just missed, but are often just met or exceeded by a small amount.[33]

Feedback Loops

When financial engineering is used, a chain reaction usually ensues. Burnish one quarter's results, and that becomes the yardstick by which the markets evaluate the next. The need to deliver the higher targets instigates another round of creative engineering. And so on, until the magnitude of the engineering becomes just too big.

Green Tree's financial engineering gave it the ability to book huge profits and, for a time, show stellar growth. Investors rewarded the stock—then demanded more growth. That translated into the need to deliver more loan volume to meet even higher growth expectations. Delivering more loans required ever more aggressive lending practices, which in turn led to more bad loans. Eventually, the consequences of the bad loans grew too large to ignore, and Green Tree imploded.

Tyco International Limited is another company that was caught up in a positive feedback loop, driven in its case by a dependence on growth by acquisition. Between 1992 and 2001, Tyco spent more than $60 billion to acquire more than one thousand companies. Sales soared from $3 billion to $38.5 billion, which rocketed the share price upward but also required more growth to keep it aloft. Speaking to *Chief Executive* magazine in 2001, Tyco CEO Dennis Kozlowski boasted that acquisitions had evolved into a disciplined and routine activity under his watch. "It's just part of our ingrained culture," Kozlowski said. "All of our senior operating people are geared toward looking for acquisition opportunities."[34]

For a while, the markets bought the story. Kozlowski was lauded as a cost cutter who was knitting the many acquisitions into a successful conglomerate, much like General Electric. He even landed on the cover of *BusinessWeek* with the title "most aggressive" CEO. True to that image, cost cutting in the form of extensive layoffs, plant closings, and business consolidations was typically announced within weeks of the change in control, and sometimes even before. When Tyco acquired ADT Limited, for instance, it eliminated one thousand of eight thousand jobs; at AMP Incorporated, eight thousand of forty-eight thousand workers were cut. Accounting that pushed the envelope was also the norm. Big restructuring charges, huge write-downs, and aggressive accounting of acquisition charges set the bar as low as possible so newly acquired companies could make quick and profitable turnarounds.

An overview of Tyco's $9.5 billion acquisition of CIT Group Incorporated, then the largest independent commercial-finance company, gives a sense of the pattern. Tyco's acquisition of CIT closed in June 2001. In the month before the closing, CIT posted $221.6 million in downward adjustments to earnings. Largely as a result, in the four months after the closing, CIT earned $252 million, as compared to $81.3 million in the five months prior to the closing. "This is one of the most startling examples of financial engineering you can hope to find," one analyst said.[35]

CIT proved to be the high-water mark for Tyco. While Tyco was previously very guarded about its acquisition accounting, it had to keep filing separate financial reports for CIT because of its reliance on public debt markets, and Tyco's accounting was for the first time clear for all to see.

The accounting fueled general concern about Tyco, producing a downward spiral. The doubts drove down Tyco's share price. This caused downgrades in CIT's credit rating, which threatened CIT's core lending business and further deflated its parent. By January 2002, Tyco's stock price had fallen 90 percent. Later that year, Tyco divested CIT through an IPO and posted a $6 billion loss. Tyco struggled for years with $20 billion–plus in debts from its acquisition binge and, in 2007, broke itself up into three independent companies. (For more on how poor a job Tyco did integrating its numerous acquisitions, see chapter 3 on rollup strategies.)

In 2006, the U.S. Securities and Exchange Commission accused Tyco of improper acquisition accounting during the period from 1996 to 2002, including "undervaluing acquired assets, overvaluing acquired liabilities, and misusing accounting rules concerning the establishment and use of purchase accounting reserves." In accounting parlance, Tyco improperly "spring-loaded" its results. The SEC complaint also asserted that "Tyco improperly established and used various kinds of reserves to make adjustments at the end of reporting periods to enhance and smooth its publicly reported results and to meet earnings forecasts." In response to the SEC charges, Tyco admitted no wrongdoing but agreed to an injunction and a $50 million civil penalty.

In either a sad coda to the Tyco story or a further indicator of the company's management culture at the time, Kozlowski was convicted on June 17, 2005, on twenty-two counts of grand larceny for taking $150 million in unauthorized bonuses. He was also convicted of fraud against the company's shareholders for an amount of more than $400 million. He was sentenced to serve from eight years and four months to twenty-five years in prison. Mark Schwartz, Tyco's CFO under Kozlowski, was convicted on similar charges and received the same sentence.

Tough Questions

The vagaries of markets, regulators, media, and shareholders make the potential consequences for faulty financial engineering very high. Corporate brands and reputations, built over decades, can be destroyed in a few accounting entries. Entire businesses can crash into the chasms left by a few risky exposures. A slew of corporate officers have received massive fines and even jail time after falling down the slippery slope of creative engineering. These doomsday scenarios should motivate managers, board members, and investors to show great skepticism when dealing with financial engineers bearing ideas that promise high returns for low risk, or that in some other way seem too good to be true.

To avoid getting caught up in excessive financial engineering, you should start with two broad questions: Can the strategy withstand sunshine? Can the strategy withstand storms?

To put the sunshine question a different way: How would others react if the strategy was announced on the front page of your company Web site or was the subject of a front-page article in the *Wall Street Journal*?

Writing in the *Harvard Business Review*, former General Electric general counsel Ben Heineman argued that the key to avoiding integrity land mines is to change the yardstick. He noted that GE, in annual legal and financial compliance reviews, now looks at its own business practices and asks not just whether they are legal but whether they are reasonable and ethical in the light of day. For example, are disclosures of interest rates on loans and credit balances hidden in credit-babble, or expressed in plain English?

As our friend John Perry Barlow has observed, information yearns to be free. In the age of the Internet, bloggers, and twenty-four-hour cable news channels, his observation will probably apply to your strategy as well: Someone will tell the world what you're doing. Could your company survive the resultant challenges?

In asking whether your strategy could survive storms, we're not talking about pleasant afternoon showers. Rather, we're talking about dreaded twenty-, fifty-, or even hundred-year floods.

The autopsies of many financial engineering failures conclude that designers did not foresee some external circumstance, some occurrence that fell well outside of recent experience and seemingly reasonable expectations. Green Tree Financial, for example, did not foresee that interest rates would decline or that competitors would target Green Tree, the industry leader, by offering aggressive refinancing terms to Green Tree borrowers. Revco's LBO deal designers did not anticipate that competition would erode traditional drugstores' market share, or that recession would help topple Revco off the high tightrope on which its leverage placed it. Yet any solid strategy must be able to withstand adversity, which means that strategists must look into the abyss, assess how their designs would perform under harsh conditions, and explicitly decide whether the risk is worth the return.

Writing on the topic of leverage to his shareholders, Warren Buffett reacted to a hypothetical of a "1% chance that some shock factor, external or internal, would cause a conventional debt ratio to produce a result falling somewhere between temporary anguish and default." "We wouldn't have liked those 99:1 odds," he wrote, "and never will. . . . A small chance of distress or disgrace cannot, in our view, be offset by a large chance of extra returns." He continued: "If your actions are sensible, you are certain to get good results."[36]

After the broad questions, there are a few specific questions to explore. One set would prompt the sort of analysis we described concerning Revco, to see what the chances are that cash flows would likely allow for required debt payments.

If you're tempted to indulge in creative accounting: Will that accounting generate positive cash flow or just make the profit-and-loss statement look better? If you won't get cash flow, then run.

Another question is even more basic: Does the strategy make any sense? In Green Tree's case, that would mean asking whether it's really appropriate to offer a thirty-year loan on an asset with a ten- to fifteen-year life. For Spiegel, the question would have been: Can I lend to risky customers while expecting a lower rate of default than companies that lend to the highly creditworthy expect?

The final question is the most basic: When does it stop? If you're going to take an aggressive approach to accounting as Green Tree and others did, and you're going to build ever greater expectations among investors, how do you get off the treadmill and get back to some sustainable approach to reporting your finances?

THREE

Deflated Rollups

Buying a String of Rock Bands to Form an Orchestra

Aristotle said, "The whole is greater than the sum of its parts," but we're pretty sure Aristotle never saw a rollup. (No, Alexander the Great's military conquests don't count. He got to lop off people's heads when things didn't go right.)

Rollups are an intriguing concept. It makes sense that many industries are too fragmented, that you can operate more efficiently by taking dozens, hundreds, or even thousands of small businesses and combining them into one large one. That large company would have increased purchasing power. It would be able to raise capital at lower cost. It would have greater brand recognition and would be able to advertise more effectively, on a regional or national basis. The rollup could attract better talent because there would be more career opportunities. It would operate more efficiently because it could spread headquarters expenses across a much bigger revenue base. What's not to like?

Rollups have been tried at least since the late 1960s and early 1970s, when Wayne Huizenga made a splash by buying garbage-hauling businesses and combining them into Waste Management. The rollup idea really grabbed hold in the 1990s, when more than one hundred went public as large collections of funeral homes, dry cleaners, flower wholesalers, bus lines, home builders, and air-conditioning repair services. For much of 1998, an average of five rollups *a week* were making initial public offerings. And rollups continue to appear; as of this writing, for instance, many companies are attempting rollups that will let them provide a broad array of services in online advertising.

As great as the concept is on paper, however, rollups, like athletic contests, don't happen on paper. In the real world, rollups haven't worked so well. Sometimes, rollups look like an attempt to stitch together a bunch of rock groups to form an orchestra.

Research says more than two-thirds of rollups fail to create any value for investors. A Booz Allen study of rollups found that almost half had lost more than 50 percent of their market value between 1998 and early 2000, despite the stock-market boom during those years. The study found that companies tended to outperform the S&P 500 until they reached $500 million in annual revenue, at which point investors began probing more deeply and the concept fell apart. A separate Booz Allen study followed eighty-one rollups from January 1993 to December 2000. Only eleven outperformed the S&P 500. Twenty were in or near bankruptcy. According to a senior partner at Booz Allen, "If every time one of those went public you put a dollar into it, and you put another dollar into the S&P 500, you would have $92 in those companies versus $264 in the S&P."[1]

There are some success stories, including SYSCO Corporation, which rolled up businesses that provide food service to institutional customers, such as universities, hospitals, and corporations. It began as a combination of nine food distributors in 1969 and has maintained a steady, sometimes rapid diet of acquisitions for much of the time since then. The company reported roughly $1 billion of earnings on more than $35 billion of sales for the year ended June 30, 2007, and had a market value of more than $20 billion as of this writing. Waste Management has a market value of more than $18 billion. AutoNation, which rolled up car dealers, has a market value of more than $3 billion. All good stuff.

But successes are hard to find, and even some of the poster children for rollups had disasters along the way. The SEC accused Waste Management's senior management of inflating earnings by $1.7 billion during the mid to late 1990s. The executives agreed to pay almost $31 million in personal fines to settle the charges. The accounting fraud, to hide significant problems at Waste Management, was the biggest in U.S. history until MCI Communications Corporation (itself a rollup) and Enron came along. AutoNation had to abandon the core of its rollup strategy—that it would be a nationwide seller of used cars—in 2000. AutoNation also gave up on the idea of a national brand; its more than four hundred car dealers operate under some twenty regional names.

We thought we found a consistent success in Steve Harter, who is sometimes called "the father of rollups" because he financed half a dozen in the 1990s through a fund called Notre Dame Capital and sold two at lofty prices. But closer inspection shows his success stems from timing, not from any magic when it comes to building businesses. One of Harter's claims to fame is U.S. Delivery Systems Incorporated, a rollup of courier services. U.S. Delivery opened for business in 1993 and was bought at the peak of its success by Corporate Express Incorporated, in 1996 for undisclosed terms. Corporate Express, also a rollup, briefly soared as it continued its rapid-fire acquisitions, but then saw its stock lose more than 80 percent of its value as problems surfaced. Harter's other claim to fame is Coach USA Incorporated, a rollup of bus lines that Stagecoach Group bought for £1.2 billion in 1999, the equivalent of $1.94 billion. But, in 2005, Stagecoach's CEO said that within six months of the acquisition Stagecoach found serious problems at Coach that almost forced Stagecoach to put itself up for sale. "We bought the wrong company," he said.[2] Three of Harter's other rollups filed for bankruptcy, and one seems to have come close.

The typical response to rollup failures resembles that of an article by three Booz Allen consultants in the firm's magazine, *Strategy and Business.* "Our analysis clearly indicates that the problem is not the concept but the execution," they wrote. Their statement jibes with the general emphasis on execution these days—that anything is possible if you have enough discipline, enough leadership, enough attention to detail. As you'll see from our research, though, a deep look into rollups shows the real issue often is fundamentally flawed strategies.

Before exploring the strategic mistakes in detail, we should mention two related caveats.

First, we write this chapter at least as much for investors as for operating executives. While the whole book tries to help investors pick their spots, this chapter emphasizes that focus because executives can sometimes make a lot of money off failed rollups even when investors lose. Thus, executives may have incentives to take risks that investors should shun. The reason investors can get sucked in is that rollups often look great early on. The concept makes sense, growth is unbelievable, and problems haven't surfaced yet. Those putting the rollups together may cash out before failure looms, so they make bundles while any investors who hold on too long lose their shirts. For instance, Jonathan Ledecky started numerous rollups that have an abysmal record, yet he has come away with what he estimates to be hundreds of millions of dollars and owns a big chunk of the Washington Capitals hockey team. (He has said the problems at the rollups came after he left an operational role or occurred at businesses where he was merely a passive investor. Responding to a class action by shareholders, he denied using any accounting trickery to boost a stock price and let him cash out before problems became apparent.)[3]

Second, with rollups, investors shouldn't always believe what they're told. A certain amount of skepticism is, of course, called for when investing, but that's especially the case with rollups, because—much to our surprise—we found that many rollups end in fraud. In addition to the fraud cases we've already mentioned, MCI, Philip Services Corporation, Westar Energy Incorporated, Tyco, FPA Medical Management Incorporated, JWP Incorporated, and many other rollups wound up involved with fraud charges.

Rollups have to keep growing by leaps and bounds, or investors disappear, and the financing for the rollup goes with them. Any sort of setback can derail the whole strategy, especially if acquisitions are made with stock; you can't keep buying if the currency that you're using, your stock, takes the kind of hit that high-growth companies take when they miss their goals. So, executives will sometimes go to any length—even fraud—to prevent reporting a setback.

We decided as a rule to avoid writing about situations where fraud brought a company down. There just isn't much to say about fraud other than "Don't do it." But the link between fraud and rollups is strong enough that investors should be extra careful.

So, having dispensed with the caveats, here is a look at a funeral-home colossus that shows just how many problems can crop up with rollups.

Loewen Group—R.I.P.

Those accustomed to the hushed tones and soft lights of the world of funeral homes would have had a hard time imagining the scene in the cramped Mississippi courtroom in 1995. The plaintiff's lawyer was delivering his closing arguments in a civil case against Loewen Group Incorporated that covered a, well, deathly boring topic—prepayments for funerals—and involved less than $1 million of revenue. But you wouldn't have guessed the circumstances as you watched Willie Gary work himself into a lather.

Gary claimed that what Loewen had done to his client was the second coming of the Japanese attack on Pearl Harbor—never mind that Loewen was based in Canada and had no connection with Japan. Gary said the jury had to help his client defeat Loewen, just as the client had defended his country by shooting down seven Japanese planes as a Marine fighter pilot in World War II. Sounding much like Shakespeare's version of Henry V talking to his troops before the battle of Agincourt, Gary told jurors to act "so in years to come anybody should mention your service for some fifty-odd days on this trial, you can say, 'Yes, I was there,' and you can talk proud about it." Gary added: "Your service on this case is higher than any honor that a citizen of this country can have, short of going to war and dying for your country."[4]

Loewen was growing so fast as it rolled up the funeral-home industry that it paid little attention to what it saw as routine commercial disputes, like the one in Biloxi, Mississippi, but it was about to get its introduction to southern justice.

The judge let Gary get away with his rants—and more. The jury bought every word. "It was bad," said Glenn Millen, the jury foreman. "If we'd had guns in there, we'd have probably been shooting."[5]

The jury came back with a $500 million judgment against Loewen. That judgment was almost equal to Loewen's annual revenue at the time. To appeal, Loewen had to post a bond equal to 125 percent of the judgment. Loewen said it had no choice but to settle. It ended up paying the plaintiff $240 million.

A judicial panel later labeled the handling of the trial a "disgrace" and a "manifest injustice."[6] But too late.

Loewen would recover solidly enough to surpass $1.1 billion in annual revenue—only to collapse again. Loewen filed for bankruptcy in 1999 and was bought at a distressed price by Service Corporation International in 2006.

Loewen Group traces its roots back to the 1950s, when A. T. Loewen opened a funeral home in Steinbach, Manitoba, a mostly Mennonite prairie town of a few thousand, forty miles north of North Dakota. The business generated just $23,000 of revenue a year, and A. T. had a wife and twelve children to support, but the family somehow made do. One of the younger children, Ray, liked being called out of school to help with funerals. Ray decided to become a minister and earned a degree in theology from a small school in Saskatchewan, but then A. T. got sick and couldn't continue running the funeral home. Ray dutifully took over in 1961.

The bright young man approached the work professionally, even though that meant he soon realized he needed to fire his brothers. Ray, who describes himself as easily bored, soon hatched a plan to form a chain of funeral homes. He found few takers. Most funeral homes were family businesses, and the families wanted to keep their livelihoods, not cash out.

Loewen and his wife moved to an area just outside Vancouver, British Columbia, in 1969 and bought another funeral home, while continuing to manage the one in Manitoba. He evolved an approach that he called succession planning. He'd offer to buy other funeral homes, promising to keep running the businesses much as they'd been run previously and to keep family members employed. He argued that his approach would ease the transition from one generation of funeral-home managers to the next. By 1975, he owned fourteen funeral homes.

At that point, he'd developed enough of a presence that he was asked by the Social Credit Party to run for the British Columbia legislature. He won and served for four years. He also started a business to develop and manage real estate and built half a dozen high-rise apartment buildings, but skyrocketing interest rates clobbered the real estate market in the early 1980s, so he resumed his focus on his funeral homes. He bought a few more, reaching a total of twenty by 1985. Then, what seemed to be some bad fortune presented him with his big chance.

Loewen financed his acquisitions with a line of credit from Canadian Commercial Bank, which went bankrupt. The receiver appointed to run the bank called all its loans. Loewen had to find a new source of capital.

Loewen Group decided to make a modest initial public offering, to raise more money for purchases. The plan was to spend $14 million on acquisitions in 1986, tapering down to $10 million in 1987 and $4 million in 1988. But that plan soon went by the boards. Loewen Group's IPO made it far more aggressive about purchases, and Service Corporation International had popularized the concept of funeral-home rollups in the United States, so family owners were more willing to sell. When Loewen Group's earnings rose and its stock price climbed, Loewen Group issued more shares, which led to more purchases and higher earnings, which led to more stock sales, which led . . . Loewen Group wound up on a treadmill of acquisitions and never got off.

By 1989, Loewen Group owned 131 funeral homes. In 1990, the company more than doubled that, spending $185.3 million to buy 135 additional homes. Earnings climbed 30 percent or more each year, and analysts waxed enthusiastic about the growth potential for the funeral-home industry because of what some called the "golden era of death," a decades-long stretch when baby boomers would drop like flies.

Obscured behind the growth, though, was the fact that Loewen Group couldn't do much to improve the operations at its funeral homes. The company as a whole might be growing earnings, but the individual homes weren't. The growth rates could last only as long as the acquisitions kept coming.

Loewen Group could do a few things. While funeral homes on average earned 10 percent of revenue after tax, Loewen Group imposed a 25 percent target from day one. That usually forced the home's director to cut some staff and eliminate perks such as cars and free dry cleaning. Loewen Group also provided some efficiencies through "clustering." It would buy several homes in the same area, so they could share the costs of embalming facilities, hearses and their drivers, receptionists, and a few other things. Loewen Group never said just how much the clustering saved. A competitor once indicated that the clustering meant that its fixed costs accounted for just 54 percent of revenue, well below the industry average of 65 percent,[7] but it isn't clear how much of that difference came from lower costs and how much from the ways that big companies found to increase revenue (for a time).

In any case, clustering was the main benefit, and many families had already done something similar by establishing several homes in an urban area. Loewen Group's sales pitch about letting families stay involved after selling their funeral homes meant that Loewen Group typically left existing managers in place, and they ran things pretty much as they always had. They weren't very sophisticated about business, either. Ray Loewen once surveyed 160 managers who had sold him their businesses, asking how many had ever run a business based on a budget. The answer: four.[8]

While the clustering helped, it provided modest benefits and only on a regional basis. Outside a radius of thirty to sixty miles, Loewen Group found that clustering didn't matter. The heavy regulation of the funeral-home industry also tends to keep economies of scale local; knowing how to comply with the rules in Biloxi doesn't help much in Butte. There wasn't any benefit to be had from a national brand. In fact, Loewen Group tended to hide the fact that it had bought a home, so the home could continue to represent itself as a local business and take advantage of all the ties it had cultivated over the years. While Loewen Group gained some pricing leverage with suppliers, it wasn't much. There are some twenty-two thousand funeral homes in the United States alone, so Loewen Group was way too tiny to exert much pressure. It's not as though it suddenly became Wal-Mart and could beat on suppliers for better prices. Loewen Group's cost of capital was lower than it had been for the individual funeral homes, but, again, not a lot. Funeral homes are very steady, low-risk businesses—only eight out of every ten thousand fail in the United States each year—so they could already borrow at low rates.

Meanwhile, as the industry consolidated, the prices of funeral homes kept rising, and Loewen Group became known as the company that would pay top dollar because it was so determined to keep expanding. Ray Loewen is "a very, very, very strong personality that basically felt his firm was the best and was going to be the biggest," said Ken Sloan, an executive who worked with him. "Nothing was going to stand in the way of him achieving it."

The one area where Loewen Group could goose the results of the homes it acquired was price. Loewen Group typically became the biggest player in the markets where it bought homes, so it could sometimes ignore competition. Besides, people tend not to shop around during the emotional time that follows a death. They pick a funeral home based on some prior experience or a referral. So Loewen Group jacked up prices. While funeral homes typically marked up the cost of a casket by 100 percent to 200 percent over the wholesale price, Loewen Group's markups were 300 percent to 500 percent.[9] Loewen Group also introduced methods to shame the bereaved into buying more expensive products and services. If you wanted a cremation, you had to check a box opting for "Basic Disposal" of your loved one. If you decided you wanted the low-end casket, you had to tell the funeral-home director you wanted the "Welfare Casket."[10]

While those price increases went straight to the bottom line, they eventually led to a backlash that hurt business. In addition, the resentment about pricing figured prominently in the lawsuit Loewen Group lost in Biloxi—and you have to get markups on a lot of pine boxes to cover a payment of a quarter of a billion dollars.

That lawsuit, tried in 1995, stemmed from a routine purchase. Loewen Group bought a few funeral homes from the Riemann family in Gulfport, Mississippi. It thus found itself in competition with one Jeremiah "Jerry" O'Keefe, who owned funeral homes in neighboring Biloxi.

When Loewen Group came to town, O'Keefe attacked. He mailed around a series of flyers saying that Riemann was hiding its foreign ownership. Then he got hold of the fact that Loewen Group had borrowed some money from the Hongkong and Shanghai Banking Corporation. It was a relatively small amount of money, and HSBC is based in England and Hong Kong, but O'Keefe somehow decided that the loan meant Loewen Group was controlled by Japanese interests. He set up billboards around Biloxi and Gulfport that showed the O'Keefe name underneath Mississippi and U.S. flags, and the Riemann name underneath a Canadian and a Japanese flag.

Loewen Group got O'Keefe really riled when it bought two other local funeral homes, where O'Keefe had an exclusive arrangement to sell "preneed" insurance, which covers funeral costs. Loewen Group kicked O'Keefe out and let the Riemanns sell insurance at the homes instead. O'Keefe complained, and Ray Loewen invited him to visit him in British Columbia. Ray Loewen's m.o. was to negotiate over a sumptuous meal on his 110-foot yacht, the *Alula Spirit*, in the sound off Vancouver. The two agreed on a deal. Ray Loewen would sell the Riemann insurance business to O'Keefe. The Riemanns complained. Although Ray Loewen is described as a deeply religious man, who often opened meetings with a prayer while everyone held hands around the boardroom table, he deferred to the Riemanns and essentially backed out of his deal with O'Keefe. O'Keefe sued.[11]

Lost in the swirl of its incredibly rapid growth, Loewen Group didn't grasp that it was about to get into a decidedly unfair fight. In addition to being a war hero and longtime fixture in the business community, O'Keefe had served four years in the state legislature and was a former mayor of Biloxi.

Beyond the silly talk about Japan and Pearl Harbor, O'Keefe's lawyers laid out what they contended were unfair business practices designed to make Loewen Group a local monopoly. The lawyers got racial about it, too. In front of a black judge and a jury with eight black members, the lawyers laid out voluminous evidence of Loewen Group's price increases and argued that the company was gouging the black community.

When the verdict came back, Loewen Group appealed to the Mississippi Supreme Court and asked that it not have to post the full $625 million bond. Loewen Group found some sympathy and won a stay. At the same time, though, Loewen Group was arranging a new round of financing for more acquisitions, and the company declared that none of the funds would go toward any bond in Mississippi. People in Mississippi took the statement as an affront, as though Loewen Group wasn't taking the judgment seriously. Days after the statement, the Mississippi Supreme Court removed the stay without explanation.

Despite the $240 million payment, Loewen Group was determined to press on. The company spent $620 million on acquisitions in 1996 alone and $546 million in 1997. Profits still looked healthy. The stock bounced back to where it was before the settlement. Ray Loewen, personally, still showed up on a list of the fifty wealthiest Canadians, with a net worth of $428 million.[12]

Service Corporation, which had been continuing its own aggressive rollup, offered to buy Loewen Group. When Loewen Group refused, Service Corporation raised its bid to $3.24 billion, a 50 percent premium over the stock price on the day the first bid was announced. Ray Loewen valued his independence, however, and convinced the board to reject the offer.

The expansion rolled on, and Loewen Group added a host of seasoned executives to make sure it stayed disciplined. Among them: the former president of a large paper company; a senior vice president of finance and administration from a major Canadian broadcaster; and a senior vice president of operations from a retail chain of 1,200 drug stores.

In 1998, revenue reached $1.14 billion. At year-end, Loewen Group owned 1,110 funeral homes and more than 400 cemeteries in the United States and Canada, plus 32 funeral homes in the United Kingdom.

But the wheels had come off.

A slight decline in the death rate in 1997 meant that Loewen Group's established funeral homes performed 3.2 percent fewer services than in 1996, and the situation worsened in 1998. Loewen Group also said in 1998 that it was having trouble integrating acquisitions and that problems had surfaced in its cemetery business. Those may not seem like catastrophic problems, but, for Loewen Group, they were. The rapid-fire acquisitions had left the company with a structure so ungainly and poorly integrated that it couldn't react quickly to problems. In addition, the acquisitions had piled $2.3 billion of debt on it. Even a modest decline in cash flow meant Loewen Group couldn't meet its obligations. The company went from a $42 million profit in 1997 to a $599 million loss in 1998.

In October 1998, Ray Loewen resigned as CEO. Although he still held 18 percent of the company's stock, he soon had to surrender those shares to a bank to settle a personal loan.[13] The bank then forced him out as chairman. By this point, the stock had fallen more than 90 percent from the price that Service Corporation had offered for Loewen Group slightly more than two years earlier.

John Lacey, a turnaround specialist, replaced Ray Loewen as chairman in January 1999. In April, he complained that he found 1,300 corporate entities that he had to deal with. "We had about 85 people in our tax department trying to file returns on all of them," he said. "There were no administrative synergies. There were silos of management that didn't talk to each other. It was singularly the biggest mess I've ever seen."[14]

The company filed for Chapter 11 bankruptcy protection in June 1999. It sold hundreds of funeral homes and other operations to reduce debt and refinanced the debt that remained. Reconstituted as Alderwoods, the company emerged from bankruptcy in 2002. A much smaller company, it eked out a $10 million profit on $741 million of revenue in 2003.

This time, when Service Corporation came calling, the company listened. Alderwoods sold itself to Service Corporation in 2006 for $856 million, about a quarter of the offer of nine years earlier.

Service Corporation, by the way, had its own near-death experience in the late 1990s. After seeing the stock plummet 70 percent in 1999, the company drastically scaled back operations to cut its debt. But SCI is another story for another venue.

RED FLAGS

Loewen aptly demonstrates the four kinds of failures that our research found in rollups:

- Rollups went for scale that wouldn't produce economies. Sometimes, rollups wound up with *diseconomies* of scale.
- Rollups required an unsustainably fast rate of acquisitions.
- Companies didn't allow for the tough times—and it seems that every rollup runs into tough times at some point.
- Companies assumed that they could get the benefits both of decentralization and of integration. The rollups often found, however, that they could choose either decentralization or integration but not both.

Scale Without Economies

It's a truism of economics that with scale comes efficiency. We all learned that in Econ 101. Even people who don't know anything about business or economics know the term "economies of scale." But, 'tain't necessarily so.

The biggest problems, when it comes to economies of scale, occur in the estimates of efficiencies. Routinely, companies assume that they will generate enormous back-office savings. Instead of having thirty legal departments, thirty human resources departments, thirty accounting departments, thirty purchasing departments, and thirty marketing departments, the rollup will have one of each. But, as we all know, operations are rarely that clean.

In the funeral-home industry, the argument was that operating one thousand homes was no more complicated than operating one. Yet, as Ray Loewen's successor as CEO found at Loewen, each of the thousand-plus homes was operated as almost a stand-alone business. To the extent that any efficiencies existed, they occurred within clusters of a dozen or so homes, not across the whole empire.

The lack of efficiencies is especially acute when a company decides to leave local management in place—usually to try to keep customers from defecting. Outsourcing Solutions Incorporated, for instance, tried to roll up collections agencies. But it pretty much let the agencies keep operating as they always had. The company filed for bankruptcy in 2003 (making it harder for *its* creditors to collect).

Even when a company tries to consolidate processes, the complexity of the work can derail the attempt. So can opposition by important parties. MedPartners Provider Network Incorporated, for example, attempted a massive rollup of small physician practices in the 1990s. The idea was that MedPartners would take the administrative load off doctors, letting them do the work they were trained for—treating patients—rather than having them be executives running small businesses. MedPartners was also going to introduce procedures that would let doctors handle records much more efficiently. But MedPartners found a complete mess when it tried to integrate all the disparate IT systems of the thousands of practices it acquired. And good luck convincing those irascible, opinionated human beings known as doctors that they should adopt electronic note-taking in the 1990s, when they thought illegible scribbles on paper charts were the state of the art. Imagine trying to tell doctors to follow corporate procedures, when they knew full well that they were acing college while the managers dictating procedures to them were struggling to get by.

MedPartners grew from an annual run rate of $1.2 million in 1993 to $6 billion in 1997 and arranged to sell itself to a rival, but when accountants looked beneath the covers they found that MedPartners had wildly overstated its profitability. A claimed $54 million profit in the third quarter of 1997 was eventually restated as an $840 million loss. MedPartners began scaling back operations. The company proceeded to lose $1.26

billion on $2.6 billion of revenue in 1998—almost 50¢ lost on every dollar taken in. MedPartners then got out of the physician practice–management business altogether.

Sometimes, rollups didn't just discover that the promised efficiencies were missing; they found inefficiencies. In other words, instead of having economies of scale, the rollups found themselves with diseconomies of scale. Solectron Corporation, for instance, thought it could become a well-oiled machine when it attempted a rollup in contract manufacturing for electronics companies. Solectron hoped to expand the array of manufacturing services it could offer and broaden its geographic reach. In practice, Solectron became focused on expanding revenue at any cost. Craig London, Solectron's executive vice president of marketing, strategy, services, and corporate development, said this about Solectron's emphasis on new business: "If the rabbit was running, we shot at it. It didn't matter whether the rabbit had two legs, one leg or three ears. And a lot of the time it turned out to be a skunk."[15]

Solectron underestimated the cost and complexity of the expansion and became less nimble—a bad thing in a business that operates on short turnaround times and demands great agility. Far from being able to focus on a manageable number of small tasks and do them repeatedly, getting better each time—the basis for economies of scale—Solectron found itself having to improvise all the time. Not much efficiency in that. In addition, Solectron had taken on a hugely complex manufacturing system. It was shipping parts back and forth around the world, trying to optimize operations for its customers, who can be highly sensitive both to cost and to speed of delivery. For good measure, many of Solectron's manufacturing facilities were in low-cost countries such as China, where electricity, roads, and other aspects of the infrastructure are iffy and where government bureaucrats can unexpectedly complicate matters. Solectron wound up with a bloated bureaucracy that focused so much on the added capabilities that relations soured with many existing customers. Solectron took more than $4 billion in write-offs in 2002 and 2003 and was later acquired by Flextronics International Limited.

When Northwestern Corporation, historically a provider of electricity and natural gas, tried two rollups simultaneously it, too, found inefficiencies. The company bought twenty-six local phone companies and ninety

HVAC (heating, ventilation, and air-conditioning) companies in the late 1990s and installed a new billing system at the telecom business in a bid for great efficiencies for all the acquired companies. But Northwestern found itself unable to generate any bills for a month. For five months in 2002, many bills were incomplete and inaccurate. It didn't help that Northwestern didn't know anything about either telecom or HVAC, or that Northwestern learned that its long-term relationships with its energy customers didn't make them any more likely to buy phone or HVAC services from Northwestern. In 2002, Northwestern wrote off essentially all of its investments in the telecom and HVAC ventures. The write-offs totaled hundreds of millions of dollars. Northwestern itself, which had been highly profitable as an energy company, filed for bankruptcy-court protection in 2003 with a negative net worth of almost $500 million.

In addition to claiming back-office efficiencies, the rollups we studied generally claimed that their increased size would improve their purchasing power, but they often were proved wrong. Despite all its purchases, Loewen, for instance, never amounted to more than 5 percent of the funeral homes in North America, so it just didn't have much bargaining power.

National Equipment Services Incorporated had similar issues. It bought forty-two equipment-rental companies between 1996 and 2001 with the idea that, among other things, it would increase its purchasing power. The problem was that the equipment-rental industry consisted of twelve thousand companies. Basically, NES went from being a gnat to being a mosquito, maybe a fly, but didn't gain enough size to fundamentally change relations with suppliers. NES also failed to build a national brand, create significant efficiencies in the back office, or provide business-changing advice on best practices to the companies it was buying. An economic downturn created more stress than the business could handle, and NES filed for bankruptcy protection in 2003.

FPA Medical Management, a rollup of physician practices à la MedPartners, also found it didn't get the bargaining power with hospitals and insurers that it expected, even though it peaked at 7,900 doctors treating 1.5 million patients in 29 states. In addition, like MedPartners, FPA found its information systems so overloaded that headquarters could barely function. To try to hide the lack of profitability, FPA increased the pace of its growth, but the haste to make acquisitions led FPA to purchase some lemons. FPA also increased the pace at which it took on debt. The company couldn't handle the stress and filed for bankruptcy in 1998. The CFO was later convicted of committing fraud to hide FPA's lack of cash. He was sentenced to fifty-one months in prison and ordered to pay $36 million in restitution to investors.

Other dynamics can also be at work that make it impossible to assume that size equals power. Compaq Computer Corporation, though not a rollup, provides a stark example.

In the early 1990s, no-name personal-computer start-ups were undercutting the prices of the giants, among them Compaq Computer. Compaq's chairman, legendary venture capitalist Ben Rosen, wondered how that could be, given that Compaq negotiated so hard to get the best prices from component suppliers and should have far more purchasing power than the start-ups. He challenged the CEO, Rod Canion, who had been a seasoned computer-industry executive before cofounding Compaq in 1982 and who had done the seemingly impossible by taking leadership of the PC industry away from the once-untouchable IBM in less than a decade. Canion, a disciplined executive, had done his homework. He showed Rosen how Compaq's component prices compared with those of IBM and other industry leaders and assured Rosen that Compaq was getting the best prices available. But Rosen, who financed Lotus Development Corporation, Compaq, and many other successful PC-industry start-ups, was suspicious.

Working without the knowledge of his friend Canion, Rosen put together a team that would pretend to be a PC start-up and would see what prices they could get. Meeting with suppliers in hotel rooms during the mammoth Comdex computer trade show in Las Vegas in November 1990, the team found it could handily beat the prices Compaq was getting.

Why? Because of the peculiar economics of the computer industry. Let's look at Intel Corporation. To launch a faster generation of central processor, Intel had to build a more advanced manufacturing facility, to allow for ever tinier electronics on the chips, produced in ever more sterile clean rooms. In those days, a new plant cost in the hundreds of millions of dollars. (These days, the plants cost billions of dollars each.) As

Intel negotiated contracts with its major customers, such as Compaq, Intel included the cost of the plant in its calculations. Now, fast-forward a few months into the production of the new generation of chips. Intel has recovered all its fixed costs. It also has become far more efficient at manufacturing the new chips. Initially, almost all production is waste, but a few months later almost every one of these little masterpieces of electronics works perfectly when it comes off the line. Intel, which had negotiated a price of, say, $100 per processor, could now produce each chip for a few dollars. Intel was by now so efficient that it was making many more processors than its major customers had ordered. What to do? It could offer the excess chips at bargain prices to the major customers—but then it would have to cut prices on all the chips, and why do that? Or, Intel could sell the chips in hotel rooms in Las Vegas to start-ups at bargain prices—and still get a markup of five or six times the cost of production—without lowering the prices to big customers. The choice was obvious. The result was at odds with common sense: The companies with the least scale were getting the best prices. And this was true for all PC components: disk drives, memory chips, everything.

When Rosen showed the board that Compaq wasn't close to getting the lowest prices for its components, Canion resigned.

These economics, by the way, can't be dismissed as applying just to computers. They apply to some extent to all electronics products, as well as products with a significant electronic component. In addition, many other industries face versions of this when dealing with excess inventory and with the marginal costs of production. Whatever the particular situation, the point is: Claims of increased purchasing power are open to challenge.

So are claims about the flip side of purchasing power: pricing power. In theory, a company should be able to raise prices as it grows in size and squeezes out the competition. But, sometimes, just enough competition remains and keeps a lid on prices, or customers are obstinate about not paying more, or something else goes wrong.

Loewen found it had pricing power, but not as much as it thought. Loewen and the other funeral-home rollups eventually sparked a backlash in the 1990s that made consumers more cost-conscious and wound up costing Loewen dearly in the lawsuit it lost in Mississippi.

Maxicare Health Plans Incorporated had the same experience a decade earlier. By the end of 1987, Maxicare owned or managed 33 HMOs in 26 states, with a combined enrollment of 2.3 million members, and was the nation's largest for-profit HMO. Maxicare then tried to push through a sharp price increase—and customers left in droves. Maxicare, which also overpaid for acquisitions and lost control of costs, sold off most of its HMOs in 1989 and 1990 and filed for bankruptcy protection in 2001.

Rollups generally assumed their cost of capital would be lower than for smaller entities, but the rollups found this wasn't always the case, either. Maxicare, for instance, had a low cost of capital—until it didn't. Just as its acquisition spree was getting into full swing, Standard & Poor's downgraded some Maxicare debt, and the rollup never again had an advantage in terms of cost of capital.

JWP started off with the kind of great credit rating and low borrowing costs that you'd expect for a long-established, consistently profitable, hopelessly boring water utility. But then JWP went further and further afield. Relying on its expertise with maintenance as a utility, JWP initially moved into maintenance of telephone lines and electrical and lighting systems. Finding itself operating in computer rooms, JWP expanded into computer installation and related technical services. Eventually, JWP moved into the personal-computer retail business, buying Businessland Incorporated in 1991. Over time, JWP's credit rating deteriorated, and it lost its advantage on cost of capital. JWP never achieved much integration of its purchases, and it lacked the expertise to handle problems that cropped up in many of them—for instance, it bought the Businessland computer retailer just as the business was collapsing. JWP filed for bankruptcy protection in 1993.

Some companies, like JWP, compounded the problems in their search for economies of scale by trying to roll up markets with which they weren't familiar. Northern Border Partners was a gas pipeline company, so it thought it was just making a small move up the food chain when it tried a rollup that would let it gather and process the gas that Northern Border's pipelines would then transport. But the company didn't know enough about gathering and processing and overpaid for a series of acquisitions. The company lost hundreds of millions of dollars.

That's all we'll say here on how JWP and others got into trouble by moving into related—but not related enough—markets. We provide a full treatment of how moves into adjacent markets can trip up companies in chapter 5.

Some rollups also made life more difficult for themselves by trying a sort of supermarket approach—essentially attempting a synergy and rollup strategy simultaneously. Rather than roll up lots of physicians practices or telecom companies, they'd buy a lot of companies that, they hoped, would cover all the needs of a particular type of customer. For instance, U.S. Office Products Company tried to serve small to midsize businesses by buying 230 companies across the country that fit into several areas, including office supplies, travel services, coffee, printing, and educational materials. The company was founded in 1994, went public in 1995, had a market value of more than $3 billion in 1998, and went bankrupt in 2001. But we won't focus here on why combining a coffee service with office supplies didn't provide enough synergy to make a large business. We treat that in chapter 1.

Unsustainable Pace

Part of the problem for rollups is that they are searching for efficiencies in the midst of the most inhospitable environment imaginable. Assuming they really want to catch investors' attention, the rollups are growing 100 percent to 1,000 percent a year, at least for the first several years. They're growing by buying a company or two or four a month, and having to go through all the cultural and operational issues that accompany a takeover. Rollups conjure up the classic Silicon Valley definition of a start-up: that of someone jumping out of an airplane without a parachute and having to build a plane around himself before hitting the ground. (The one difference is that, when Silicon Valley start-ups fail, they mostly go unnoticed because they've only burned through a few million dollars of money from venture capitalists, who are almost certain to recoup their money on some other start-up. Rollups typically involve much more money, usually raised in the public markets, because they're buying up established businesses, so their failures are usually much more explosive and take many more people down with them.)

For the first part of a rollup's life, all that matters is growth. Growth,

growth, and more growth. Investors know that the accounting for profitability is going to be hard to decipher, because of all the charges and adjustments that come from integrating lots of businesses, so they focus on the one number that's easy to see: revenue. As long as a rollup keeps growing by leaps and bounds, it's fine.

Senior executives, not being stupid, thus focus on the next deal. They know that, at some point, when the rollup reaches more of a steady state, they'll have to show consistent profitability. But, when in doubt, they're going to spend their time thinking about buying that next company or ten, for at least the first few years.

As a result, the acquisitions can keep coming at a rollup faster than it can handle. Loewen certainly had that problem.

Some companies are so distracted by the emphasis on acquisitions that they never even make much of an attempt to reap their economies of scale. Tyco spent $63 billion acquiring more than one thousand companies between 1994 and 2001 as it tried multiple rollups in home-security alarms, special electronic connectors, fire-protection equipment, and specialized manufacturing. Tyco bought companies so fast that it sometimes bought additional plants in an industry even though other of its plants had excess capacity.

But there was so little emphasis on integrating the acquisitions that headquarters staff was just 250 people. There wasn't even a corporate chief information officer. "These businesses were never deeply integrated," says Chris Coughlin, Tyco's CFO.

The rollup strategy came apart in 2002, and Tyco reported a $9.3 billion loss that contained numerous write-offs—among other problems, at the height of Tyco's acquisition spree, it spent $24 billion to buy businesses that, its financial statements indicate, had a tangible value of just $4 billion. Tyco's market capitalization declined by $90 billion in 2002. Tyco has since spun off its health-care and electronics businesses. Both those companies, plus Tyco itself, announced further plans to unwind much of the rolling up Tyco had done previously.

Execution error, you say? Surely that was part of Tyco's trouble. But Tyco was never going to be able to effectively integrate as many companies as it bought, so it would have needed to scale back its ambitions at the same time it stepped up its focus on integration. (For more on Tyco's other failings, see chapter 2, on financial engineering. We generally limit ourselves to using a company as an example in just one chapter, but Tyco was such a sprawling, spectacular mess that it warrants two looks.)

The speed of acquisition can mean that rollups overlook problems at the companies being bought. They just don't have time to do enough due diligence, especially because sellers can be crafty about hiding problems. DaVita Incorporated, a rollup of dialysis centers, bought a company that led to its reporting $110 million in charges and to coughing up $40 million of bad receivables. (DaVita also found itself unable to collect payments in a timely manner because its information systems couldn't keep pace with its growth.) DaVita narrowly avoided bankruptcy in the late 1990s.

Kent Thiry, who was brought in as CEO to rescue DaVita, says there are limits to how fast a company can grow, partly because managers can only develop their skills so rapidly. "Just because someone can manage a 1,000-person factory doesn't mean he can manage a 5,000-person factory," Thiry says. "Maybe he can grow into that larger role if you give him a year or two, but he won't be able to run that 5,000-person operation immediately." Thiry notes that the mistakes didn't just cost the company and its investors; they also cost the business's managers, almost all of whom he quickly fired. He notes, too, that, once he got the pace of expansion under control, DaVita thrived. As of this writing, it has a market capitalization of more than $5 billion.

When a rollup is in buying mode, everybody knows it. So sellers start asking for steeper and steeper prices. That can mess up the rollup strategy, which may be based on some price standard set when the strategy is formed. In the 1980s, as Gillett Holdings Incorporated and others tried to roll up the market for local television stations, the stations began demanding prices equal to twenty-one times their annual revenue, way up from before the rollups began. Gillett Holdings bought twelve stations in twelve months in the mid-1980s. Ignoring warnings from junk-bond king Michael Milken that it was overpaying, Gillett then purchased Storer Communications Incorporated, which owned six local stations. The high purchase prices led to a debt load that reached $1.2 billion and caused problems almost immediately. In 1991, Gillett filed for bankruptcy. The next year, its principal owner, George Gillett, filed for personal bankruptcy and lost his collection of 30 sports cars and his 235,000-acre ranch in Oregon. (His fortunes have since rebounded through investments in ski resorts.)

Once a company gets going on a rollup, it's hard to stop. After you've promised Wall Street that you're going to triple in size every year for the next five years, you can't just say, "Oops, never mind." Even if you have a good reason—you need time for integration and for due diligence on the next round of purchases, or the prices of acquisition candidates have become impossible—the drop in growth will hammer your stock, and your rollup will fall apart.

The problem is exemplified by a conversation relayed to us by George Churchill, a partner at our former firm, Diamond. The conversation was with the head of strategy at a rollup he was advising. The rollup had just reported a surprisingly strong first quarter in 2007, mostly because the benefits from a major deal kicked in sooner than expected, but the head of strategy looked glum. The conversation went like this:

CHURCHILL: "What's bugging you?"
ROLLUP: "We need to raise expectations for Q2."
CHURCHILL: "Why? I don't see much more coming from [the major deal]. Where are you going to find the growth?"
ROLLUP: "I have no idea."
CHURCHILL: "Then why raise expectations with the Street? Tell them you executed well, and maintain the same targets for Q2 and Q3 so you can continue on the original plan."
ROLLUP: "We can't tell them we no longer believe in the business!"

The rollup did raise expectations and got a nice bump in the stock price. Six months later, the rollup acknowledged that it couldn't meet those expectations. The stock fell below where it had been in the first place.

When the Going Gets Tough

By their very nature, rollups are financial high-wire acts. If companies are purchased with cash, debt piles up. If companies are purchased with stock, the stock price needs to be kept high to keep the string of acquisitions going. Yet strategists often underestimate what relatively small changes in the business environment can do to rollups' borrowing costs or stock price.

All it took to finally, well, bury Loewen was a small decline in the death rate. Because of bad contingency planning, all it took to send Gillett into bankruptcy was a 30 percent decline in the price of television stations over several years. A bit of economic softness was enough to push National Equipment into bankruptcy in 2003. The economic stress associated with the bursting of the dot-com bubble added to the problems at Harter's companies and helped push three of them into bankruptcy in 2001 even though the three—Transportation Components Incorporated, Metals USA Incorporated, and Physicians Resource Group Incorporated—had no ties to the "new economy."

Centralization or Integration, but Not Both

When attempting a rollup, companies face trade-offs between centralization and decentralization. The literature emphasizes the need to centralize, and that's certainly required if rollups are to realize the efficiencies they seek and are to achieve economies of scale. But centralizing can mean lost revenue, at least initially. The guy who ran the local office-supply store before it was rolled up may have long-term relations with his customers. He may know some quirks about how his customers like to place orders and may have worked out some special payment arrangements, to help customers during times of the year when cash flow is poor. Maybe he's a figure of some local prominence—a former star of the high school football team who played a few games in the NFL. Changing the name of his business, running his business from headquarters, and enforcing standardized procedures could chase away some of his customers and cause a drop in revenue, at least in the short term. Certainly, competitors will do everything they can to use the takeover as a way of trying to win away customers, perhaps arguing that locals should support their neighbor's small business rather than some behemoth based thousands of miles away.

The problem for those deciding whether to proceed with a rollup is that the trade-offs are sometimes ignored. Strategists may assume they'll get all the efficiencies that are theoretically possible with a rollup, yet can mitigate or even eliminate any drop in revenue. Booz Allen consultants, while arguing for an "acquisition engine" that will integrate businesses quickly and tightly, insist that rollups "should not tolerate any loss of customers during the transition."[16]

Well, it happens.

Loewen suffered on both sides of the equation. It gave up efficiencies by trying to keep its funeral-home operators in place and letting the businesses run much as they always had. At the same time, as Loewen found in Mississippi, competitors will use a rollup as a reason to try to steal customers—though few, it's true, will go to the lengths of portraying a quiet Canadian company as a Japanese company that should be shunned because of World War II.

Tough Questions

We'll phrase these in terms that operating executives might use, but note that potential investors in a rollup should be asking themselves variants of almost all these questions. Many of these questions may seem obvious, because they're the sort that ought to be covered in any due diligence. But the questions need to be asked, and with more than the usual urgency. The questioning needs to be colored by the fact that so many rollups have failed; the assumption should be that the rollup won't work, unless there is compelling evidence to the contrary.

Because of the potential for diseconomies of scale, you need to look for all the areas where complexity will hinder your ability to act efficiently and, before you plunk down the money for acquisitions, try to quantify what those inefficiencies will cost you. Will your information systems break down, à la FPA and DaVita, if you increase the size of your business by a factor of one hundred, or whatever the right number is? What other systems might break down? How much of senior management's time is going to go to putting out fires, to coordinating activities, and so on?

Don't just think about the long term, either. You need to ask yourself how much business you'll lose in the short run, as competitors use the confusion associated with a takeover to try to poach your business. Ask yourself what you'd do to attack your business, if you were a competitor.

If you're moving into a regulated industry, you need to look carefully at what regulations might change and how they'd affect the business. It's easy to get blindsided when you're a newbie.

You also need to cast a skeptical eye on all the economies of scale that you're expecting. You may think your cost of capital will decline, but will it really? By how much? How do you know? You may decide that your pricing power will increase, but why? Be specific about how much you think you'll be able to raise prices, by product and market. See if there isn't some way to test your assumption before going ahead with the rollup. Do the same with purchasing power. Try to predict how much you'll save on each supply or service you buy. If possible, test your assumptions. Be skeptical.

What will you have to spend, both in time and money, to get the efficiencies you expect from a takeover? Remember that many companies say they'll achieve integration quickly yet, years later, are still working on the issues.

Try to identify who has a vested interest in keeping you from achieving all the efficiencies you expect. Also, list those important players, such as the recalcitrant doctors at MedPartners, who may have habits that aren't easy to change.

Given that rollups often require an unsustainably fast rate of acquisitions, you need to start looking for problems before you even start. Estimate what percentage of your acquisitions will have significant problems. Make a prediction and debate it. Then track what the actual number turns out to be and, if necessary, adjust your prediction as time goes on. Ask yourself how much prices of acquisitions will rise over time, as your rollup intentions become clear. If others are rolling up the industry, too, or might follow your lead, then you need to assume even greater price increases. Decide ahead of time what the maximum price is that you'll pay based on cash flow, earnings, revenue, or whatever—and stick to that maximum. Otherwise, you'll wind up like Loewen, buying everything in sight.

Because just about every rollup has a hiccup or two along the way, you need to be explicit about just how big a hit you can withstand. If you're financing the rollup with debt, what will happen to you if you have a 10 percent decline in cash flow for two years? Twenty percent? Fifty percent? If you're buying companies with stock, what do you do if the stock price drops by 50 percent?

Given the history of fraud in rollups, you also need to be sure you've thought about how to prevent people from cooking the books when the bad times come.

If you're counting on getting full benefits from both decentralization and integration, you need to think again. If you're going to leave local management in place, you need to discount the gains you expect to get from integration. Local managers typically don't completely buy into the rollup's processes or don't have the business acumen to fully implement the processes, so integration will suffer. On the other hand, if you're planning to replace local managers in the name of efficiency and of having everyone buy into your processes, then you need to assume some loss of revenue. You should, of course, do everything you can to prevent any loss of revenue, but you'll still lose some; the prior local managers of the business surely have some connections and have some expertise about the local market, or they wouldn't have survived as long as they did. You also have to realize that if you're going to try to guarantee no loss of business, you need to account for costs elsewhere because you'll get drawn into offering discounts to keep customers who are on the fence and may even start a price war.

Finally, when is enough enough? In other words, what is the end game? How big do you need to get? Can you, in fact, stop?

If you look at all the answers to these questions and still decide to proceed, then ask yourself: How slowly can I go (given that many of a rollup's problems typically come from excessive speed)? Do you have to be a national rollup, or would a regional one make more sense? If you need to be national, can you at least start as a regional rollup to work out the kinks? At what point are you going to double back and check on the assumptions you've made about efficiencies, pricing power, and everything else?

If you can slog through all the questions, designed to provoke qualms, and still come away enthusiastic about your rollup, then good luck to you.

FOUR

Staying the (Misguided) Course

Threat? What Threat?

Aviation investigators have a euphemism: "controlled flight into terrain." What they mean is that a pilot took a perfectly functioning plane, in good conditions, and flew it into the ground, usually the side of a hill or a mountain.

Executives sometimes do this, too. They, like the pilots, have warning signs that they're about to crash, but they do it anyway.

Obviously, no one intends to crash, whether you're talking about a plane or a business. But executives can kid themselves into thinking that a problem isn't as severe as it really is or delay any reaction for so long that, before they know it, they're face-to-face with that mountain.

Our research found numerous examples. We found retailers that could see Wal-Mart coming after them with its low, low prices but failed to react. We saw manufacturers fail to grasp how much outsourcing to China and other developing countries would restructure their industries. We saw loads of technology companies that didn't see that they were about to become obsolete.

In most cases, executives told themselves that they were making needed improvements to their core businesses, that they were staying the course. In fact, they were just tinkering as a way of staying in denial about a threat that put that very business in doubt. Executives were rearranging the proverbial deck chairs on the *Titanic.*

It isn't that the coming problems were hard to discern. They were evident to outsiders. But insiders couldn't quite fathom that their very existence could be threatened, usually after a long history of success. When problems became apparent to those in the trenches, information about them got filtered out before reaching those who were in a position to address them. Even when the problems crystallized for those in the executive suite, managers sometimes held on to the old business as long as possible, temporizing to preserve profit margins in the short term rather than make some drastic move that could address the long term. And even if everyone up and down the line saw the problem, it was still hard to see the solution. That's because it's hard to explore options that attack core assumptions and values, such as those about what customers are actually buying, where profit comes from, the business model, and the very notion of being an independent, growth-oriented company. The solution in the cases we unearthed often would have been to sell the company or go out of business—if you're a paging company, and cell phones are about to supersede you, there isn't much you can do about it—but winding down a business is the last thing an executive would consider doing. Selling at a distressed price isn't far behind as an unpleasant option.

Our research didn't find as many examples for this chapter as for others, but we still believe that ignoring a threat is a very common problem that needs to be addressed. We believe the relative paucity of examples stems partly from the nature of corporate reporting. Companies report what they did, not what they didn't do. So finding errors of omission is inherently harder than finding errors of commission. In addition, even when companies seemed to ignore threats for too long, we sometimes used those examples elsewhere. Under pressure, companies almost invariably took *some* action, and they sometimes made mistakes that seemed to fit better in other chapters.

A study published in 2004 found that just about every company is in danger of ignoring imminent threats. In the study, only 17 percent of managers felt that their company would react quickly enough and aggressively enough to a structural change in their industry that constituted a major threat. Some 20 percent said their companies were the embodiment of "paralysis by analysis." Roughly 16 percent said their companies would decide that the crisis would disappear; therefore, the companies wouldn't even discuss the possibility of trouble. Almost 39 percent said their companies would take action, but said the action would be too slow and too late. Because of this lack of forceful action, 92 percent of those surveyed said their company had recently been surprised by at least one event that could affect their organization's long-term positioning.

Another study, published in 2007, found that 60 percent of executives felt their primary source of competitive advantage was eroding. Some 65 percent said they needed to fundamentally restructure their business model. Roughly 72 percent said their main competitor five years down the road would likely be different from the main competitor at the time of the survey.

Research published in 2003 found that major slumps in earnings are becoming more common. The research, by Gary Hamel and Liisa Valikangas, found that in each year from 1973 through 1977, an average of thirty-seven Fortune 500 companies were entering or in the midst of a five-year, 50 percent decline in net income. From 1993 to 1997, the average number of companies suffering through such an earnings contraction had more than doubled, to eighty-four, even though the United States was smack in the middle of the longest economic boom in modern times.[1]

The lessons that come out of the cases in this chapter, for how to face up to an imminent threat, should be useful to many, whether at the top levels of a business or in middle management, because, it seems, we're all always in danger of ignoring approaching peril.

The story of Eastman Kodak shows just how devastating it can be when a company reacts too slowly—and just how hard it is to react, even when the threat is blatantly obvious. Kodak failed to avoid the digital-photography revolution even though Kodak had made a detailed (and accurate) analysis of the threat as far back as 1981, according to material provided by our friend Vince Barabba, who was an executive at Kodak at the time (and who provides considerable additional detail in his book *Surviving Transformation*). Kodak kept its plane on autopilot until it flew into the side of the mountain.

Kodak: Focusing on the Negatives

Kodak has been an American institution for more than a century. Its bright yellow boxes have delivered vivid memories of the most important moments in people's lives. The time when a loved one is being unbearably cute even goes by the name "a Kodak moment." As a company, Kodak thrived for more than a century. It was part of the "Nifty Fifty," a group of stocks that were known as sure bets and that soared in the 1960s and 1970s, and the company prospered into the 1990s. Kodak, together with Xerox Corporation, pretty much built an entire American city, Rochester, New York. The company was such an icon that Neil Armstrong took a roll of Kodak's Ektachrome film to the moon with him in 1969.

Kodak was started by an enterprising young man named George Eastman. He was a bank clerk in Rochester in the late 1870s and was planning a vacation to Santo Domingo. A coworker suggested he take photos. Eastman bought a camera, film, and the chemicals and equipment needed to develop the images. But the system was too bulky. Eastman promptly canceled his travel plans and spent his vacation trying to find a way to make photography more convenient.

Although we tend to think of photography as some semimagical, modern phenomenon—what could be more hip than snapping a friend's picture with a cell phone and e-mailing it around?—the roots of photography actually reach into antiquity. A Chinese philosopher named Mozi mentioned in the fifth century B.C. that it was possible to use a pinhole to let light project an image onto a small, flat surface. Aristotle showed that he also grasped the idea in the fourth century B.C. In the fifteenth century A.D., Leonardo da Vinci became the first to describe a pinhole device, which he called a *camera obscura*, Latin for "dark chamber"; he was careful to note on his drawing that the idea was "not invented by us." People sometimes used the devices so they could draw an image accurately. It took centuries to figure out the processes that allowed for images to be captured chemically, but as far back as the Civil War those processes were already two decades old. Photography was in its second generation and was in wide use.

The system Eastman bought used wet chemicals on a glass plate to capture an image, but Eastman eventually found a description of a simpler, dry process used in England. He spent his evenings after work trying to replicate the process in his mother's kitchen. After three years, Eastman was satisfied that he had a dry-plate process that worked. He obtained a patent and founded the Eastman Dry Plate Company in 1881. Cautiously, he initially kept his day job at the bank, but sales were strong enough that he quit later that year to work full-time on his company.

Eastman Dry Plate innovated in various processes that let it produce film plates more efficiently, but Eastman saw that, as far out there as photography was technologically, plates were becoming a commodity business. (A saying in the technology world is that "it can take hundreds of PhDs to develop a product that eventually gets priced like bushels of corn.") Eastman also saw that the dry-plate process was still awfully cumbersome. Cameras were huge. The glass plates were heavy—and eminently breakable. It took considerable resources, time, and expense to transfer images from the film to paper. Photography was limited to professionals and serious amateurs such as Eastman.

So Eastman developed paper film that could be sold in a roll, greatly cutting the weight and expense of film. The rolls of paper film couldn't match the quality of the glass plates, so serious photographers shunned paper film. Rather than give up, though, he saw the potential for the paper film in an untapped mass market: rank amateurs.

In 1888, Eastman introduced the Kodak camera. (Eastman, who thought *K* was a strong letter, came up with the name with his mother at her kitchen table using an anagram set, a popular game of the time.) The camera sold for $25 and came with one hundred frames of film. A buyer would take the pictures, then send the whole camera to Eastman Dry Plate, which would develop the film and send the camera back, loaded with a fresh roll of film. Eastman Dry Plate charged $10 for developing. The system was an immediate hit. Demand for the cameras and its film was so strong that the company struggled for a decade to keep up.

Some competitors sniffed at the inferior quality of the paper film, which soon morphed into the sort of celluloid film that is still available today. Rather than switch to rolls, the companies tried to improve on glass-plate technology. One, for instance, tried to simulate the convenience of rolls of film by inventing a device that carried twenty plates. After a plate was exposed, a mechanical arm would remove it and replace it with a fresh plate. The mechanical device was huge and awkward and never could have competed with paper film. Companies that focused on improving glass plates continued to serve the professional market for fifteen to twenty years, and sales were steady, but the companies missed out on all of the phenomenal growth in the photography market and eventually faded away.

Despite the original Kodak's success, Eastman Dry Plate quickly replaced it. The company introduced the "No. 1" camera, which incorporated a simplified shutter system and other redesigns that reduced manufacturing costs. In 1898, Eastman introduced the first of his series of "Brownie" cameras. These sold for just $1 each. Rolls of film were 15¢.

Eastman cemented his lead. By 1902, Eastman's company, renamed Eastman Kodak to acknowledge the role of the Kodak camera, sold 80 percent to 90 percent of the world's celluloid film.

A threat emerged in the early 1900s, when German inventors began producing color film. The quality didn't come close to matching that of existing black-and-white film, but Eastman didn't repeat the mistake many glass-plate makers had committed. He didn't dismiss the incipient technology. He was convinced that it would eventually render black-and-white film obsolete. He carefully monitored the Germans' process and invested heavily in research and development at his own labs. He failed repeatedly, but eventually, in the 1920s, he came out with a high-quality color film. Eastman maintained his stranglehold on the film market.

The market for film stayed stable for decades, though not as many decades as you might think. The march toward digital photography began way back in 1951 in a laboratory set up by Bing Crosby. The lab found a way to capture images digitally on videotape. The research was aimed at the new market for television, but capturing bits is capturing bits. The basic means for taking digital still photographs had been uncovered.

In the 1960s, NASA improved the technology to allow for transmission of pictures from space. It used the growing power of computers to enhance the images. Work on spy satellites furthered the development of digital photography. By 1972, Texas Instruments Incorporated had patented a filmless electronic camera. In 1981, Sony Corporation introduced the first commercial electronic camera, the Mavica. The race was on.

Shortly before the Mavica's introduction, Kodak's various partners—photo finishers and film retailers—became worried enough about the long-term viability of film that they asked Kodak what the future held. Kodak, which had already been working on digital technology in its labs, conducted a thorough review by challenging technical and market assumptions and determined that, until 1990:

- "The quality of prints from electronic images will not be generally acceptable to consumers as replacement for prints based on the science of photography," by which Kodak meant traditional film and prints.
- "The consumer's desire to handle, display, and distribute prints cannot be replaced by electronic display devices."
- "The incompatibility of electronic-imaging systems to the full range of VCR and video disc devices in the market will be a barrier to widespread amateur acceptance of those systems." In other words, even if consumers didn't have a strong preference for prints, it was going to be hard to hook the cameras up to electronic displays.
- "In-home, personal electronic print systems will not be competitive in terms of price and quality with commercial print-making services."
- "Electronic systems (camera and viewing input device for TV) will not be low enough in price to have widespread appeal."

In sum, Kodak decided that traditional film and prints would continue to dominate through the 1980s and that photo finishers, film retailers, and, of course, Kodak itself could expect to continue to occupy their long-held positions until 1990.

Kodak was right—and wrong.

Everything Kodak said about the 1980s was correct. Digital cameras, electronic displays, and printers still didn't work well enough to pose a threat to Kodak, the photo finishers, and film retailers. The new devices were also too expensive.

But the game didn't end at the close of the 1980s. In fact, the game was just starting. In the next decade, numerous technologies came together to erode, or even erase, the advantages of traditional film. The quality of digital cameras greatly improved. Prices plunged because the cameras generally followed Moore's Law, the famous prediction by Intel cofounder Gordon Moore in the 1960s that the cost of a unit of computing power would fall by 50 percent every eighteen to twenty-four months. Cameras began to be equipped with what the industry called removable media—those little cards that hold the pictures—so pictures were easier to print or to move to other devices, such as computers. Printers improved. Their costs dropped, too. The Internet caught the popular imagination, and people began e-mailing each other pictures rather than print them. Companies sprang up that let people post pictures on Web sites, again obviating the need to print them.

Many Kodak senior managers used the 1981 assessment to hold to their beliefs, formed long before the study was conducted, that the company could ride out the storm. While Kodak had identified all the relevant factors affecting how quickly digital technology would be adopted, managers' interpretation of the assessment allowed them to reinforce their strongly held beliefs rather than to point out what to watch out for.

Kodak's labs spent the 1980s doing some research on digital technology, but without much enthusiasm. Steven J. Sasson, an engineer who invented the first digital camera at Kodak in the 1970s, told the *New York Times* that his bosses were dismayed at the prospects. "It was filmless photography," he said, "so management's reaction was, 'that's cute—but don't tell anyone about it.' " In 1986, it produced the first working version of the type of sensor that is at the core of today's digital cameras. But despite having a solid decade following 1981, Kodak did not take advantage of its early warning and did little to ready itself for the onslaught of digital technology because it consistently tried to hold on to the profits from its old technology and underestimated the speed with which the new would take hold. Kodak decided it could use digital technology to enhance film, rather than replace it. Kodak decided it could tinker with its business model but didn't need to overhaul it or replace it. In the process, Kodak just ensured that it would be neither fish nor fowl.

In fact, Kodak made the very mistake that George Eastman had avoided twice. He gave up a profitable dry-plate business to move quickly to film. He also moved rapidly to color film, even though it was demonstrably inferior to black-and-white for almost twenty years.

Instead of preparing for the digital world, Kodak headed off in a direction that cost it dearly. In 1988, Kodak bought Sterling Drug for $5.1 billion. In one of those classic semantic leaps that we describe in chapter 5 on ill-fated moves into adjacent markets, Kodak had decided it was really a chemicals business, not a photography company. So, Kodak reasoned, it should move into adjacent chemical markets, such as drugs. Well, chemically treated photo paper really isn't that similar to hormonal agents and cardiovascular drugs. The customers are different. The delivery channels are different. The regulatory environment is different. The approach to research and development is different.

Kodak lost its shirt. It sold Sterling in pieces in 1994 for about half the original purchase price.

With the diversification failing, and with worries about the digital-photography threat growing, Kodak's board had a chance to take a stand in 1990 when longtime CEO Colby Chandler retired. The choices to replace him came down to Phil Samper and Kay Whitmore. Whitmore represented the traditional film business, where he had moved up the ranks for three decades. Samper had a deep appreciation for digital technology and what it could do for photography. The board chose Whitmore. (Samper demonstrated his grasp of the digital world by heading off to be president of Sun Microsystems Incorporated, then CEO of Cray Research Incorporated.)

Whitmore lasted all of three years, before the board fired him in 1993. This time, the board went for a technologist and, amid much hoopla, hired George M. C. Fisher. Fisher had a spectacular run as CEO of Motorola Incorporated and was being talked about as one of the great executives of all time. Roberto C. Goizueta, a Kodak director who was chairman of Coca-Cola Company, said of Fisher's hiring: "When we began this search, our No. 1 candidate was God, and we stepped down from that."[2]

Fisher promised to carry Kodak into the digital world. But most of Kodak didn't want to go there. Fisher said in an interview, in the paraphrase of a *New York Times* reporter, that Kodak "regarded digital photography as the enemy, an evil juggernaut that would kill the chemical-based film and paper business that had fueled Kodak's sales and profits for decades."[3] Profit margins on the existing business were far greater than in the digital world. Why the hurry to change?

Fisher's solution was to hold on to the film business as long as possible, while adding a technological veneer to it. For instance, he introduced the Advantix Preview camera, a hybrid of digital and film technology. Users took pictures the way they always had, and the images were captured on film. But, because the camera was at its core digital, a display on the back let users immediately see the picture they'd taken. Users would then decide whether they wanted that image printed and would press buttons that would instruct the photoprocessor on how many images of that photo to print. In other words, a customer was buying a fully digital camera but was also going to pay Kodak for rolls of film. There was no benefit to the consumer. Once you've captured an image electronically, there's no need for the film. Kodak spent more than $500 million developing Advantix, which flopped.

Trying to move Kodak's traditional retail photoprocessing systems into the digital world, Fisher installed tens of thousands of Image Magic kiosks. Customers could use the kiosks to view images they'd stored online, then enhance them and print them. These kiosks came just as numerous companies introduced inexpensive, high-quality photo printers that people could use at home, which, in fact, is where customers preferred to view their images and fiddle with them. Another flop.

Fisher also tried to insert Kodak as an intermediary in the process of sharing images electronically. He formed partnerships that let customers receive electronic versions of their photos by e-mail and gave them access to kiosks that let them manipulate and reproduce old photographs. Yet customers can, of course, do those sorts of things without Kodak's blessing. You don't need Kodak to upload photos to your computer and e-mail them. You don't need Kodak to remove the red-eye from photos; any software package can do that these days. Fisher also formed a partnership with AOL called "You've Got Pictures." Customers would have their film developed and posted online, where friends and family could view them. Customers would pay AOL $7 for this privilege, on top of the $9 paid for the photoprocessing. But why pay AOL $7 when sites such as Snapfish were allowing pictures to be posted online free? And who needs photoprocessing, anyway?

Sure, in the early days of a technology, customers will pay for handholding and for services that they haven't yet figured out how to do for themselves. But there's a long history in the technology world of people moving up the learning curve and doing things for themselves that they used to pay others to do for them. Look at AOL, which provided a sort of Internet for newbies and which has struggled for years as those newbies have grown in confidence and learned to venture online on their own. There's also a long history of products that were once sold separately that are now essentially free. Look at the word-processing software and spreadsheets for personal computers that sold for several hundred dollars apiece in the 1980s and that now come bundled with a new computer. Look at all the early PC software add-ons, such as calculators and calendars, that have long since been absorbed into the operating system.

Fisher promised early on that Kodak's digital-photography business would be profitable by 1997. It wasn't. For good measure, Kodak's rivals in the traditional film business started a price war that caught Fisher by surprise. Kodak, the film industry's high-cost producer, laid off nineteen thousand employees, more than 20 percent of its workforce.

As it happens, another fateful event took place in 1997: Philippe Kahn's wife had a baby.

Kahn, a serial entrepreneur, found himself with some time on his hands while sitting in a hospital while his wife was in labor. Kahn had been a story in the early days of the personal computer because he founded Borland Incorporated, which provided software development tools. He had famously founded the company while an unemployed mathematician and illegal immigrant from France. The way he tells the story, the U.S. government eventually caught up with him and talked about kicking him out of the country, then realized he employed several hundred well-paid Americans and decided to give him a green card instead. After Borland ran into problems, Kahn founded Starfish Software Incorporated, which provided synchronization capabilities for wireless devices. Then, as he sat in the hospital thinking about the pictures he was going to take with his digital camera, he wondered why he had to take them back to his computer to upload them and send them around. Why couldn't he just send them straight from his cell phone? Over the next few days, Kahn jerry-rigged a system to do just that. The cell phone camera was born.

Kodak didn't just lose out on more prints. The whole industry lost out on sales of digital cameras, because they became just a feature that was given away free on cell phones. Soon cameras became a free feature on many personal computers, too.

With the move to digital now fully under way, Kodak and Fisher had run into what some in the technology world call "the Las Vegas business model." The name comes from the fact that it's hard to be just a hotel or a restaurant in Las Vegas, because the casinos are happy to give rooms and food away if it'll increase their gambling revenue. You can have a great hotel or a great restaurant, but it's hard to compete with free.

What had been so profitable for Kodak for so long—capturing images and displaying them—was going to become essentially free. Yes, people had to buy the initial devices: the cameras and cell phones. But then the ability to share images was going to be provided by companies other than Kodak at no additional charge, as part of Internet and cell phone services.

It's not as though Kodak didn't have any warning. *BusinessWeek* wrote this in 1997:

"While Fisher is still struggling to reinvent Kodak as a digital company, serious questions remain about whether that business . . . can ever pan out."

Fortune wrote this even earlier, in 1995:

"The conversion from film to electronics may take 30 years or ten years or (watch out!) five years. . . . Hardware prices will fall enough to make digital imaging as common as home computers. . . . Fisher's goal is to make sure Kodak can survive the ambush, whenever it comes. Not an easy task. Some 45 percent of the company's $13.5 billion in revenue and 75 percent of its profits come from traditional photography in North America. That means Kodak's biggest profit maker will be at ground zero when digital competition strikes."

Fisher's response in the article? "But Kodak has to grow."

And yet it didn't. Kodak's revenue today is about equal to the 1997 total of $13.41 billion.

Fisher stepped down as CEO at the end of 1999, at age sixty, with a year to go on his employment contract, amid speculation that the board pushed him out the door.

Fisher vociferously denied that he was asked to go and argued that he had done everything he could to position Kodak for the digital future. When he was reminded that he'd promised that Kodak's digital-photography operations would be profitable by 1997, yet racked up $100 million in losses in 1999, Fisher replied combatively: "You call it losses. I call it investment."[4]

The new CEO was Daniel Carp, a Kodak lifer who had been with the company twenty-nine years and had no background in technology. Carp, like Fisher before him, came in with grand promises. The 2000 annual report bragged about all the prospects for digital photography, a category Kodak named with the clunky neologism "infoimaging." The report described infoimaging as a $225 billion-a-year market and claimed that Kodak technology "touched" 75 percent of all images on the Web and is "the catalyst for value creation for virtually every company who produces info-imaging products and services." Carp vowed that Kodak's sales would grow 8 percent to 12 percent a year and that profit would climb 10 percent annually for the following five years. Carp's worst-case scenario, as laid out for *Forbes*, was that the photography world would go digital much faster than Kodak anticipated, in which case profit would rise "only" 8 percent a year.[5]

Didn't happen. In 2000, Carp's first year as CEO, profit was about flat, at $1.41 billion. Then profit plunged 95 percent, to $76 million in 2001. That's about what profit averaged from 2002 through 2005, when Carp, too, retired early, at age fifty-seven.

Carp had pursued Fisher's basic strategy of "enhancing" the film business to make it last as long as possible, while trying to figure out some way to get recurring revenue from the filmless, digital world. But the temporizing didn't work any better for Carp than it had for Fisher.

Kodak talked, for instance, about getting customers to digitize and upload to the Internet more of the 300 million rolls of film that Kodak processed annually, as of 2000. Instead, customers increasingly skipped the film part. In 2002, sales of digital cameras in the United States passed those of traditional cameras—even though Kodak in the mid-1990s had projected that it would take twenty years for digital technology to eclipse film. The move to digital in the 2000s happened so fast that, in 2004, Kodak introduced a film camera that won a "camera of the year" award, yet was discontinued by the time Kodak collected the award.

Kodak staked out a position as one of the major sellers of digital cameras, but being "one of" is a lot different from owning 70 percent to 80 percent of a market, as Kodak had with film, chemicals, and processing. Besides, Kodak expected gross profit margins of just 15 percent on digital products, versus the 60 percent it enjoyed on its traditional film, paper, and chemicals. In 2002, competition in the digital market was so intense that Kodak was losing $60 on every $400 camera it sold.[6]

There are signs that growth is already slowing in sales of digital cameras. The ubiquity of cell phone cameras is cutting into sales of the low-end, snapshot cameras that would find their way into a pocket or a purse. Meanwhile, quality has increased so much at the high end that many people have as much camera as they'll ever need and aren't tempted to upgrade each time a camera comes out with more megapixels. In addition, customers are more often sharing images by e-mailing them or sending them to a friend's cell phone, without ever printing the images. After all, there's only so much room on your refrigerator for photos of your nieces and nephews; you can get a chuckle out of the photo of six-month-old Johnny with sand all over his face without printing it and giving it primo refrigerator space.

Under Carp, Kodak bought Ofoto, which lets customers post photos online in the hopes of selling prints to them or their friends. But others staked out the territory long before Kodak, so Ofoto is just one among many.

Carp stayed hopeful to the end. When a reporter suggested to Carp that Kodak might sell itself to Yahoo! or Hewlett-Packard, Carp glared and said, in essence, "Over my dead body."[7] In 2003, Carp said, "People are no longer saying film is dead. That's a major change. . . . There are still ways to expand the life of film and expand the category. . . . Investors now see digital really evolving, but it's not an on/off switch."[8] In 2005, accepting an award from the Business Council of New York State, Carp said he had successfully managed Kodak's transition from film to digital, a challenge that he described as "the most liberating, most exhilarating and most enriching phase in my career."

Except that he hadn't managed the transition, at least not according to his successor, Antonio Perez. Perez took over from Carp in May 2005 and promptly instituted what he called a four-year plan to make that very transition.

In all, Kodak has lost 75 percent of its stock-market value over the past decade, falling to a level about half of what it was when the reporter suggested to Carp that he might sell the company. As of 2005, Kodak employed less than a third of the number who worked for it twenty years earlier.

We're not saying Kodak's situation was easy. Far from it. We're just saying Kodak could have handled its situation much better. It could have sold itself in the 1980s or 1990s at a far higher valuation than it now has, and let the acquirer deal with the switch to digital technology. Kodak could have streamlined operations aggressively, not piecemeal. Kodak could have milked all the cash possible from its business, while winding down the traditional film business. Kodak could have moved faster into the digital world, capturing a greater share of sales of cameras and printers and, perhaps, the revenue from picture Web sites and cell phone cameras—surely, Kodak's labs had access to the same technology that Philippe Kahn did.

To see what might have been, look at Kodak's principal competitors in the film and paper markets. Agfa temporized on digital technology, then sold its film and paper business to private-equity investors in 2004. The business went into bankruptcy proceedings the following year, but that wasn't Agfa's problem. It had cashed out at a halfway reasonable price. Fuji did even better. It gave up its old business and moved into the digital world. By the end of 2003, for instance, the company's traditional products—film, paper, and chemicals—accounted for just 42 percent of revenue, compared with 61 percent at Kodak. In the process of attacking the digital world, Fuji developed technologies that were fundamental to flat-screen displays, which have been in great demand as they have become popular both as computer monitors and as televisions. In that same decade when Kodak lost three-fourths of its market value, Fuji's market value *increased*.

RED FLAGS

As Kodak demonstrated ably, companies that face a looming threat often make three mistakes:

- They tend to see the future as a variant of the present and can't bring themselves to imagine truly radical threats, the kind that might wipe out their whole market.
- They tend to consider whether to adopt a new technology or business practice based on how the economics compare with those of the existing business—not accounting for the possibility that the new technology or approach to business will eventually kill the economics of the existing business and require an entirely new business model.
- They tend not to consider all their options. They focus on shoring up the existing business and ignore the possibility that perhaps they should sell that business or at least cut back significantly.

The Future as a Variant of the Present

Even though Kodak saw the threat from digital photography clearly, more than twenty-five years ago, executives never quite internalized how severe that threat was. They had grown up with prints. They loved prints and the bright yellow boxes they came in. They assumed everyone loved prints as much as they did. So what they saw when they looked at the digital threat was a world that, while changed, would still be centered on prints.

They could imagine that people might want to make some prints on their own, at home. They could imagine that people might want to avoid the waste of printing bad photos. They could imagine that people wanted better prints, without red-eye, cropped as they pleased, with exactly the right lighting.

What Kodak couldn't imagine was a world where images were evanescent expressions, sent as a lark via e-mail or cell phone and never printed. Kodak executives couldn't fathom a world where images became the wallpaper on a cell phone or computer screen but never touched paper, or where lots of images were uploaded to a Web site and viewed but never turned into 4" × 6" chemically coated glossy pieces.

That Kodak saw the future as a variant of the present is why the company came up with its neither-fish-nor-fowl strategy, in which it assumed digital was just a new way of producing prints rather than potentially a powerfully different animal altogether. Viewing the world through the prism of prints is why Kodak consistently underestimated the speed with which digital would overtake film and prints.

The music industry has made the same sort of mistake, by assuming for the longest time that people would buy full CDs (including the dog songs that nobody liked) and do it through traditional distribution channels. The industry couldn't envision a world in which Steve Jobs ruled, in which songs could be purchased individually for less than $1, and in which the only distribution channel that was needed was a cord to connect your iPod to your computer.

While not all the details about the industry's transformation had been clear—especially the Steve Jobs part—it had been apparent for years that music was vulnerable, because it was just a stream of information like many others whose profitability had been attacked by the Internet. We personally warned the number two executive at a large, privately held music distributor whom we interviewed for a report we published in 1997 because we were stunned to see how blasé he was about what the Internet could do to his business within a few years. (We promised anonymity at the time, so we won't name him or the company here, either.)

Because most music companies are part of conglomerates, it's hard to demonstrate just how profoundly the industry has been hit, but here are three data points: 1) Music industry revenue fell 15 percent in 2007 even though digital downloads rose 45 percent;[9] 2) The company whose senior executive we interviewed has since gone public and records well north of $1 billion in sales each year but, as of this writing, carries a market valuation of less than $30 million; 3) The executive we interviewed has long since left the company.

Leaving aside the world of technology, Safeway Incorporated was also guilty of seeing the future as a version of the present when it made disastrous acquisitions in the 1990s. Wal-Mart had already entered the grocery business. It had been identified as the catalyst in twenty-five of the latest twenty-nine bankruptcies of retail chains,[10] and it was establishing itself as a monster in groceries. Its ruthless pressure to cut costs let it push prices so low that few could compete. Yet Safeway followed the traditional grocery-industry approach of trying to spread its geographic reach and wipe out competitors so it could increase prices, rather than find some way to either compete with Wal-Mart on price or differentiate itself through quality, service, or some other means. Safeway bought Dominick's Supermarkets Incorporated and Randall's Food Markets Incorporated for $4 billion in the late 1990s to expand its geographic reach. Safeway later wrote off some $2.4 billion related to the acquisitions.

Our favorite bit of wishful thinking came from Jamie Kellner, chairman and CEO of Turner Broadcasting System Incorporated, in 2002. Rather than accept that TiVo and other digital video recorders were forever changing the traditional model of TV ads, Kellner fought a rearguard action, telling viewers: "Your contract with the [TV] network when you get the show is you're going to watch the spots. Otherwise you couldn't get the show on an ad-supported basis. Anytime you skip a commercial . . . you're actually stealing the programming."

Kellner briefly relented: "I guess there's a certain amount of tolerance for going to the bathroom."[11]

Making the New Measure Up to the Economics of the Old

If Kodak had been starting from scratch, it would have salivated at the prospects for digital photography. It would be able to sell cameras in all forms, from inserts in cell phones and personal computers on up through professional models with expensive, interchangeable lenses. Kodak could sell printers and software that let people enhance their photos before printing them. Kodak could sell prints.

But, compared with the traditional film business, digital was never going to measure up. Digital wasn't going to deliver the 60 percent gross margins that were possible in film, paper, and chemicals—especially when digital was in the early stages and Kodak was *losing* $60 on every $400 camera it sold. The biggest problem was that there wasn't recurring revenue. Once you sold a camera and maybe a printer to a customer, you were pretty much done.

So Kodak fell into a trap. It continued to make short-term evaluations on profitability and slowed its move into digital, rather than bite the bullet and either move to a totally new, digital business model or sell the company.

This is a common trap. Clay Christensen, Stephen P. Kaufman, and Willy Shih wrote in *Harvard Business Review* that widely used financial tools, designed for tough analysis, actually lead companies into this trap. For instance, the authors say companies often ask whether a move into a new business will leave the company better off or worse off. The problem is that the analysis almost always assumes that the business will maintain a steady state, absent any change in strategy—not that the business will plummet because of the sort of fundamental challenge that digital photography poses. Ignoring the likelihood of a significant decline, if nothing is done, encourages companies to avoid radical change.

Studies find that securities analysts reinforce this trap. They all develop a basic financial model for an industry, and they aren't quite sure what to do when companies stray from that model, as they must if they're trying to make a switch like the one from film to digital technology. So analysts tend to punish companies when they move into uncharted territory. If companies pay too much attention to analysts, they can become even more likely to hold on to a dying business model for too long.[12]

Polaroid Corporation fell into the same trap that Kodak did. While product managers were enthusiastic about the prospects for digital photography in the early 1990s—they figured they, of all people, should own the market for truly instant images—senior executives wondered why they would trade the 60 percent gross margins of their existing business for what they calculated as the 38 percent margins they could get selling digital hardware.

Polaroid actually had a war chest it could have spent on digital, courtesy of Kodak. Kodak had tried to move into Polaroid's instant-camera business in the mid-1970s; Polaroid sued for patent infringement and, after the case spent years wending its way through the court system, was awarded $925 million in damages in 1990. Instead of moving into digital, though, Polaroid made some short-term moves to shore up its existing, more profitable business. It expanded overseas, reasoning that less-developed countries would have less of the infrastructure needed to develop film and would be more inclined to go for instant pictures. It moved into the toy market and popularized cameras like a Barbie model. Polaroid's biggest success was the I-Zone, often sold at supermarket checkouts, which produced postage stamp–sized photographs with adhesive backs that could be used as stickers. Though the photos were of poor quality, kids found them cool, partly because the cameras came in colors with names like Go Grape Sorbet and Wicked Wasabi. Britney Spears used the camera onstage to snap pictures of fans.

But Polaroid's successes were short-lived. Kodak, Fuji, and others followed Polaroid into developing countries and set up photoprocessing centers, undercutting Polaroid. And buyers of Polaroid cameras as toys or sticker makers deserted as fast as they arrived. The I-Zone fad lasted for just parts of 1999 and 2000.

Polaroid also tried to produce 35mm instant film, to compete with the 4" × 6" photos that regular film produced. In addition, Polaroid worked on video that would develop itself in minutes. Neither worked. Polaroid's 35mm pictures couldn't match the sharpness of regular film. The self-developing video produced too much heat to work properly; having it develop mostly sent out plumes of smoke, while melting parts of the images.

In the meantime, Polaroid had been hurt by the spread of one-hour photoprocessing; the quality of the prints was so much better than what Polaroid produced that many customers were willing to wait that hour. In addition, digital hit Polaroid faster than it did Kodak. While people associated Polaroid with birthday parties, in fact, many of its cameras were used for commercial purposes, such as insurance claims adjusters who needed a picture of a damaged car. Commercial users were among the first to go digital.

Having delayed dealing with digital because its economics didn't measure up, Polaroid declared bankruptcy in 2001.

In his book *The Innovator's Dilemma*, Clay Christensen shows just how common a trap it is for companies to ignore new technologies partly because their economics don't measure up to the old. He shows how disk-drive makers that led the market in one generation of technology repeatedly failed to see the prospects for the next generation. He shows how every maker of mainframes was slow to move into the market for minicomputers, and how all the minicomputer makers initially mishandled the market for personal computers. Importantly, Christensen also shows that the dilemma he describes about oncoming threats reaches beyond the technology world into heavy industries such as earthmovers and steel.

Not Considering All the Options

Kodak's approach to the coming threat of digital photography was summed up neatly by CEO George Fisher's statement, "But Kodak has to grow," and by successor Daniel Carp's glare when the possibility of selling Kodak was raised.

It was hard for Kodak executives to even consider that something might replace those colorful prints they loved so much. It was almost impossible to consider selling the company or just milking it for cash as the film business wound down.

And yet.

As numerous outside analysts noted at the time, once digital started to grab hold, there was never any chance that the new technologies would do anything but savage Kodak. The only questions were how quickly the problems would appear and how completely the use of traditional prints would go away.

Kodak would have done best if it had been willing to sell itself before the beginning of the new millennium—in other words, after the depths of the digital threat had become clear but while Kodak still carried a market valuation north of $20 billion. Failing that, Kodak could have recognized the shift to digital earlier and tried to dominate niches where film and prints would still be used—such as grandmas and certain commercial applications—while rapidly scaling back investment in the future of film and trying to find profitable parts of the digital market. In other words, no Advantix cameras or Image Magic photoprocessing equipment that cost a lot of money while failing to extend the life of the film market.

Paging company Mobile Media Communications Incorporated had even less of an excuse than Kodak, because pagers were essentially a fad that lasted only several years, not more than one hundred years, like film cameras. It shouldn't have been that hard for Mobile Media to see that cell phones were going to supersede pagers. Sure, pagers were cool there for a while. It wasn't just repairmen who consulted them to get updates on their next assignment. Almost every self-respecting executive had one clipped to his belt, so everyone could see he was a with-it type who could be reached immediately about any urgent news. Besides, cell phones were still bulky and calls expensive in the mid-1990s, when pagers were in their heyday. But cell phones, being electronic, follow Moore's Law, so they were always going to get small and cheap. Pagers were destined to be the electronic version of pocket protectors, making wearers look geeky—not like those sleek cell phones or BlackBerries, which could send and receive text messages and do much, much more. Yet Mobile Media, like Kodak, never considered any options other than growth.

Mobile Media looked great in 1995 when it went public and promptly bought two big rivals. It bought Dial Page Incorporated's paging operations for $189 million. A month later, Mobile Media bought BellSouth Corporation's paging arm for $930 million. Mobile Media had doubled in size, becoming the second-largest paging company in the nation. It turned its attention to integrating the acquisitions to become a hyperefficient national player. The company, like others, also focused on what it saw as the next generation of technology: two-way paging. At that point, someone sending a page either left a phone number on the pager or had an operator send a text message. The person receiving the message couldn't respond via his pager. So companies were trying to remedy that lack.

Integrating the companies turned out to be much tougher than expected. Problems with the combined phone networks meant that operators sat around waiting for calls that never came through. Customer service deteriorated to the point that nearly 4 percent of customers left in the first quarter of 1996. "You could page yourself, and it would take seven to ten minutes" for the page to come through, said Kenneth A. Toudouze, a Dallas securities analyst and Mobile Media customer.[13]

In May 1996, Mobile Media issued a press release with the headline: "Acquisition Integration Running Ahead of Schedule." But in June, the company was so stretched that it had to ask bankers to relax covenants on its line of credit. In July, the company began missing payments to suppliers. The whole thing snowballed.

Hellman & Friedman, the highly regarded San Francisco–based investment firm that made its name taking Levi Strauss & Company private in 1988, led the board on a purge of senior executives.[14] When that didn't work, Mobile Media filed for bankruptcy, in January 1997.

Actually, Mobile Media was lucky. Although it had focused on absolutely the wrong issues—achieving scale and moving to a new generation of paging, when pagers were about to become obsolete, at least as a mass market—the company's problems with its acquisitions pushed it into bankruptcy early enough in the death throes of the paging industry that Mobile Media managed to sell itself to Arch Communications Group Incorporated in mid-1998 for $649 million. It was Arch that bore the full brunt of the decline in paging.

From 1999 through 2003, more than two-thirds of those who used pagers gave them up. With volumes so low, many manufacturers, including Motorola, stopped producing pagers. Arch, which had bought dozens of paging companies as it tried to achieve scale, filed for bankruptcy in December 2001. Almost every other paging company has also filed for bankruptcy. The only companies that did well during the decline of the paging market were those, such as BellSouth and Dial Page, that saw the freight train coming soon enough that they sold and got out of the way.

By rights, MicroAge Incorporated should have been one of those that saw the freight train coming in the market for personal-computer retailers in the late 1990s. The company had already been run over once and had gone through bankruptcy proceedings, before becoming a Fortune 500 company as a retail chain with $3 billion in sales of personal computers and related equipment. So MicroAge should have been more sensitive than most and should have been ready to move when the retailing of personal computers became so cutthroat that it was almost impossible for specialty retailers like MicroAge to survive. Yet, facing the threat posed by Dell Incorporated's direct-order approach and by mass-market retailers such as Best Buy Company, MicroAge couldn't bring itself to get out of its market of long standing, even though a new direction held great promise.

MicroAge was founded in the earliest days of the personal-computer industry. Actually, the PC retailer was founded even before PCs existed, at least as we know them today. The company began in 1976 when two Arizona bankers, Alan Hald and Geoffrey McKeever, became interested in an article in *Byte* magazine that said people could buy kits and assemble what were grandly known as microcomputers—"grandly," because the computers didn't even have a screen or a keyboard, let alone a disk drive or any of the other appurtenances that are commonly associated with PCs these days; input and output were handled through a series of toggle switches. Hald and McKeever bought a kit and built their PC/microcomputer, then decided they could build a business.

They did, but they expanded too fast and went into bankruptcy court. They emerged in time, however, to benefit from the huge interest generated by the introduction of the IBM PC in 1981. Getting ahead of the curve, McKeever and Hald began negotiating partnerships with major computer companies. One, with Hewlett-Packard Company, led the two companies to develop products and services that let customers use networking technology to improve the efficiency of their businesses. MicroAge also sold franchises, and, between 1984 and 1985, saw the number of MicroAge stores soar from 36 to 178. MicroAge did well in the following years, but, by 1989, it decided it had to make a wrenching change. Competition had increased to the point where gross margins had become very thin. MicroAge had to find ways to cut its fees, or it would put its franchisees out of business. Hald and McKeever made the tough decision to slash their markups, and business boomed. Within a few years, MicroAge had more than 1,500 stores carrying its name.

"If you don't figure out how to improve what you do each year, you're going to be out of business fairly quickly," McKeever said at the time.[15]

MicroAge plunged further into the networking business and found a receptive audience. Networks were notoriously fickle in those days, and companies were delighted to offload the installation and maintenance to a company that knew how to do the work and would troubleshoot problems. By the mid-1990s, sales were approaching $3 billion a year, and MicroAge had posted thirty-six consecutive quarters of profit in a difficult business.

By the late 1990s, however, the specialty computer-retailing business was untenable. Consumers had become comfortable enough with PCs that they were willing to buy them over the phone or online, straight from the manufacturer; retailers could no longer justify their markup. Consumers were also willing to go to nonspecialists, the big consumer-electronics chains, to buy computers. These chains didn't make any money on the computers, either, but the computers rounded out their product lines and had to carry just a small share of the overhead rather than covering the entire expense of separate stores.

This time, Hald and McKeever couldn't make the tough decision. They actually had a plan in place that would have jettisoned the retail business and moved MicroAge fully into networking, which was still a highly profitable business. But they couldn't pull the trigger. They kept trying to make retail work. When it didn't, the company went into bankruptcy again, in 2000, and this time was liquidated.

While technology companies such as Kodak, pager carriers, and MicroAge sometimes seem to hit the wall at a million miles per hour because of the rapid changes in technology, old-line manufacturing businesses can also get caught if they focus too long on the details of their day-to-day business and ignore a threat for too long. Pillowtex Corporation is a prime example.

Pillowtex, whose roots go back 120 years, was incorporated in Dallas in 1954 to manufacture bed pillows. The company soon began acquiring manufacturing plants throughout the country to establish a sophisticated "hub-and-spoke" network of manufacturing and distribution. The company developed a reputation for having a creative sales force and for setting trends on products. Pillowtex grew steadily and, by 1990, was known in the pillow industry as "the gorilla."

Declaring that it wanted to be "the largest and most profitable maker and seller of pillows, comforters and bed pads," Pillowtex made numerous acquisitions and invested heavily in technology. By the mid-1990s, all but 10 percent of Pillowtex's customers were ordering without paperwork; when a cashier scanned a Pillowtex item in the checkout line, a replacement order was automatically generated.

By 1995, Pillowtex's annual sales had reached almost half a billion dollars. It was the leading manufacturer of what were known in the industry as "top-of-the-bed" products, including blankets, pillows, mattress pads, and comforters. Through its subsidiary, Fieldcrest Cannon, Pillowtex was also the leading U.S. manufacturer of towels. Its many well-known home textile brands included Royal Velvet, Cannon, and Charisma. Pillowtex's customers included practically every major North American retailer, from department stores and mass merchandisers to catalogs to large institutional organizations such as the U.S. Postal Service. The company offered more than ten thousand products.

But a threat had taken shape in 1994. Based on international trade agreements, the United States had begun a decade-long phaseout of quotas that had limited the import of goods that would compete with Pillowtex's products. Increasingly, goods were going to come pouring into this country at prices that Pillowtex couldn't possibly match.

The response was clear: Outsource production to developing countries and take advantage of low labor costs. In whatever industry, almost every company facing a challenge like Pillowtex's has outsourced.

Pillowtex, however, redoubled its acquisition efforts, hoping that scale would let it become so efficient it could handle the competition from imports. The company's SEC filings from the late 1990s barely even mention outsourcing as an option. Instead, the filings highlight the $240 million that Pillowtex was spending on new, efficient machinery for its U.S. plants in 1998 alone.

Annual revenue reached $1.7 billion, but customers weren't willing to pay the prices that Pillowtex needed to charge. In 1999, the *Motley Fool* noted that inventory had risen 25 percent in one quarter while sales were up just 1 percent. "The company's plants appear to be busy making things; they just aren't what customers want," the *Fool* wrote.

With imports killing Pillowtex's prices, CEO Charles Hansen Jr. was asked in mid-2000 whether the company would consider a bankruptcy filing. "No way in hell," he replied.[16] Yet, by that fall, Hansen had resigned, and Pillowtex soon filed for bankruptcy.

During an arduous bankruptcy process, Pillowtex managed to close numerous plants and shed half its assets. The company also convinced lenders to slice its $1.1 billion debt to $205 million. Pillowtex had Wal-Mart as its biggest customer and had substantial financial backing, so executives were optimistic. The new president and chief operating officer, Tony Williams, announced that he had plans for making the company even more efficient than it had historically been, by trimming product lines, reorganizing manufacturing processes, and shortening cycle times to eliminate excess inventory.

But Pillowtex still hadn't faced its fundamental problem: Overseas manufacturers had far lower labor rates.

By 2003, Pillowtex was back in bankruptcy. This time, the company liquidated. Although part of the company's rationale for keeping manufacturing in the United States was to protect American jobs, the company dismissed 6,450 workers in the Southeast in the liquidation. The firings were the largest in the history of the U.S. textile industry.

Tough Questions

The problem is that acknowledging a threat isn't the same as dealing with it. Discussions within a management team (at every level, up and down the organization) can become an echo chamber, where everyone repeats reassuring comments and decides that a threat can be managed without too much disruption. So companies facing a threat need to find ways to get out of the echo chamber and evaluate their situation objectively, using outside perspectives from customers and various experts.

One way is to seek out those who disagree with your company's assessment of the threat and ask whether they might be right, at least on some aspects of the threat. Kodak, for instance, could have taken advantage of the articles in *Fortune* and *BusinessWeek* in the mid- to late 1990s that said Kodak was extraordinarily vulnerable to the switch to digital photography, that the switch could happen quickly, and that it might not be possible for Kodak to produce a business model that would be profitable in the new era. Rather than adopt a bunker mentality and decide that uninformed outsiders were picking on the company—the natural tendency at every company—Kodak could have assigned someone to line up all the evidence in support of the *BusinessWeek* and *Fortune* articles. Kodak could have used that evidence to challenge the strategy that assumed film would be profitable for a long time to come. While it's impossible to know just how Kodak would have responded to the challenges, at the least Kodak would have seen the weaknesses of its strategy more sharply and sooner.

The press is an obvious source when looking for disagreement. So are securities analysts, who tend to be ostracized when they attack a company's strategy but who can, in fact, be very useful if their concerns are explored in detail. Other analysts and competitors can also provide useful critiques.

As a threat unfolds, the tendency is for companies to assume that they have a good handle on how the problem will progress. Even when surprises develop, companies use twenty-twenty hindsight to say that, well, they really knew the surprise might be coming. So the only real way to know whether you have a handle on the speed of a threat's progress is to develop a sort of diary with a very specific set of predictions, so you can see whether you're right or whether the threat is coming at you faster than you expected.

Based on its assessment of digital photography in 1981, Kodak could have felt pretty confident that it understood where digital photography was going for the entire decade, but it should then have continued to monitor the explicit assumptions upon which it had based that assessment of the expected conditions for 1990. By monitoring the underlying assumptions, Kodak would have been able to determine how quickly each barrier to the adoption of digital photography would fall—how soon it would be possible to print high-quality photos on personal printers, how soon it would be easy to e-mail photos around, how soon it would be easy to display digital photos on computer screens and other electronic media, and so on.

It's crucial that these assessments be extremely detailed and based on data or judgments from outside the corporation. In Kodak's case, predictions about personal printers could have been based on the dots per square inch that could be produced on them, on their prices, on the number sold, and on other measures that could be quantified. If the projections were based on fuzzy numbers or subjective evaluations, Kodak could have held on to the notion for years that personal printers weren't very good and that, by extension, Kodak was on top of the digital threat. By contrast, precise predictions would have shown Kodak that the threat was materializing surprisingly fast.

In evaluating how quickly a threat is coming, you should also consider that there may be a flash point at which the new technology or business model takes over. In other words, the threat's progress may be linear for a time, but then the threat may suddenly take over the whole market. This happened with cable television, for instance. The industry steadily added households for years. Then everything came together, and penetration went from 20 percent to 60 percent of U.S. households in five years.[17]

It's rarely certain that a flash point will occur, so companies may still be able to maintain their complacency despite the prospect that a whole market may virtually disappear in short order—as Kodak did well into the 2000s. But the history of companies in similar situations can provide some clues. And, at the least, raising the possibility of a flash point should produce some contingency planning about what to do if one occurs.

Taking into account the predictions about the speed of a threat's onset and whether its progress will stay gradual or reach a flash point, companies should develop a business model for how their company might look once the threat hits. The model will, of course, be sketchy because it won't be clear how the future will look. Still, the model would force companies to put key assumptions on the table for debate. That way, companies could keep coming back to revisit those assumptions and revise the business model as the future becomes clearer. Companies would also have a way of testing to see whether they are just taking actions to shore up the short term without addressing the long term—in fact, the short-term actions sometimes make it harder to move to the long-term solutions, as was the case when Kodak kept wasting cash on film, photoprocessing, and film-camera technology that had no place in a digital business model.

If Kodak had done a digital business model, it would have had to make assumptions about how much profit it could still get from film in, say, 2010, how much from chemicals, how much from its new digital business, and so forth. It would then have been able to see that its assumptions looked increasingly unrealistic and would have felt a greater sense of urgency.

Even with a sense of urgency, companies need to ask themselves whether they are considering all their options. Typically, there are blind spots that prevent them from doing so. To try to remove those blind spots, companies should periodically force themselves to go through an exercise like one Michael Porter has laid out for evaluating how to proceed in a declining business.

The model is simple. It is based on two questions. First, does your industry have a favorable structure for decline? In other words, is your industry like steel, which would still offer profits while revenue declined? Or is your industry like traditional photography, which would mostly disappear once digital took hold? Second, can you compete successfully for the remaining demand? In other words, are you like Kodak, with a great brand? Or do you not only lack a brand but also lack other assets, such as a low cost structure?

If you can't compete and are in an industry with a crummy structure, Porter says to sell, sell, sell—as soon as possible. If you can't compete but are in an industry with a good structure, Porter says to sell pieces of the business selectively while seeking to get the most cash flow possible by eliminating or curtailing new investment, maintenance, research, and advertising while reaping the benefits of past goodwill. If you, like Kodak, can compete but are in an industry with a bad structure for handling decline, Porter says to seek niche markets that have high returns and that aren't declining as fast as the rest of the market. He says to move into those niches aggressively while getting out of the rest of the market. If you can compete and are in an industry with a good structure, Porter says to exert leadership. He says to establish cost leadership while avoiding destabilizing activities such as price wars.

Porter says that a study of sixty-two companies in eight declining industries found that those that followed his approach had a 92 percent chance of playing the market right, while those that didn't follow his approach had just a 15 percent chance of success.[18] We can't vouch for the numbers, but an approach such as his would certainly help companies consider all their options, including: getting out of part or all of a threatened market; winding down the business while extracting as much cash as possible; or selling the company outright.

One note: It's much easier for a boss to insist that all options be considered than it is for the person running the business to do so. That's true whether the person running the business is the CEO or a department manager. The person running the business always has incentive to maintain his empire. Usually, he's been involved in building the business, and he's reluctant to say its days have passed. So bosses need to give a shove in the face of any possible threat. That includes boards of directors, which need to insist that CEOs consider dismantling or selling a business before the threat becomes so great that its value plunges. That way, it's much more likely that your company will be like BellSouth, which sold its paging business before the cell phone killed the industry, and not like Arch Communications, which kept buying paging companies right up until the end.

FIVE

Misjudged Adjacencies

The Grass Isn't Always Greener

"Expanding into adjacent markets is the easiest way to grow," according to legendary General Electric CEO Jack Welch.[1] But it turns out that even the easiest is not so easy.

Adjacent-market strategies attempt to build on core organizational strengths to expand the business in a significant way while taking minimal risk. The strategy might entail selling new products to existing customers or selling existing products to new customers. Sometimes it could mean selling new products to new customers. A move into adjacent markets generally seems quite sensible and is often regarded as the logical next step when organic growth in existing markets slows. "Long-term winners sustain their growth by edging out from their core," said George Day, a professor at the Wharton School.[2]

At GE, Welch combined the concept of adjacent markets with another of his key management principles, that GE business units had to either dominate their markets or get out of them. "Challenging the organization to continually redefine their markets in a fashion that decreases their share opens their eyes to opportunities in adjacent markets," Welch said.[3] GE managers turned to adjacency strategies as one of their primary methods for satisfying GE's thirst for growth. For example, in the late 1990s, GE Aircraft Engines redefined its market from one of selling aircraft engines and replacement parts to that of providing the services necessary to keeping airplanes aloft. To meet that need, GE sold "power by the hour," which packaged equipment, maintenance, certification, and

financing. GE Aircraft Engines' market share, revenue, and profit margin grew tremendously.

Empirical research supports Welch's view about the potential of adjacent markets. Perhaps the most thorough study is by Bain Company, and reported in Chris Zook's *Beyond the Core.* Bain's five-year study of 1,850 companies concluded that most sustained profitable growth comes when a company pushes out the boundaries of its core business into an adjacent space.

Unfortunately, the research also shows that adjacency moves usually fail. Of the companies Bain studied, 75 percent saw their moves into adjacent markets fail. Only 13 percent achieved what Bain called "even a modest level of sustained and profitable growth." These companies grew earnings and revenues at least 5.5 percent a year (adjusted for inflation) and earned their cost of capital over ten years. A far smaller number achieved "sustainable growth performance far in excess of their peer groups."

Easy enough, right? Just look at the successful companies to see what they have in common and emulate them.

The problem is that the only thing the successful companies had in common is, well, that they were successful. Each built on core strengths. Each found rich veins of profitability. Each achieved market-leading economics. At a more detailed level, each evolved an approach that improved with multiple attempts and, over time, crystallized into a fairly repeatable process. But each approach was different, driven in large part by unique organizational and competitive circumstances. None offered a formula that others could simply follow.

There's another problem, too. Adjacency moves are not only hard to pull off; they are risky. Another Bain study looked at the twenty-five most costly business disasters from 1997 through 2002 (excluding those caused by the dot-com bubble). That study concluded that in 75 percent of those failures, the root cause or a major contributing factor was an attempt to enter an adjacent market. Those twenty-five companies lost $1.1 trillion in stock-market value, about 88 percent of their total.[4]

Our research, likewise, found dozens of examples where a seemingly innocuous strategy for entering an adjacent market led to catastrophe.

The trick, of course, is to know which is which. Which adjacent-marke strategies will succeed? Which will fail?

As it turns out, the failures have a number of common charac
so even if you can't know for sure which strategies will be big su
you can at least avoid many of the strategies that are doomed to f
explain what those common characteristics are, we'll begin with the
of Oglebay Norton, a cautionary tale that shows how an ill-thought-
move into an adjacent market can bring down even a firm with a lo
storied history.

Oglebay Norton: From John D. Rockefeller to Gordon Lightfoot

For most of its first 150 years, Cleveland-based Oglebay Norton Company served the regional steel industry and rode the ups and downs of that industry. It wasn't always pretty, but it worked. Then Oglebay decided to move into limestone, and—poof!—the company was pushed into bankruptcy in 2004.

Oglebay began business in 1854 as an iron-ore trader. Later, Oglebay operated its own iron-ore mines and managed others' mining operations. In the 1890s, it garnered a contract to operate vast iron-ore properties in Minnesota. In 1921, Oglebay expanded into shipping. It operated one of the largest shipping fleets on the Great Lakes, mostly hauling ore and other minerals for the steel industry.

Along the way, Oglebay had brushes with history. Not long after its founding, it had the distinction of employing John D. Rockefeller as a $3.50-a-week bookkeeper. "The three and a half years of business training I had in that commission house formed a large part of the foundation of my business training," Rockefeller wrote. Oglebay operated the SS *Edmund Fitzgerald*, a freighter that sank in Lake Superior in 1975 and was immortalized in the Gordon Lightfoot song, "The Wreck of the *Edmund Fitzgerald*." In 1985, Oglebay lost the country's first sexual harassment class-action lawsuit. The suit was brought by female mine workers at Oglebay's Eveleth mines and captured in the 2005 movie *North Country*.

By 1997, the regional steel business was in clear decline, and Oglebay had undergone a slow diversification away from it. After 143 years in the business, Oglebay sold its last iron ore–mining operations. "Iron ore was

a tough, competitive, low-growth business," said R. Thomas Green Jr., the CEO at the time.[5] The sale left Oglebay with about 1,200 employees and annual revenue of $170 million. Green invested the proceeds into Oglebay's industrial-sands division, hoping to capitalize on a boom in oil exploration, construction, and golf courses.

Slow-growth, steel-related businesses still supplied 60 percent of Oglebay's revenue. Oglebay's shipping division, for example, mostly hauled iron ore, coal, and limestone for major steelmakers and accounted for about half of the company's total revenue. As Green acknowledged at the time, "Shipping remains strong, but it's not a growth business."[6]

Under Green—a thirty-two-year employee and the last direct descendant of the Oglebay and Norton families to run the company—Oglebay had delivered five consecutive years of earnings growth and increased stock prices. Yet, in late 1997, Oglebay's board, no doubt envious of the economic boom around them, replaced Green with John Lauer. Lauer, a former president and chief operating officer of BFGoodrich, came onto the scene with a splash worthy of the dot-com times. It didn't seem to matter that he was taking over the helm of a company about as far from an Internet-related business as one might imagine.

Lauer said in a company press release, "My objective will be to create an aggressive but doable growth strategy." That "doable growth strategy" called for Oglebay to have a $1 billion market value in three years, a fivefold increase. In that time, Lauer planned to grow revenues more than threefold, to $600 million.

With a flourish that led the AFL-CIO to declare him a "CEO pay hero," Lauer crafted a five-year contract with no cash pay. Instead, he was granted an options package that gave him rights to buy as many as 383,000 shares, equal to 8 percent of the company, if he met performance targets. Lauer also bought $1 million of Oglebay stock at market value, which was in the mid-$30s. "When we put the deal together," Lauer said, "the way we designed it was that I wouldn't get credit for market momentum. I'd get credit for true growth."[7]

Lauer's strategy was to leverage Oglebay's shipping business and mining experience to get much farther away from the declining steel market and move into a market with better prospects. Put that way, the strategy sounded logical enough at the time.

Lauer focused on limestone. Oglebay already hauled limestone for steel mills. The material had growth opportunities beyond steel, including applications in road construction, environmental applications such as cleaning power-plant emissions and water filtration, and consumer lawn and garden applications. Rather than just transporting limestone, Lauer would buy up quarries within a region to become a dominant supplier. With quarries located fairly close to customers, Oglebay's lower shipping costs would give it a competitive edge over rivals based outside the region.

By mid-1998, within six months of his arrival, Lauer had made three major acquisitions and doubled Oglebay's size. The stock market initially responded with enthusiasm, briefly bidding Oglebay's share price to $50.50. But all of the acquisitions were financed through debt; none of the sellers would take Oglebay stock. In a foreshadowing of the troubles to come, Oglebay's debt increased by $250 million to just over $300 million. By the end of 1998, Oglebay's share price was down to the mid-$20s.

Oglebay completed a number of other acquisitions through the end of 2000. The company acquired its way to be the fifth-largest producer of limestone in North America and one of the top twenty-five mineral producers overall. Revenue grew quickly, with limestone now representing about half of Oglebay's total. Oglebay ended 2000 with $393 million in revenue—not the $600 million Lauer predicted, but still more than twice the level before Lauer arrived.

Debt grew even faster, though, reaching $379 million and leaving the company dangerously leveraged. Because of the debt load, net income for 2000 was just $15 million. As one analyst put it, "The company is poised for tremendous growth . . . or an ugly fall."[8]

He turned out to be half right. The ugly fall was a definite possibility, but the potential for growth was quite limited.

In its rush to grow, Oglebay paid peak prices for its acquisitions, both because the market for minerals was hot and because of Oglebay's desire to corner local supplies—after one company was purchased in a market, the others knew they could raise their asking prices. To justify those high prices, Oglebay made ill-considered judgments about the strengths of its core business, about the strengths of the new limestone business, and about the dynamics of the limestone market.

Oglebay assumed that it would be able to integrate its acquisitions and improve its efficiency, but it had never accomplished such a task before and didn't have the expertise to do so. Oglebay also overestimated the pricing power that its limestone business would have. Being the fifth-largest producer of limestone just didn't carry much weight. In addition, Lauer's hopes about the power of being an integrated producer and shipper of limestone didn't pan out. With the decline of the steelmakers, there was lots of extra capacity available to ship limestone around the Great Lakes. Oglebay didn't get as much shipping business as it had hoped, and it couldn't raise prices. In addition, Oglebay's background in shipping iron ore didn't prepare it for one aspect of the limestone market: Limestone often needed to travel on rivers to get closer to customers. That meant being loaded on six-hundred- to seven-hundred-foot river-class vessels. But Oglebay's fleet was mostly thousand-footers designed to transport iron ore on the Great Lakes.

The minerals industry was, in fact, enjoying brisk sales, even in the face of an economy that started slumping in 2000. For example, market leader Vulcan Materials Co. had record sales in 2000, then posted a 7 percent increase for 2001. Martin Marietta Materials Incorporated, another competitor, reported a 13 percent increase for 2001. But Oglebay didn't share in the good times. Struggling to integrate its acquisitions and hampered by an enormous debt load, Oglebay's mineral sales were flat or down in 2000 and 2001.

Oglebay was being crushed from other directions, too. Low lake levels, higher fuel prices, a collapsing steel industry, and the loss of one of its largest customers to competition grounded Oglebay's shipping business. A downturn in construction and changes in oil and gas exploration struck its industrial-sands business.

Lauer began glossing over problems. John Weil, a former board member, reported that Lauer would forecast record earnings—but his numbers wouldn't include major costs, such as routine off-season maintenance at Oglebay's largest limestone operations. More fatally, Weil recalls, forecasts did not take into account that the economy was showing signs of softening.[9]

Although it takes a lot to stand up to a dynamic CEO, Weil and another board member, Brent Baird, challenged Lauer. Baird says that the first time he raised his concerns, Lauer talked about growth and diversification. The next time Baird asked questions, Lauer got "nasty." Weil recalled that Lauer's response to Baird's skepticism was, "Why'd you hire me if you wanted me to be a custodial manager?"

Baird, who joined the board in 1990 and was once the second-largest shareholder, said he supported the first one or two acquisitions but started asking questions as the acquisitions and debt mounted. Lauer "would buy almost anything," Baird marveled. "And it was all with borrowed money."[10]

Douglas Barr, a former major shareholder, said he initially "thought Lauer's plan was fine. Everyone agreed [iron-ore mining and shipping] was probably not long-term." However, he continued, "If you need a new car, it's a prudent thing to go out and get one. But you don't buy eight of them and pay sticker price for each."[11]

Oglebay had weathered challenges before. You don't last 150 years in the steel business—or any business, for that matter—without overcoming problems. So Oglebay had tried-and-true methods it could use to outlast the latest problems, and it used some. It moved, for example, to pool its Great Lakes shipping fleet with that of American Steamship Company, a similar-sized rival. The arrangement allowed the two fleets to operate more efficiently by coordinating dispatching and other fleet operations. Oglebay also cut costs by closing some regional headquarters and discontinuing several underperforming operations. It also sold some business units.

But none of this was sufficient under the weight of more than $400 million in debt. In October 2001, Oglebay stopped paying dividends. The stock price went into free fall.

The rest was just a slow march to the end. Oglebay directors appointed a new president and chief operating officer in November 2001. By January 2003, Lauer was out as CEO. In April 2003, with the stock trading at $3, Lauer resigned as chairman. The company declared bankruptcy on February 23, 2004, with $440 million of debt. Shareholders like Douglas Barr, whose family had three hundred thousand shares and whose wife was a great-granddaughter of cofounder David Z. Norton, recouped pennies per share.

Oglebay Norton would emerge from bankruptcy but never recover its footing. By August 2006, Oglebay had sold its Great Lakes fleet piecemeal to retire a part of its significant debt. In October 2007, Oglebay agreed to be acquired by Carmeuse North America, a subsidiary of Belgium's Carmeuse Group.

RED FLAGS

While Bain found that successful adjacency strategies are one-offs, not capable of being used as a template for other companies' moves into adjacent markets, our research found four patterns that show up in many strategies that fail. They are:

- The move is being driven more by a change in a company's core business rather than by some great opportunity in the adjacent market.
- The company lacks expertise in the adjacent market, leading the company to misjudge acquisitions and mismanage the competitive challenges of the new market.
- The company overestimates the strength or importance its core business's capabilities will have in the new market.
- A company overestimates its hold on customers, leading to expectations of cross-selling or up-selling that won't materialize.

Fleeing from the Core

In theory, what's going on in the core business should have no bearing on the assessment that's made of a new opportunity. In practice, however, it seems that the worse the current business looks, the more likely a company is to make a bad bet on an adjacent market.

That certainly happened with Oglebay Norton. The company might well have taken a more considered look at the limestone business, spotting the potential problems before plunging in. But Lauer was so intent on transforming the business to reduce its reliance on steel that he bought businesses too quickly and paid too much.

FLYi Incorporated felt similar pressure. It had prospered for years as a regional airline that operated flights along the East Coast in what's known as a code-sharing arrangement with United Airlines Incorporated and Delta Air Lines Incorporated. The arrangement meant that customers of the bigger airlines could book an entire itinerary through them even if that meant going to a city where Delta and United didn't fly. FLYi would operate the flights to the smaller cities and would give United and Delta a share of the revenue for steering the business in its direction. Then, United filed for bankruptcy in 2002. It tried to renegotiate rates with FLYi. FLYi could have accepted a lower share of revenue and attempted to cut costs. As it happened, FLYi also had a chance to sell out to fellow regional carrier, Mesa Air Group Incorporated, which made an unsolicited $512 million buyout offer. Instead, FLYi decided to remake itself as an independent carrier.

FLYi thought it had plenty of expertise. After all, it had operated an airline for years. It was just going to operate that same airline while dealing directly with customers, rather than working under the umbrella provided by United and Delta. Yet, as many analysts predicted at the time, FLYi was woefully unprepared for the ferocity of open competition in the airline business. FLYi, which defiantly named its new incarnation Independence Air, promised to be "the polar opposite of the lumbering, arrogant major carriers." But those major carriers were not so lumbering when it came to slapping down this upstart. As a FLYi court filing explained, "These competitors . . . have reacted by matching fares, reducing restrictions [on airline tickets], offering additional frequent flier incentives, increasing advertising, and by taking aggressive steps to reduce their own costs."[12] Desperate for cash flow, FLYi's only option was to rely on money-losing fares that were often as low as a Greyhound bus ticket. Smelling blood, competitors matched those fares route for route, never letting them rise to sustainable levels.

Besides, FLYi's aircraft weren't cost-efficient for an independent airline. FLYi's planes had been selected based on the numbers of passengers it could get through its arrangements with United and Delta. The planes weren't suited for the larger loads that FLYi would attempt to serve as an independent carrier. As a result, FLYi's planes cost about three times as much to operate per seat per mile as those of JetBlue, a direct competitor.

FLYi also lacked expertise in direct-to-consumer marketing, sales, and service, because it had always piggybacked on others' reservation systems. FLYi encountered problems with ticket sales, and customers complained of poor service. Yet FLYi couldn't afford to back off and take the new business slowly while it learned the ropes. It had leases on eighty-seven small regional jets. It could not afford to keep any idle. So FLYi began life as an independent carrier with service to thirty-nine cities, too many for a newcomer to handle without major logistical problems.

In 2005, a little over a year after commencing service, FLYi declared bankruptcy. In its final year of operation, FLYi lost almost $250 million.

One of the company's largest shareholders says he warned FLYi executives not to become an independent carrier. "They had opportunities to preserve value, and they decided to completely shun them," he said. "Their argument to me was that renegotiating with United 'would have produced a lousy margin, and we couldn't have made any money.' That may be true. But versus what? Versus the negative operating margins" they wound up with as an independent?[13]

In retrospect, the Mesa offer looks awfully good—and, even at the time, FLYi should have known that becoming an independent wasn't the way to go.

Similarly, Xerox went into financial services because of problems with its core business, copiers, in the early 1980s. Xerox's revolutionary Model 914 plain paper copier was, at its peak, the bestselling industrial product of all time. It enjoyed 95 percent market share and 70 percent gross margins. But by 1982, Xerox's U.S. market share had dwindled to 13 percent.

In a desperate attempt to offset the failing copier business, Xerox decided to move into what it considered to be an adjacent market. But the way Xerox formulated its strategy practically guaranteed that it would move into businesses where it had no expertise and thus would have a high likelihood of failure. Rather than risk a repeat of the problems it was having keeping up with foreign manufacturers of copiers, Xerox decided to move into a market that would not involve manufacturing and that had little foreign competition. Yet Xerox's management team's whole recent experience had been developing expertise in just those areas that Xerox decided to avoid—manufacturing and confronting foreign competition.

Rather than trying to build on some core competency, Xerox decided to leverage its balance sheet. Xerox moved into financial services, based on two strains of logic. Xerox reasoned that many of its customers financed their purchases, so it wouldn't be much of a stretch for Xerox to add other kinds of financing. In addition, Xerox hoped the financial-services business would generate cash that it could then use to finance research and development of copiers.

Xerox spent more than $2 billion to acquire Crum & Forster Incorporated, a property and casualty insurer; Van Kampen Merritt, an investment adviser; and Furman Selz Incorporated, a brokerage house. After some initial problems, the investment seemed to pay off. In 1988, the financial-services arm accounted for half of Xerox's profit. A significant portion of that profit came from financing Xerox equipment sales. But because Xerox didn't have the experience to properly vet the acquisitions, it had bought headaches as well as cash flow. Several Crum & Forster units had been guilty of sloppy underwriting before the acquisition, and the problems were surfacing as claims mounted. For good measure, the whole industry went into a downturn. As one reporter described it at the time, Xerox management "turned pale" as they tallied up the potential losses.[14] Unwinding the problems required Xerox CFO Melvin Howard to take personal charge of the insurer, commuting for a year between Xerox headquarters in Stamford, Connecticut, and Crum & Forster's headquarters in Morristown, New Jersey.

Xerox wrote off almost $800 million in 1992 and said it intended to leave the financial-services business. Actually doing so would take another five years. During that time, the financial-services business lost $2.8 billion.

"Whether it was mainframe computers or financial services," one analyst observed at the time, "Xerox tended to buy the wrong company at the wrong price and then run it into the ground."[15]

Even if Crum & Forster hadn't cratered, Xerox had overstated how much cash it could get from its financial-services business. What Xerox didn't realize was that, even during periods when the financial-services arm delivered strong results, most of the cash flow was unavailable. Insurers, for instance, typically have to retain considerable cash to meet regulatory requirements.

Ironically, once senior management returned its full attention to the copier business, drastic cost cutting and innovative products revived it.

Lack of Expertise

From a distance, everything looks easier. But once you move into a new market, you're no longer at a distance. You have to deal with the new business, up close and personal, warts and all.

Oglebay learned that the hard way when it had to face up to soft demand for limestone, the complexities of shipping it, and the stiffer-than-expected competition.

Avon Products Incorporated had its own tough lesson in the 1980s. The problems actually began with an acute insight and a big success: Avon saw that, with more women out working, fewer prospective customers were at home to buy beauty products from its famed door-to-door sales force. Avon decided to add health-care products to the traditional line of Avon cosmetics, reasoning that it might be able to sell more products to each customer, even if the customer base was shrinking. Sales boomed. Avon then went one step too far, by taking a larger step into health care. In 1984, Avon bought Foster Medical Corporation, a medical equipment–rental company. In 1985, Avon bought Retirement Inns of America Incorporated and Mediplex Group Incorporated, both of which operated nursing homes. The strategic rationale, as expressed in Avon's annual report, was that health care fit into the company's "culture of caring." Maybe, but the strategy was a disaster. The move did nothing to build on Avon's core asset, its sales force, and Avon simply didn't have the expertise to manage the new acquisitions. In 1988, Avon took a total charge of $545 million for dismantling its health-care business.

While Avon thought its decision to sell health-care products meant it knew something about other parts of the health-care business, the equipment-rental business faced regulatory issues Avon didn't foresee. The acquisition initially seemed brilliant, because Foster Medical revenues proceeded to double for each of the next two years. But the growth was short-lived. In fact, it was partly an illusion. In 1985, the government changed reimbursement policies for home oxygen therapy, a treatment that represented more than $100 million in annual revenue for Foster and more than 20 percent of its profit. Doctors had to recertify patients to qualify their treatment for reimbursement. Foster—now overseen by a cosmetics company that lacked experience in regulated environments—failed to do the necessary paperwork to recertify patients. Much of the revenue booked in 1986 was disallowed because the government wouldn't reimburse Foster. Even once Foster adapted to the regulatory changes, its reimbursements continued to be squeezed. Avon sold Foster in 1988.

Avon's lack of industry insight also played out in the inept management of Mediplex Group. Mediplex was a profitable system of twenty-seven long-term-care and substance-abuse centers when Avon bought it in 1985 for $245 million. On Avon's watch, however, Mediplex failed to navigate the quickly changing health-care space. Profits turned to losses. Four years after the acquisition, Avon sold Mediplex back to the previous owners for $48 million. Within a few years, the new owners had the business nicely profitable once more. In 1994, they sold Mediplex again, this time for $315 million.

American Standard Companies, a maker of plumbing supplies, air-conditioning systems, and automotive systems, also fell victim to a lack of expertise. American Standard was solidly profitable, but in our growth-oriented investment culture it was hard to get too excited about the prospects for toilets. So, in the sort of strategic-planning exercise that many companies undergo, American Standard looked for faster-growing markets and then tried to find a way into them. Health care certainly seemed to fit the bill. It was riding a decades-long, demographically powered growth curve. Medical devices offered the promise of patent-protected revenue streams, and big industrial companies such as GE, 3M Company, and Siemens AG had shown that manufacturing expertise and deep pockets could eventually overcome a lack of initial expertise in medical devices. Once American Standard identified an in-house manufacturing technology that held potential for medical devices, it decided to make the leap into the new market.

The company thought it could take the laser technology used in its ceramics manufacturing and apply it to small medical diagnostic devices. In 1997, judging the technology viable, American Standard combined several acquisitions into a new medical systems group to commercialize the new devices.

But American Standard management lacked experience in diagnostics, so it couldn't manage the businesses it acquired. The hoped-for new product, an in vitro diagnostics device targeted for laboratories and small hospitals, was rife with problems. American Standard also struggled with regulatory control that it had never previously experienced. The company didn't have the right kind of investors, either. Its investors were looking for consistent quarterly earnings and dividend growth. The investors wanted nothing to do with the long product-development cycles and heavy up-front investments that came with medical devices.

In late 1999, after racking up $30 million in losses, the company sold its medical systems group for a fraction of what it invested and took a $126 million write-off.

It's not just health care that trips up newcomers, either. CanWest Global Communications Corporation, one of Canada's largest media companies, decided in 1998 to move beyond distribution. The company decided to produce original film and television content for both its Canadian and international channels. CanWest found, however, that operating television stations was much different from the creative side of the business. European customers didn't take to the new content. In 2004, the company discontinued film production and recorded total losses of $294 million.

Overestimating the Core's Strengths

When railroads failed to foresee the impact of the automobile in the early 1900s, they lost their position as the go-go stocks of the era and never regained it. The conventional wisdom has become that the railroads' problem was that they saw themselves as being in the railroad business; they should have seen themselves as being in the transportation business. How many times have we heard that bromide? "Railroads weren't in the railroad business. They were in the transportation business."

That's fair enough—until you think about it for a minute. Just what exactly did railroads and automobiles have in common? Not much. The railroads sold tickets for pennies apiece; they had no experience selling consumer items for hundreds of dollars each. The railroads had limited experience with consumer tastes; decorating a passenger railcar didn't have much to do with designing a roadster that some young swell could use to go sparking with his lovely damsel. The customer bases were very different; everybody rode the trains, while, for a long time, only the affluent could afford cars. The distribution channels were different; railroads sold tickets in offices, while cars needed to be displayed in stores or on lots. The technology was different; the coal-fired engines used on trains bore little resemblance to the internal combustion engine used in cars.

All the railroads really had to bring to the car business were brand names and cash. The odds are high that any move into cars would have reached the same end that almost every other carmaker reached—the railroads' ventures would have been acquired by Ford Motor Company or General Motors Corporation or one of the other handful of carmakers that survived the early days. Sure, the railroads could have done a better job of foreseeing the impact of cars and perhaps could have sold out before railroad stocks suffered. But to imply that railroads should have dominated the car business strikes us as naïve.

Yet companies continue to make that sort of railroad-to-transportation semantic leap and use it as justification for a move into adjacent markets. In the process, those companies overestimate what their core business can provide in the new market.

Studies suggest that these overestimation problems are common. Building on existing assets gives managers a false sense of security. Some capabilities are indeed built upon, but other critical variables are different. Chris Zook, in *Beyond the Core*, calls this the "trap of false enthusiasm," referring to adjacency moves for which managers feel confidence because they are close to their core business while not realizing that the differences are significant enough to be problematic. Overestimation may actually occur more often in successful companies, based on what Stanford researchers William Barnett and Elizabeth Pontikes call the "Red Queen" syndrome. The term comes from Lewis Carroll's *Through the Looking Glass*, in which the Red Queen says, "It takes all the running you can do, to keep in the same place." Applied to a business setting, the Red Queen syndrome occurs at companies that work incredibly hard to adapt to their environment. That's why they're successful. The problem, as expressed by Barnett and Pontikes, is that the adaptation means the companies are less prepared for other markets, which operate under different rules—and, here's the key part, they don't know it. In fact, companies with success in one market become overly confident that they'll be successful in the next market, even though their Red Queen adaptations make it more likely that they'll fail.

Oglebay Norton succumbed to the Red Queen syndrome when it overestimated the value of its expertise in shipping steel, not realizing that shipping limestone had important differences, because of the need to transport it away from the Great Lakes and onto rivers.

Comdisco Incorporated is an even better example. It thrived for more than twenty-five years, primarily as a lessor of mainframe computers. It withstood withering competition from IBM, as powerful an adversary as has ever existed—well into the 1980s, the rule of thumb was that IBM accounted for half the revenue of the entire computer industry, two-thirds of the profit, and three-quarters of the stock-market capitalization.

In 1994, CEO Ken Pontikes died unexpectedly. Pontikes had founded the company in 1969, and his family owned 25 percent of the stock, so his son Nick was groomed for the top job. Nick became CEO in 1999.

Much had changed in the five years since Ken Pontikes died. After many years during which the death of the mainframe was greatly exaggerated, technology changes meant that the mainframe leasing business was clearly past its prime. In 1994, 75 percent of Comdisco's profits came from leasing mainframes. By 1999, the share was just 10 percent.

Nick Pontikes, a former investment banker, began acting like, well, an investment banker. He sold the mainframe-leasing business to IBM for $485 million. He also did the classic sort of analysis that bankers and strategists do to identify markets with better growth prospects—leaving for later the question of whether a company has the capability to succeed in the high-growth markets. Pontikes decided he would move Comdisco into telecommunications. He reasoned that the company's long history of dealing with complex mainframe technology would carry over into the telecom marketplace. Pontikes also moved the company into venture capital. He felt that Comdisco's experience with sophisticated leases gave it the financial expertise to manage investments.

Pontikes had made the Red Queen mistake. (Oddly enough, he is a second cousin to Elizabeth Pontikes, coauthor of the Red Queen work; she says their fathers grew up together on the west side of Chicago. We're not saying, though, that her work should have given him pause. She is much younger than he is, and she did her work well after the problems occurred at Comdisco.)

Nick Pontikes seriously misjudged the dynamics of telecommunications. Comdisco entered the market with a service called Prism and a promise that it would become "a leading integrated telecommunications provider." Prism planned to build a nationwide network offering voice, data, video, Internet, and secure business applications via high-speed Internet access. Comdisco couldn't afford to spend the tens of billions of dollars that would be necessary to build a thoroughly nationwide network from scratch, so it piggybacked its services on existing local telephone company networks. Regulators required that operators of those existing networks had to provide access to new services like Prism—but, as Comdisco learned, regulators couldn't make the operators *like* what Prism was doing. Many of those companies were either offering or planning to offer similar services, so they had every incentive to make Prism fail. The network operators worked only to the letter of the law. The service they provided to Prism customers was awful, resulting in long delays in getting service initiated. Given the competitiveness of the market, and the fact that a former mainframe lessor had no particular claim to the affections of consumers and small businesses who wanted a bundle of Internet services, Prism's service problems chased customers away.

Comdisco also faced trouble because its sales force had no experience selling to consumers and small businesses. While Comdisco executives assumed the sales force could make the transition, they didn't even *want* to make the transition. The sales force didn't even try to bundle Prism's low-cost services with the other services they were selling to corporations. Comdisco tried to gin up interest through a $12 million branding campaign that included a Super Bowl commercial. But at the time Comdisco pulled the plug in 2000, Prism's total investment of nearly $500 million had garnered it only about two thousand customers. In other words, Comdisco had spent $250,000 per customer. To shut down the business, Comdisco took a write-off of $600 million.

Comdisco's ventures arm invested nearly $3 billion in nine hundred start-ups, but it learned that wizardry with leases doesn't carry over into venture capital. The evaluation of mainframe leases depended primarily on how quickly new technology would reduce the value of existing machines, and that new technology appeared at a predictable rate. Picking winners in the venture-capital market, by contrast, involved evaluating the quality of people in the company. VCs need to have great gut instincts about radically disruptive technologies, not generate precise calculations about predictable technologies, as lessors do. The disciplines of the businesses differ, too. When Goldman Sachs evaluated Comdisco's investment portfolio in late 2000, Goldman found Comdisco had no active credit-scoring system or fundamental systems to track how its portfolio was allocated—basic tools employed by venture capitalists to estimate the risk in their holdings.[16] A Comdisco court filing said corporate executives were surprised to learn that the ventures group did little or no due diligence before funding prospects. Instead, the filing said, the VCs had a "follow the smart money" strategy, where they invested blindly in deals along with "A-list" venture-capital funds. (Comdisco Ventures executives, who sued and eventually extracted almost $30 million in unpaid bonuses from the bankrupt company, countered that senior management was fully briefed on all investments. "Whatever was being done was always reviewed by parties at levels above our clients," the lawyer for the ventures executives said.)[17]

By mid-2001, the ventures unit had written off $275 million in bad loans and set aside another $381 million in reserves. Comdisco declared bankruptcy in July 2001. The former Fortune 500 company was eventually dismantled and sold in pieces.

Laidlaw Incorporated, North America's largest school bus operator, also fell victim to the Red Queen syndrome. Laidlaw figured it could leverage its considerable expertise in logistics and move into health care. The first move was into ambulance services, where Laidlaw went on a more than $4 billion buying spree. What Laidlaw found, however, was that the new business was just too different, that expertise in logistics wasn't nearly enough.

With buses, Laidlaw negotiated a reasonably small number of large contracts. With ambulances, however, the situation was far more complicated. Medicare and private insurance plans set complex rates and restrictions, and changing Medicare regulations cut much of the reimbursement for ambulance services. Laidlaw had to negotiate contracts with innumerable city and county governmental agencies. Each had its own regulations about response times, training, and licensing. Laidlaw had to provide its service to whomever called, then hope to be reimbursed. Yet the company often could guess that it wouldn't be repaid. Sometimes paramedics can't even get needed billing information from patients, who may be unconscious or otherwise unable to communicate. In fiscal year 1998, the last year before Laidlaw discontinued its ambulance operations, bad receivables amounted to $700 million, almost 40 percent of the total billed.

Laidlaw tried to navigate the complexity by shifting its focus away from municipal contracts and lining up large contracts with managed-care plans—moving to the sort of contractual setup that Laidlaw had long followed in its bus business. Laidlaw signed a five-year, $600 million contract to provide all ambulance services to Kaiser Permanente's 8.5 million members. But not so fast. The system provoked sharp criticism from local authorities and other ambulance providers because it side-stepped local 911 contracts—those contracts specified that a caller to 911 would be handled in a certain way, but the Laidlaw-Kaiser contract required that Kaiser members' calls be routed to Laidlaw. Some cities, such as Aurora, Colorado, ended up dealing with the confusion by banning Laidlaw from responding to emergency calls.

In another run-in with regulators—of the kind Laidlaw never saw in its sedate bus business—the Connecticut state attorney general found that the company had violated antitrust laws by buying up smaller ambulance companies across the state and taking over their contracts. Laidlaw had to give up 40 percent of Hartford's 911 business and agree not to trample on the business of smaller companies.

James Bullock, the Laidlaw CEO who launched the strategy, said he thought the ambulance business was "a transportation business that was aligned with many of the skill sets associated with our bus business. We've come to realize it is quite a different business than the bus business."[18] John Grainger, who replaced James Bullock as CEO, underscored the point at a Laidlaw shareholders meeting. Grainger said Laidlaw realized too late that ambulances are a health-care business, with complex regulatory issues, and not a transport business.

When Laidlaw focused on how its logistical expertise in buses would translate to the market for ambulance services, Laidlaw also overlooked that it was missing one crucial type of expertise: the ability to consolidate numerous acquisitions. That expertise is hard to come by—witness our discussion on rollups in chapter 3—but Laidlaw just assumed the expertise was there and went about buying dozens of ambulance businesses. After several years of high-paced acquisitions, Laidlaw was the third-largest operator of ambulances. It proceeded to buy the two larger ones, including American Medical Response Incorporated, the industry leader, for $1.2 billion in cash. AMR itself was the product of massive consolidation; it was made up of 250 small ambulance operations across the country. That left Laidlaw with an enormous problem of consolidation, which turned out to be more than Laidlaw could handle.

Problems surfaced almost immediately. The ambulance industry was already in the midst of major consolidation, so Laidlaw had paid high premiums to buy companies. Many had troubles. Some were shut down soon after purchase. As a Laidlaw executive later observed, "In retrospect, it should have been done more slowly, but, when you're consolidating, speed is part of the strategy."[19]

Laidlaw tried centralizing operations such as collection centers, which did cut costs but also led to reduced revenue by diminishing the role of local contacts that generated business. Laidlaw wound up with excessive layers of management and bloated costs. Like many rollups, Laidlaw achieved scale but not the economies of scale.

In 1998, Laidlaw wrote off more than $1.8 billion for its combined health-care business.

For good measure, Laidlaw also committed the kind of mistake that we cover in chapter 2 on financial engineering. Laidlaw, a Canadian company, partially financed its U.S. acquisitions through intracompany loans to its U.S. subsidiaries from a Dutch financing subsidiary. The arrangement let the U.S. subsidiaries deduct interest payments on their U.S. tax returns. The Dutch financing subsidiary reported profits but paid very low taxes on them, taking advantage of laws in the Netherlands that were designed to attract foreign finance facilities. Essentially, Laidlaw transferred profits from a high-tax U.S. environment to a low-tax Dutch one. The problem was that a U.S. tax court ruled in 1998 that the almost

$1 billion transferred to the United States from the Netherlands was really a capital infusion, not a bona fide loan. Unlike with real loans, the principal wasn't repaid on maturity. In addition, the interest payments that the U.S. subsidiaries made to their Dutch counterpart were immediately refunded back in the form of new loans. "What these guys tried to do with the tax code is off the charts," said Robert Willens, a Lehman Brothers tax expert.[20] The tax court issued an initial judgment of $141 million against Laidlaw for "loans" made between 1986 and 1988—and investors were even tougher. Fearing even larger tax liabilities for loans made in subsequent years, investors drove Laidlaw shares down 28 percent. The doubt lingered over the company for several years. Laidlaw ultimately paid almost $300 million in back taxes and interest.

The Fickle Customer

When companies move into adjacent markets, they usually assume that their customers will come with them. When an adjacency move fails badly, it's often because companies grossly overestimated their customers' loyalty—and could have known better.

Oglebay Norton suffered a bit of this problem when it mistakenly assumed its customers would buy both its ore and its shipping services. Electrical utilities provide a more robust example, because of mistakes they made when they were awash with cash in the mid-1980s. The industry had just gone through a building boom, and rates had been set to finance even more building. But that additional capacity was not needed. Regulators across the country were making noises about reducing rates. In response, utilities everywhere went shopping. They decided they could buy businesses that would yield better returns than the utility industry did, partly because loyal customers would support the utilities' efforts. But, as the utilities learned the hard way, having a bunch of cash to spend and having a deadline for spending it may not lead to the best decisions.

Florida Power & Light, a subsidiary of FPL Group Incorporated that provides electricity to much of southern Florida, attempted to move into insurance. In 1985, FPL paid $565 million for Colonial Penn Life Insurance Company, which focused on senior citizens. FPL reasoned that there was a sizable overlap between Colonial Penn's target market and the utility's captive utility customers, and that the utility's brand recognition would help Colonial Penn's sales. In its eagerness to get into the market, FPL paid a 50 percent premium over Colonial Penn's book value. Wall Street applauded the move. One analyst noted that "FPL may decide to stuff its utility bills with promotional material on Colonial Penn insurance products, thus taking advantage of already established business relationships."[21]

But FPL soon learned that sending people junk mail didn't generate much business. People kept buying insurance from their insurance company, not their electric utility.

Florida Power & Light has been known for good management. It has been on *Fortune*'s list of Most Admired Companies and has won the prestigious Deming Award for quality control. But FPL added little to Colonial Penn's management skills, and Colonial Penn suffered from industrywide pressure that stemmed from litigation and natural disasters. Colonial Penn was hurting more than most, having recently lost a key marketing alliance with the American Association of Retired Persons.

FPL sold Colonial in 1991 for $128 million, less than a third of the insurer's book value, and took a $689 million write-off. "Now it's time to focus efforts on the utility," FPL chairman James L. Broadband said.

FPL's strategic rationale for adding an insurance company to an electric utility wasn't even close to the flimsiest among utilities of that era. An executive with Florida Progress Corporation, another Florida utility, for example, explained his company's purchase of a life-insurance company by saying, "Utilities tend to be very good at all different kinds of service. So, it seemed logical to steer our diversification activity toward other kinds of service businesses."[22] Florida Progress also joined a group seeking to buy a major league baseball franchise. Its rationale? The proposed stadium would be a big user of electricity.[23]

The mistakes by electric utilities continued well past the 1980s. In the late 1990s, Montana Power Company expanded into telecommunications, initially by creating a microwave communications system to save on internal telecommunications costs. The company expanded this service and sold telecommunications services to external customers. Eventually management came to believe that the telecommunications business had more value than the monopoly electricity business. In 2000, Montana Power sold its energy assets for more than $1 billion and used the proceeds to build a nationwide fiber-optic network. The company laid almost twenty-four thousand miles of fiber, under the brand name Touch America. Unfortunately, many others were also laying fiber at the same time, and software advances were dramatically expanding the capacity of existing cables. The company soon found itself with massive overcapacity and a lack of customers. Touch America filed for bankruptcy in 2003. Its core assets and businesses would eventually be sold for less than $30 million.

But, while electric utilities may have a monopoly on a local market, they don't have a monopoly on assuming too much loyalty by customers. In the late 1980s, Blue Circle Industries PLC, one of the world's biggest cement makers, moved into property management, brick production, waste management, industrial minerals, gas cookers, bathroom furnishings, and lawn mowers—seeing all of those markets as being adjacent to the cement market and assuming its customers would see things that way, too. Blue Circle's rationale went like this, according to a retired senior executive: "We started out believing that our business was not just the cement business but the supply of building products, *one* of which is cement. This led us into the bricks business and then soon after that into cooking appliances and central heating boilers—after all, these are all products you need when you build your house with our bricks and cement. The culmination of this strategy was our move into lawn mowers, based on the logic that you need a lawn mower for your garden, which is after all next to the house our materials built!"[24]

As you can imagine, the idea that Blue Circle should sell lawn mowers because they would be used near its cement was a disaster. Blue Circle's strength in cement did nothing to help it in selling gas cookers, bathroom furnishings, and lawn mowers, whose only connection to Blue Circle's core business was a semantic one. Blue Circle later unwound its diversification moves. In the meantime, it lost ground to its competitors in the cement market and was acquired by Lafarge SA in 2001.

Norelco made almost the same mistake when it decided that its electric razors meant that it could also sell coffeepots, toaster ovens, and can openers, as well as home-security systems and vacuum cleaners. The reasoning was that Norelco would just move from the bathroom to "other rooms of the house." But razors had nothing to do with kitchen appliances or home-security systems. Dick Kress, who had achieved stardom because of his successes with electric razors during the eighteen years he was president of the Norelco division of North American Philips, left the company. Norelco discontinued all his attempts at product extensions.

Tough Questions

So, how do you know if you're going to be like Jack Welch and march triumphantly into adjacent markets, or if you're going to be like Avon, Comdisco, Laidlaw, and many others in our database, and fall on your face?

Look, first, at your motivations. If you're moving into new markets because of some long-term negative trend in your core market, then look again. The odds have greatly increased that you are taking too much risk with the move into a new market. You should consider reversing the normal imperative and adopt this one: Don't just do something; stand there.

Don't just look at the similarities between your core market and the adjacent one. That's too easy, especially if you're willing to indulge in semantic games and talk about ideas like a "culture of caring." Look at the differences. Be systematic. How do the sales channels differ in the new market? How do the customers differ? How do the products differ? Are the regulatory environments different? Oftentimes, in failure cases such as Laidlaw, the core and adjacent markets may sound similar—transportation is transportation, right?—but may have differences that overpower the resemblances.

When you assemble your business plan, build in a significant margin for error. Some experts suggest, for instance, that you need to believe you have a 30 percent advantage on costs before entering a new market. Otherwise, you probably won't wind up with an advantage at all. That's because, lacking a detailed understanding of the adjacent market, you'll surely make some mistakes and underestimate certain costs. In addition, you'll incur unexpected costs that are hard to quantify, because the managers of the existing business are going to have to spend time learning how to manage the new business and will make errors along the way.

In addition to looking at the upside, explore the downside. What if the economy goes seriously south? What if the sector you're moving into goes into decline? What if your expectations about opportunities for efficiency and revenue growth don't happen? How much do you have to be off in your estimates of cost savings or revenue increases for the adjacency strategy to be a bad idea?

Don't just look at the assets that you bring to an adjacency. Look at what you lack. What don't you know about your new market? What don't you know about making acquisitions? What might you not know that you don't know?

When you look at the assets you may buy, think about what problems you'll buy along with those assets. How many of your acquisitions will be lemons? Don't say none will be, because that's wrong. Rather, pick a percentage and debate it. Then track the results and debate and revise your estimates as you go along. These problems are the sorts of things that should show up in a normal due-diligence process but that often don't, because, by the time a company gets to due diligence, it's hoping to confirm that the strategy is a good one. That's why it's important to turn the usual process on its head and actively look for problems.

Consider whether your customers will really follow you into your new market. Maybe, if you're Avon, you can add health-care products to the bags that your sales force carries, but why, if you're a utility, would your customers buy life insurance from you? There's way too much competition in the market to assume that kind of blind loyalty.

Try to find a company that did something similar to your strategy—whether through this book or some other means—and use that company's experience to challenge your assumptions.

As Avon, Laidlaw, FLYi, and many other companies have shown, just because a market is adjacent to your core market doesn't mean you'll have any success in it.

SIX

Fumbling Technology

Riding the Wrong Technology

In a cynical mood, we once decided that marketing is when you lie to your customers; market research is when you lie to yourself. That thought came to mind in studying strategic failures that stemmed from a fundamental misreading of technology trends.

The temptation to kid yourself about technology is great because the Holy Grail for every company is a killer app, a breakthrough product so enticing that it drives demand for a whole new category of products and services. Every company wants to launch the next Walkman or iPod, or to grow to be the next Bloomberg L.P., eBay Incorporated, or Google Incorporated. The garages, coffee shops, and juice bars of Silicon Valley have been filled with entrepreneurs chasing this dream for decades. A whole venture capital–fueled ecosystem has evolved to nurture and realize this ambition.

The hunger to create killer apps is not limited to start-ups; it exists in the boardrooms and cubicles of the corporate world, too. The desire has even spread to companies that wouldn't be thought of as high-tech—think dolls connected to the Internet—as technology plays an increasing role in all industries.

And why not? Breakthrough offerings can bring disproportionate rewards. While 85 percent to 90 percent of corporate developmental budgets go toward incremental improvements, these projects tend not to change competitive balance or profitability. Competitors are usually making the same moves, leading to relative competitive equilibrium and even gradual declines in profitability as customers reap the benefits of continuous improvements through lower costs. By contrast, a study by W. Chan Kim and Renée Mauborgne, the coauthors of *Blue Ocean Strategy*, found that 14 percent of a sample of business launches that attempted substantial innovations accounted for 61 percent of all the profits. These are the launches that create "blue oceans," which Kim and Mauborgne define as untapped market spaces where innovators create and capture new demand. Because the space is uncontested, innovators capture the initial period of highly profitable growth. Not all blue oceans require technology innovations, but the markets that killer apps create are, by nature, blue oceans.

While the rewards of success are great, attempts at gaining an edge through technology often end in failure. Recent studies by the Government Accountability Office and the National Institute of Standards and Technology show that almost a third of all software projects are never completed. More than half of the projects will cost almost twice as much as their original estimates. Experience does help; another recent large-scale study showed that experienced project managers are more likely to deliver projects close to budget, schedule, and scope expectations. Still, those experienced managers failed a third of the time.

The numbers get even worse when you move beyond garden-variety big software projects and get into efforts that are of strategic importance to a business. After analyzing numerous studies, Wharton School professor George Day concluded that companies attempting to introduce new products or technology into new markets failed a staggering 70 percent to 95 percent of the time. Even efforts to introduce new products or technology into existing markets failed 45 percent to 65 percent of the time. While there is a large body of research and methodology to guide the execution of technology-dependent strategies, such strategies are inherently risky.

We have no issue with many of the failures covered in these studies. When the rewards for success are so great, it makes sense that companies will take lots of stabs at achieving those rewards and will sometimes fail.

What surprised us, however, was the number of technology-dependent strategies that were ill conceived from the get-go. No amount of luck or sophisticated execution could have saved them. To keep pursuing the strategies that produced these failures—some of them spectacular—companies had to go to great lengths to kid themselves. They misjudged trends that were clearly working against them or even ignored fundamental physical limitations, such as the inability of a weak radio signal to pass through thick walls. This group of failures should have been stopped somewhere along the way.

The storied Pony Express was actually such a failure. The Pony Express assembled 50 riders, 500 horses, and 190 relay stations over 2,000 miles between Missouri and Sacramento to speed mail service in 1860, in the face of the inevitability that telegraphs and trains would soon surpass it. The Pony Express operated for only about a year. It shut down two days after the transcontinental telegraph reached Salt Lake City, Utah.

Much more recently, Motorola's launch of its Iridium satellite telephone venture shows just how thoroughly companies can lie to themselves and how disastrous the consequences can be—the phone system cost $5 billion to develop but went bankrupt less than a year after it began service, and its assets were auctioned off for $25 million. While Iridium is widely cited as a corporate failure, the lessons have been widely misread. It tends to be treated as a failure of execution or of marketing when, in fact, Iridium's failure stemmed from a flawed strategy. The case offers important lessons about the mistakes that even the most technologically savvy companies can make in evaluating the potential of new technologies.

Iridium Crashes to Earth

Motorola company lore has it that Barry Bertiger, a Motorola engineer, conceived of the satellite phone system that became Iridium when his wife, Karen, complained that she couldn't reach her real estate clients via her cell phone while on vacation in the Bahamas in 1985.

She was thwarted because, in the mid-1980s, cellular phone systems had numerous limitations. Network coverage was limited, as cellular systems mainly served major metropolitan areas and the highways that connected them. Roaming, the ability to make and receive calls outside of one's home region, was difficult at best. Roaming was nearly impossible when the caller traveled from one country to another. The prospects for quick solutions to cellular's problems were dim because phone companies, in many cases, didn't have agreements to route traffic to each other and, in fact, used different, incompatible technologies.

Karen Bertiger could have used the existing Inmarsat Satellite System, but that would have required a briefcase-sized phone with poor audio quality and annoying transmission delays. Inmarsat used geostationary communications satellites, meaning that they stayed over the same spot on the earth while they orbited 22,300 miles above it. Because of their enormous altitude, geostationary satellites can cover a large area of the earth's surface, so covering the entire globe required a small number of satellites. The downside, however, was that sending signals such a long distance required cumbersome phones with directional antennae and large batteries. The distance also introduced inevitable transmission delays, because of the time it takes the signal to travel up to the satellite and back down again.

Karen Bertiger could have, of course, gone back to her air-conditioned hotel room to make her calls. But, as the vagaries of business history would have it, she wanted to stay on the beach.

In the best tradition of problem solving, her husband took her complaint as a challenge. When he returned to his job at Motorola's satellite group in Phoenix, he and several fellow engineers designed a global satellite phone system that could connect callers anywhere on the planet. The original design called for seventy-seven satellites, and the system was dubbed Iridium for the seventy-seventh element in the periodic table.

To deal with the transmission delays and large batteries that limited the utility of the Inmarsat system, the Iridium design called for satellites that orbited a mere 420 miles aboveground. Iridium bypassed the problems of incompatibilities and the lack of call-sharing agreements; Iridium routed calls between its own satellites and used earth-based gateways to connect to plain old telephone services or individual cellular systems.

Iridium required very sophisticated hardware and software. The system would have to coordinate calls between a constellation of satellites that, from an earthbound perspective, were constantly whizzing by overhead. Phones had to find the satellites, which then had to switch calls with other satellites, which then had to decide how to route calls to ground-based systems, depending on where the other party to the call was and what type of the phone was on the other end.

Still, Motorola had a world of expertise in handling complicated switching tasks, and, if the difficulties could be surmounted, Karen

Bertiger and everybody else could conduct their business while soaking up rays and sipping umbrella drinks.

After fourteen months operating as a secret "skunk works" project, Bertiger and Raymond Leopold, the chief technical officer of the unit, won a hearing to senior management. Robert Galvin, then chairman and CEO, was immediately enthralled. Leopold recalled an early meeting at which Galvin asked Motorola president John Mitchell, "John, can you write the check faster than I can?"[1] Another version of the story is that Galvin was even more forceful, telling Mitchell, "If you don't write a check for this, John, I will. Out of my own pocket." Mitchell, not surprisingly, agreed.

Part of the enthusiastic reaction stemmed from the fact that military spending was set to decline, so Motorola, like all defense contractors, was looking for ways to commercialize expertise, such as considerable satellite technology, that it had developed doing military work. But Galvin's reaction was much deeper than that. It went to the core of how Motorola saw itself.

Founded in 1928, Motorola led the way in car radios—the name comes from a combination of "motor" and the "ola" suffix that was popular for a time—and pushed the limits in a host of other electronic technologies over the years. When Iridium came along, Motorola was a leader in two-way radios, televisions, computer chips, and mobile phones.

Motorola had just $10 million in sales when Bob Galvin joined his father's company in 1940. Over the next fifty years, Motorola enjoyed a 15 percent annual growth rate and reached $10 billion in yearly revenue. Galvin wanted to reach $100 billion by 2005. "And if we reach $100 billion, why not $200 billion by 2010, then $400 billion, and eventually $10 trillion?" he asked.[2]

Galvin attributed Motorola's success to engineering prowess and high aspirations. Writing in a journal for research managers, Galvin declared that "allowing engineers and scientists to accomplish the job is what lies at the root of our success. Conversely, failure results from holding these people back." Galvin focused Motorola on "renewal." "It is the driving thrust of our corporation," he wrote. And, by renewal, he did not just mean incremental change. "We believe that its most profound meaning is to found anew—to create something that was never thought of before. To that end, our most pressing objective is to create new industries."[3]

Galvin, a technology visionary who had spent thirty years guiding the company, saw in Iridium the audacity and potential of decades of earlier pioneering efforts.

After Galvin approved $6 million as seed money for the initial research, Motorola and several industrial partners spent $150 million to further develop the concept. In 1991, Motorola established Iridium LLC as a separate consortium to bring in outside partners to build and operate the system.

The initial reaction was tepid. Most of Iridium's natural partners, namely large landline and mobile-telephone operators, saw Iridium as a competitor, so they were reluctant to participate. Motorola also realized belatedly that there were huge regulatory hurdles to overcome. It had to lobby the International Telecommunications Union, an arcane and politically sensitive worldwide body composed of more than 170 countries, for a global license to the radio frequencies Iridium needed in order to operate. It then needed approval from the regulatory agency of every country in which it wanted to operate.[4] An initial equity placement failed.

It would take two years for Motorola and Iridium LLC to gain the necessary approvals and complete first-round financing. According to the *Wall Street Journal*, Barry Bertiger and Ray Leopold practically lived on airplanes in lobbying and fund-raising efforts. Bertiger made at least fifty visits to potential partners and investors in twenty-four countries. John Mitchell, Motorola's president, logged more than a million air miles. By 1993, they raised $800 million in equity, including $270 million from Motorola. Iridium completed a second round of financing in 1994, for $734 million. To Iridium's credit, it was the largest private placement equity to date. Raising equity allowed Iridium to arrange billions of dollars in debt financing, a portion of which Motorola guaranteed.

Iridium's business proposition was vague. It consisted mostly of sweeping statements, such as Iridium CEO Bob Kinzie's declaration in 1992, "We're bringing dial-tone to places no dial-tone has gone before."[5] John Windolph, an Iridium project spokesman, liked to remind skeptics, "Half of the people in the world today live more than two hours away from a telephone."[6] William Kidd, an analyst at C. E. Unterberg, Towbin, who adopted Motorola's exuberant pitch, wrote: "The target market was virtually the entire world." He noted that cellular phones, the ones that relied on towers rather than satellites to relay their signals, worked on only 15 percent of the earth's surface.

In fact, Motorola engineers were predicting as early as 1990 that handsets would cost around $3,000 each when the system debuted and that calls would cost around $3 per minute, plus fees paid to local cellular or landline systems. The engineers already knew that the phones would need "line-of-sight" connections to the satellites and therefore wouldn't work inside buildings or cars, or even in most metropolitan areas.

Many critics pointed out from the earliest days of the plan that it wasn't clear how Iridium could have a viable business model, given the system's limitations. "The issues facing Iridium are whether there is a need for it and whether there is a market for it," Herschel Shosteck wrote in 1992. Shosteck, the head of a Maryland-based telecommunications consulting firm and a consistent, widely quoted critic, wrote: "There are too many low-cost alternatives to Iridium, . . . not the least of which is regular telephone service. By the time that Iridium is due to go on line, technologies like fiber optics will link the remotest areas of the world, and even terrestrial cellular systems will be more widely diffused."[7]

Still, many equity investors and financiers were attracted by the sterling reputation of Motorola, which was one of the world's elite companies. It dominated the paging and cellular equipment businesses, both of which were booming despite early skepticism. The company had invented the Six Sigma quality improvement process, which had recently spread like wildfire across the corporate world. The company's Motorola University was seen as a model for leadership training. Under this halo, Motorola's trumpeting Iridium as a leapfrog technology in wireless communications was treated with respect. As Iridium's Kinzie said at the time, "When they [Motorola] put their name on a worldwide project like this, no matter how futuristic it is, people around the world want to share in the system."[8] One analyst probably captured the prevailing mood when she wrote, "If anybody can get it right, I think these guys can."[9] Another wrote, "Motorola won't let this fail."

Investors and financiers were also drawn to the heady expansion of wireless communications markets in general. In 1992, Motorola executives projected that cellular telephone users would increase from fifteen million to more than one hundred million by 2000.

Whenever skepticism was raised, Motorola was quick to recount the history of the cellular business. "Wireless naysayers were skeptical when

Motorola entered the cellular phone business back in 1983," said Christopher Galvin, Robert's son, who became CEO of Motorola during Iridium's build-out phase. "Critics predicted consumers wouldn't abandon their regular phones, but the number of wireless subscribers will hit 539 million worldwide in 2000. This is like déjà vu all over again."[10]

Internally, Iridium went to extraordinary lengths to try to make sure it wasn't breathing its own exhaust. To estimate potential demand for its services, Iridium engaged in extensive market analysis, including primary market research that involved screening more than 200,000 persons and interviewing more than 23,300 individuals from 42 countries and 3,000 corporations with remote operations. This market analysis was led by an internal marketing department of more than one hundred employees, many of whom had backgrounds in consulting, satellite, and telecommunications businesses. In addition, their efforts were augmented over the course of prelaunch planning and development by extensive efforts of top-tier consulting firms, including Arthur D. Little, Booz Allen Hamilton, A.T. Kearney, the Gallup Organization, and Coopers & Lybrand. The Coopers & Lybrand team, for example, worked for almost fifteen months and ranged in size from twenty to sixty people. In addition, numerous bankers and investors did their own due diligence, including Goldman Sachs, Chase Securities, Barclays, and Sprint.[11]

But much of the research confused marketing with market research. This is where the "lying to yourself" comes in.

For instance, as Motorola sought consortium investors in 1991, it commissioned Arthur D. Little to validate its internal estimates of Iridium's market. As a part of its market research, Arthur D. Little began a survey question by making this statement: "There will soon be a new personal telephone service which at a reasonable cost will provide you with the capability to be reached or to place calls anywhere in the world using satellite technology, which is not limited in coverage like a cellular phone. To access the service you would have a small handset that fits in your pocket. . . ." When asked whether they'd like such a device, respondents were quite positive, and Motorola enthusiastically reported the survey results at an investor conference.[12]

The problem with the survey question, as phrased, was that it was more marketing than market research. The responses validated the appeal of the Iridium concept but did little to validate the actual offering. For that to have happened, the respondents would have had to understand that "reasonable cost" meant $3,000 per handset plus $3 per minute plus monthly fees, that "anywhere" meant anywhere with a line-of-sight view of the rapidly orbiting satellites, and that "fits in your pocket" meant you needed a pocket that would hold a brick.

According to some experts, Iridium's market research repeatedly highlighted the vision while glossing over the known limits to the actual service. In doing so, the research consistently overestimated demand.

Still, from Iridium's standpoint, everything looked great. It had studies showing it was on to something, and it had equity investors and debt financing in hand. So Iridium began the development of its system in earnest in 1995.

The task was huge. In four years' time, project engineers had to build and launch a network of sixty-six satellites, plus spares, orbiting the earth along six different orbital planes. The satellites were complex, standing out especially for their ability to switch calls between satellites, a technology that had not been used commercially. In addition, Iridium had to develop a staggering twenty million lines of computer software to control the satellites, to manage the network, to switch calls, and to handle numerous billing and administrative functions.

In late 1996, midway through the development process, Iridium brought in Edward Staiano as CEO to drive Iridium to market. Staiano left his position leading Motorola's $11 billion cellular phone division to do so. As incentive, he was awarded more than one million options that vested over a five-year period. He had tremendous incentives to make Iridium work and no incentives to look for problems that would kill the project. "If I can make Iridium's dream come true, I'll make a significant amount of money," he said.[13] Staiano seemed well suited for the role. He had a reputation at Motorola as a hard-driving and demanding leader. One of his first major decisions was to ban all vacations at Iridium.

Still, there were serious technical glitches, schedule delays, and cost overruns. The launch of the first satellite took five tries because of problems that included software glitches and loose insulation of the launch rocket's liquid-oxygen tanks. Once in place, a number of satellites failed, and there were not enough spares. Iridium had to launch five more satellites than originally planned, two to replaced failed satellites and three as additional spares. There were also problems in testing, with call completion and dropped calls. Just weeks before the official launch date, only 70 percent to 80 percent of calls were being connected at all. Of those, 15 percent were dropped before the end of the call. Even as Iridium was preparing to launch the service, one of its main handset suppliers was still grappling with software bugs. The Iridium system ultimately cost hundreds of millions more to launch than originally estimated, therefore putting the whole venture in a very precarious debt position.

Worse, even as glitches were addressed, the serious fundamental limitations of the service were becoming apparent to all. As expected, the phones did not work inside buildings, in cars, or in dense metropolitan areas where tall buildings blocked line-of-sight access to the satellites. The satellites only handled 11,000 simultaneous calls, which wasn't a problem initially but which would ultimately limit the size of the customer base. The service was focused on voice communications, allowing only low-bandwidth data transmissions, thus missing out on the explosion in demand for data transmission being generated by the Internet. And the six-year expected life of each satellite implied huge continuing maintenance and operations costs. The handsets were a throwback to the earliest days of cellular, in both form and cost. As the engineers had long forecast, the handset would cost $3,000 and calls would cost around $3 per minute, not including monthly service fees and other calling charges (such as the costs tacked on by other telephone companies).

None of these limitations should have been a surprise, as they had been well-documented characteristics for years. But they had been overshadowed by the poetic descriptions about Iridium's anywhere-to-anywhere phone capabilities.

Iridium's limitations were ever more apparent because of the rapid improvements of its main competitor, cellular systems. Global standards were improving the ability for calls to be shared between networks. Technology was improving audio quality. Massive adoption was driving down price. As one analyst asked, "Who wants to use a phone that won't even work indoors, that weighs 16 ounces and costs $5 a minute? In the United States, it costs a dime to use a phone you carry in your pocket. Even in undeveloped countries, they usually have phones in the hotel you can use, and, even if it is expensive, so is Iridium, and at least the hotel phone works indoors."[14]

Iridium remained adamant. It cited research that showed that 250 million people used cell phones, and that about 40 million traveled and made enough money to afford the $3,000 Iridium phone and its calling charges. Craig Bond, Iridium's vice president for market development, said the company needed only a tiny sliver of the market, about six hundred thousand clients, to break even and predicted it would reach that magic number by the end of 1999. The company said Iridium would have $4 billion of annual revenue by 2005.[15]

For a while, the markets embraced the story. In 1997, Iridium issued $240 million of equity through an IPO, successfully floated $1.1 billion of high-yield debt, and arranged a $1 billion secured bank facility.

Iridium officially started service on November 1, 1998. It launched with an aggressive $140 million advertising campaign in sixteen languages across forty-five countries targeted at globe-trotting business travelers like Karen Bertiger. Ed Staiano told one reporter that it wasn't unreasonable to expect Iridium to have about forty thousand customers by the end of 1998. He also expected the company's operations to generate enough cash to exceed operating expenses by the fourth quarter of 1999.[16] As it turned out, neither Staiano nor Iridium even survived until the fourth quarter of 1999.

The immediate problem was that, ironically, after a decade of development, Iridium rushed to market before it was ready. Manufacturing delays at its two suppliers, Motorola and Kyocera, limited the availability of handsets. One influential industry analyst wrote that he bought his handset at Iridium's launch but did not receive it until January and could not get his service turned on until February. Sales and distribution were left to regional partners, many of which were not yet geared up to handle customer inquiries; it was estimated that the initial advertising barrage generated more than one million inquiries that were never pursued. Some partners, such as Sprint, which owned 3.5 percent of Iridium, were planning on selling a dual-mode service, which essentially used Iridium as an option of last resort when there was no cellular coverage. But the dual-mode phones were not yet available when Iridium was launched.

Another problem was that the handsets were extremely unattractive, especially to the elite business travelers being targeted. Looking at an early model of the handset, one Iridium marketing executive said, "It's huge. It will scare people. If we had a campaign that featured our product, we'd lose."[17]

The most fundamental problem, however, was one that better handsets, marketing, and execution could not have solved. While the vision claimed in advertising, "Anyone, Anywhere, Anytime—Iridium," was thrilling, that was not actually what Iridium provided. Rather than leapfrogging cellular, as Motorola promised investors, Iridium was a poor cousin that had to survive on the scraps of the diminishing market not yet served by cellular. That's because, in the ever-expanding service areas covered by cellular, where most of Iridium's potential customers roamed, Iridium either did not work or paled in comparison. Yet, in the market left to Iridium—the remote areas not covered by cellular—most potential users could not afford the rates that Iridium's high fixed costs and limited calling capacity demanded. Sure, great marketing scenarios could be spun about globe-trotting executives on exotic vacations, or adventurers, sailors, and workers at remote construction sites. But how many of these people are there, and how many call minutes would they generate?

The results were dismal. Rather than the forty thousand customers forecast by Ed Staiano for the end of 1998, Iridium had just a few thousand. Revenues were negligible. Iridium posted a $440 million loss for the fourth quarter of 1998. Iridium's loan covenants called for it to have more than fifty thousand customers by the end of the first quarter of 1999. Iridium had, instead, just a little more than ten thousand. It had revenue of $1.5 million in the quarter, far short of operating expenses, much less the $100 million it owed creditors on its $3.4 billion in debt. It posted a $505 million loss for the quarter. By the end of April, Staiano was gone.

Creditors gave Iridium several extensions to meet its loan covenants. John Richardson, who replaced Ed Staiano as CEO, tried to reposition Iridium for vertical markets such as oil and gas exploration and to entice customers with major price cuts. But by August, just nine months after it launched, Iridium had defaulted on more than $1.5 billion in debt and declared Chapter 11 bankruptcy.

While Iridium and Motorola had forecast that Iridium would have six hundred thousand customers by the end of 1999, at the time of the filing Iridium had about twenty thousand.

When various attempts at restructuring debt obligations failed, Iridium's assets were eventually auctioned off for $25 million, about half what it would have cost to safely destroy the satellites.

Motorola had tried to insulate itself from whatever happened to Iridium by becoming primarily a contractor to it, albeit one that had more than $6 billion of business locked up with Iridium. But Motorola would eventually write off more than $2.5 billion related to Iridium and spend eight years after the bankruptcy filing fighting off billions in additional claims by Iridium's other investors and creditors.

Motorola's market value has, as of this writing, fallen more than two-thirds from where it was at the time of the Iridium bankruptcy filing. Chris Galvin resigned in 2003, with the company under severe pressure because of problems in its cellular business. His successor, Ed Zander, briefly oversaw a revival but acknowledged a new wave of problems in 2007 and resigned at the beginning of 2008.

RED FLAGS

Iridium demonstrates the key mistakes that lead companies to ride the wrong technology into disaster:

- They evaluate their offering in isolation or at a single point in time, rather than in the context of how alternatives will evolve over time.
- They confuse market research with marketing, allowing their entrenched interests and hopes to color the analysis of true market potential.
- They find false security in competition, incorrectly thinking that the presence of rivals equates to a validation of the potential market.
- They design the effort as a front-loaded gamble, foreclosing possibilities for adaptation and severely limiting the option to stop.

Bet on the Context, Not the Vision

"Skate to where the puck is going, not to where it is," advised Wayne Gretzky, the Hall of Fame hockey player, imparting a piece of advice that is crucial in thinking about technology.

At the time Iridium was conceived in 1987, mobile phones were physically unwieldy and provided poor connections. They were usually carried in briefcases rather than pockets. They required special antennae when operated from cars. And users had to find a nearby window when inside buildings. Mobile phone service performed, in essence, much like the Iridium phones would a decade later. If offered in 1987 rather than 1997, Iridium would have provided comparable service while addressing cellular's coverage and roaming limitations. (Even then, it is doubtful whether it would have been the leapfrog technology that Motorola touted. There were serious questions about whether Iridium's capacity limitations would have allowed it to scale, and in the process drive down costs, as terrestrial cellular services did. But Iridium would have been much more competitive.)

The rest of the world, of course, did not stand still. Iridium's engineers, actually, did a very good job of delivering the long-promised function, feature, and cost characteristics. In the decade that it took for Iridium to reach the market, however, cellular technology advanced at an exponential rate—the puck moved. The cellular industry had long since reset customer expectations for price and quality. Cellular had eaten up the most lucrative geographical regions by expanding coverage. It had adopted standards that made roaming from network to network much easier. By 1998, though Iridium's vision was compelling, its service offering was not.

Federal Express also misread the relevant technology trends related to its Zapmail product, leading to huge losses.

Fred Smith built FedEx's overnight-delivery business throughout the 1970s. Smith realized early, however, that the growth of digital communications would inevitably cut into his overnight-document business, which by 1984 had grown to account for a third of FedEx's revenues and half of its shipments. Rather than wait for the onslaught, Smith invested $100 million over four years to launch Zapmail. "We could consider [digital] to be a threat, or we could attack," one FedEx executive said at the time.[18]

With Zapmail, FedEx couriers would pick up paper documents and deliver them to a nearby FedEx processing center. FedEx would fax the documents to another processing center near the destination. From there, another courier would deliver the documents to the recipient, all within two hours. The cost was $35 for as many as five pages. If the customer brought the document to the FedEx office, FedEx charged $25 and promised delivery within an hour. High-volume customers, ones that sent more than ten to twenty documents a month, could lease facsimile machines for in-house usage.

Fax machines were not new; ITT Corporation had been offering an in-office fax service for five years. But FedEx thought that it had discovered what Kim and Mauborgne refer to in *Blue Ocean Strategy* as a "value innovation," an innovative combination of value, differentiation, and cost. FedEx saw that fax machines were too expensive for most companies to acquire and that the transmission quality was too poor. It reasoned that if it developed a private fax network using specially designed fax machines and high-quality leased telephone lines, it could offer a valuable service built on the technology at a reasonable cost to customers.

Like many failures, Zapmail had the germ of a good idea. From FedEx's perspective, Zapmail was absolutely a win-win proposition. Customers, FedEx reasoned, no longer had to wait for documents to "absolutely, positively" arrive the next day when the need was so immediate that "there was no tomorrow." And FedEx could provide its service at lower cost and with higher quality than customers would have had if left to their own devices. Besides, there was no guarantee that the intended recipient would have a fax machine, so having FedEx physically deliver a document took the guesswork out of the equation. From FedEx's perspective, as one analyst described it, "Toner would replace jet fuel, bike messengers' hourly rates would replace pilots' salaries, and so on. With a much less expensive network, FedEx could attract customers with a discount on regular delivery rates, but, with the dramatically lower costs, profit margins would be huge compared to actually moving packages point to point. Lower prices, higher margins, and, to top it all off, the customer would get their documents in 2 hours instead of 24. What's not to love?"[19]

Zapmail was, however, an abject failure because it was built on the assumption that the puck wasn't going to move. While Zapmail made preeminent sense from the isolated vantage point of FedEx's existing business, it made little sense in the broader context of fax and other digital transmission trends. First, while fax machines were expensive and data transmission problems frequent when Zapmail was launched, faxes were getting cheaper and better rapidly. Zapmail's target customers soon found it cheaper to buy their own fax machines than to use the Zapmail service. In addition, widely adopted industry fax standards soon provided higher resolution, faster speeds, and greater compatibility between fax machines. But Zapmail used nonstandard fax machines. Customers who leased FedEx fax machines could only send faxes to other FedEx customers. The customers had to rely on FedEx couriers to deliver faxes to everyone else. Because of the rapid improvement of industry-standard fax machines, they soon dwarfed the number on FedEx's isolated network. One estimate is that there were five hundred thousand fax machines in the United States in 1986, of which only seven thousand belonged to the FedEx network. FedEx spent $100 million assembling its network, while no single company had to bear the expense of the much larger, more powerful public network; users were building that network at their own expense, one machine at a time.

Toby Redshaw, who was a junior member of the team, code-named Gemini, that developed the Zapmail strategy, says FedEx got itself caught up because it viewed the world through the prism of documents. It focused relentlessly on building a fax system that would deliver documents that looked like the original—even though the quality added little to the value of the documents, given that the legal system doesn't recognize faxed signatures as valid, no matter how good the fax. Redshaw, now a senior executive with Aviva PLC, said FedEx also focused on its traditional approach of point-to-point deliveries, rather than grasping the potential value of a huge network of fax machines and trying to find a way into that market. FedEx "failed to see that person to courier to machine to machine to courier to person was a very different product and customer experience than machine to machine," he says.

Redshaw says he once got so frustrated that, despite his junior status, he shut down two members of the team who were continually diverting the discussion to consider issues that ultimately weren't going to matter to customers. The project manager thanked him after the meeting, then added, "The only problem is that both of them are senior vice presidents, and now they want to squash you." In the end, of course, the senior vice presidents won—and FedEx lost.

(Redshaw also contributes a story from earlier in his career—when he was at Motorola, at it happens—to illustrate how bosses squash challenges by subordinates. "My boss had two really bad habits," Redshaw says. "First, he'd say, 'Team, I have a great idea. It's really fantastic. But before I pursue it I want to have open discussions to make sure it's really good.' Yikes. Second, if someone disagreed with him, he'd often say, 'What are you, stupid?' Actually, he'd shout it.")

When Zapmail launched in 1984, FedEx predicted it would replace as much as 30 percent of FedEx's document and urgent-letter traffic. FedEx forecast that Zapmail would generate $1.3 billion in sales, or about a third of FedEx's expected overall revenue, by 1988. Instead, FedEx shut down Zapmail altogether in 1986, after losing $317 million during the two years of service. The closure resulted in another $340 million pretax write-off.

Lies, Damn Lies, and Marketing

From the moment of its conception, Iridium's universal phone service vision was brilliant. The vision was so brilliant that it seemed to blind management and investors to the realities of the service that would ultimately be delivered, and to the competitive realities of substitute offerings. It didn't seem to matter that the fine print, throughout Iridium's development, contained numerous declarations that the service was far from universal, that the handset and other equipment would be clunky, that the cost would be exorbitant, and that there were limited opportunities for economies of scale as the offering matured.

How could so many talented, hardworking people have it so wrong? Part of the answer lies in the difference between marketing and market research, and what can happen if one confuses the two.

Henry Goldblatt, writing in *Fortune* in early 1999 just months after Iridium's launch, captured Iridium's allure—and why there were so few customers. He described telling a globe-trotting TV producer about

Iridium's ability to send and receive phone calls and pages anywhere. The producer, who took three cell phones on his long trips—each capable of working in only one part of the world—replied, "If I could have one phone I could take anywhere, I'd be the happiest man on the planet." What if it resembled a brick with a baguette sticking out of it? "Umm . . . I'd rather stick to my little Nokia."

Most Iridium users were like Howard Anderson, a Boston-based venture capitalist. Anderson paid $3,500 for his Iridium phone but did not use it for business. He took it instead on exotic excursions to South America, Australia, and Africa. He sent it into the jungles of Vietnam and Cambodia with his daughter. Of the dozens of times he tried to use it, it worked once. In his two years of owning it, he made one essential call, so his cost per call was $3,500, plus monthly service fees. But, as Anderson described it, "the amazing thing was that it worked at all." In the end, Anderson says, he bronzed the phone to remind himself "to be wary of technological feats that suck up money."[20]

What was Iridium's real market potential? Consider this relative measure raised by Herschel Shosteck, the telecommunications analyst and longtime Iridium critic: "If all of the revenue from international business travelers calling internationally from developing countries went to Iridium, Iridium would still not be able to cover its capital costs, let alone its operating costs." And, of course, Iridium could only compete for a fraction of that revenue because of its service limitations and because of pricing that dwarfed that of any available alternative.

There is a long history of market research that tells companies—incorrectly—what they want to hear. Western Union Company, which was wedded to the telegraph business, concluded in 1876: "This 'telephone' has too many shortcomings to be seriously considered as a means of communication. The device is inherently of no value to us."[21] Thomas Watson Sr., chairman of IBM, which relied on sales of mechanical business machines, said in 1943, "I think there is a world market for maybe five computers."[22] Ken Olson, founder of Digital Equipment Corporation, the leading minicomputer company, said in 1977, "There is no reason anyone would want a computer in their home."[23] IBM, which by the 1980s relied on sales of large computers, predicted right before the introduction of its personal computer in 1981 that the total market for PCs over the lifetime of the product would be about two hundred thousand machines.[24] Currently, Hewlett-Packard and Dell each sell that many PCs every three or four days.

Beware the Lemming Syndrome

Companies tend to find false comfort when others are pursuing similar strategies. There must be a viable market, they reason, if others are chasing it as well. The question then becomes one of who will win versus whether a strategy to enter the market makes any sense at all.

This lemming syndrome happened in the case of Iridium, as a number of other consortia followed Motorola's lead and jumped into the race for satellite voice and data communications. One contender was ICO Communications, created by Inmarsat PLC, the satellite phone offering that predated Iridium. Other contenders included Globalstar, a consortium started by Loral Corporation, and Odyssey, a consortium begun by TRW Incorporated. Both Loral and TRW were defense contractors looking to commercialize their military technology.

With the market potential validated in large part by Motorola's support for Iridium, these other ventures aimed to capture the satellite phone market with better technical and partnering strategies. ICO, for example, planned to keep costs low by relying on only twelve medium-altitude earth-orbiting satellites, a far smaller number than Iridium's sixty-six. Odyssey sought to limit complexity by building a service that covered just the United States. Globalstar kept costs lower by launching a smaller constellation of simpler low-altitude earth-orbiting satellites that just relayed signals to a larger number of ground relays, rather than switching them between satellites as Iridium did.

The competitive focus turned toward a mishmash of technical and operational differences, rather than the ultimate question of whether any multibillion-dollar satellite communications venture was viable. Many observers argued that the market could not support all of these ventures, so every group rushed to get to market first. In its 1997 prospectus, Iridium named the other satellite ventures as its competition and cited getting to market earlier as a key part of its strategy.

Yet the real competitor was cellular. The satellite companies had initially assumed that cellular would be limited to urban areas in the developing world, but cellular quickly spread beyond cities, eating away at satellite phones' potential markets. In the end, all of the satellite phone ventures either shut down or went into bankruptcy.

The lemming syndrome is, in fact, rather common. In the 1980s, every electronics company worth its silicon decided it would get into the market for personal computers. There were TV manufacturers such as Zenith Electronics Corporation. There were Japanese consumer-electronics companies such as Sony. There were minicomputer makers such as Wang Laboratories Incorporated. All this interest occurred even though, by 1984, it was clear that PCs were probably on their way to being commodities, with razor-thin margins. Microsoft Corporation, as the supplier of the operating system, and Intel, as the supplier of the central processor, were going to make some serious money. But among those who bundled everything together into a PC, IBM was the only one with much of a chance to make a technological breakthrough that would eclipse Microsoft and Intel and capture hefty profits. Apple Computer Incorporated had a lesser, but real, chance because it controlled all the technology in its computers. Yet as many as ten other companies convinced themselves that they could capture the market if they could just edge each other out. Each company somehow came to the conclusion that it could gain a 20 percent share of the key U.S. market.[25]

To this day, no company has a 20 percent share of the market. And even those few companies that survived the brutal competition that occurred when everyone tumbled into the market found that the PC market is no El Dorado. The market is huge but has cutthroat margins, and any mistake is costly, as even Dell has learned.

The same sort of problem afflicted telecommunications companies in the late 1990s. Everyone rushed to put fiber in the ground, hoping to beat the other guy to the punch and lock up traffic. Companies spent tens of billions on their efforts. An acquaintance of ours once bragged to us that he had tied up all of Corning Incorporated's fiber production for the foreseeable future, freezing out competitors.

In their haste to get to market, though, what people didn't realize was that there just wasn't demand for anything close to the amount of fiber being laid. People were forgetting about Moore's Law, that computer processors double in power every eighteen to twenty-four months for the same price. The upshot of Moore's Law is that the processors that route traffic over the fiber improve so fast that, even without additional fiber in the ground, the capacity of the telecom networks doubles every year and a half to two years. Actually, for a while there, the processors used in telecom were improving much faster than Moore's Law would suggest. So, while the Internet was certainly driving a surge in traffic over telecom networks, the natural progression of technology could accommodate almost all of the increase. Telecom companies took billions of dollars of write-offs on their fiber investments, and many companies—including our acquaintance's—went out of business. It's only been recently that telecom companies have started "lighting" the fiber that has lain "dark" in the ground since the late 1990s and early 2000s.

Research shows that the lemming syndrome tends to show up in two types of situations. One is when diverse competitors are facing high uncertainty about the market or technology. Lemmings, in this case, fear that competitors, especially highly regarded ones, know something they don't and swiftly follow the leader so as not to be left out. Disaster can occur when the role model is on a doomed path, and thus the others follow it over the cliff. The various competitors to Iridium, afraid that Motorola would walk away with a lucrative new market, fall into this pattern.

The other situation where the lemming syndrome shows up is when relatively evenly matched rivals imitate each other so as not to let competitors gain a differentiated position. Disaster can happen when the collective action leads to mutual harm, such as when so many telecom companies overinvested in fiber. If only one had done so, it might have cornered the market. The fact that so many followed the same path completely oversaturated the market, leading to years of losses before demand could catch up.

A Field of Nightmares

The only thing harder than starting a bold new strategy is killing one after it starts. Once a strategy is launched, there is often too much ego, credibility, and money on the line to stop. Stopping is seen as a clear failure, whereas forging on offers continued hope—even if that hope is no more than a fading long shot. The long lead times and high fixed costs associated with technology-related strategies make them especially hard to stop before total failure. Management and investors alike adopt a "field of dreams" approach, where success is hinged on a "build it and they will come" philosophy, rather than experimentation and gradual ramp-up. Then the field of dreams turns out to be a field of nightmares.

From a design standpoint, for example, Iridium was an all-or-nothing proposition. Iridium's initial market was drawn to be virtually the entire world. This required an immense investment in infrastructure, marketing, and operations before the system could be tested and the first subscriber call could be made. It required enormous management time to coordinate the numerous partners, not to mention the front-loaded effort required to negotiate and administer the 256 operating agreements with local providers in 100 countries before launch.

As a result, at least from an internal perspective, there was no logical point at which Iridium could pause and reflect and consider abandoning the venture. Iridium and Motorola didn't face up to the fundamental problems until after billions of dollars were spent and the system had gone.

Another "field of dreams" strategy was undertaken by Webvan Group Incorporated, a company that hoped to revolutionize the grocery industry by taking orders online and delivering groceries to customers' doorsteps. Launched in April 1999, Webvan promised to save time-starved consumers the trip to the grocery store. Webvan expected that it, in turn, would save itself the cost of multiple stores, relying instead on sophisticated distribution centers that served entire metropolitan regions. On the allure of its digital storefront, Webvan was able to raise almost $1 billion of venture capital and investor dollars during the dot-com boom of the late 1990s.

There's a saying in Silicon Valley that the worst thing you can do to a start-up is to give it too much money. Flush with funding, Webvan raced to build a twenty-six-city network of warehouses—even though there were few economies of scale for doing so. The consequences were disastrous. The sensible approach would have been to build a few facilities and debug them, then incorporate the learning into future facilities. Instead, Webvan took its initial flawed design and built it in every city. Lessons that could have been used to build better facilities were learned too late. For example, Webvan built elaborate on-site butcher operations in every warehouse, only to decide later that it was more efficient to have prepared meat delivered daily. Webvan built separate fresh fruit and vegetable operations in the warehouses, then realized it was better to combine them. Webvan built walk-in humidors, then phased them out. A visitor to Webvan's huge distribution center in Oakland, California, estimated that reconfigurations led to 30 percent to 40 percent of the warehouse space being left unused. The simultaneous build-out in so many markets also led to poor adaptation to local demographics and shopping patterns. Customers in congested metropolitan areas like San Francisco, for example, valued different qualities from those in cities such as Los Angeles and Atlanta, where people are more likely to drive. The enormity of Webvan's undertaking led to a plague of operational kinks. One worker said Webvan rarely went a month without a major meltdown, which could result in as many as 1,700 orders being late, incomplete, or not delivered.[26]

Webvan ceased operations in July 2001, a little more than two years after its launch, after losing about $700 million on operations. Efforts at restructuring failed, and the company assets were liquidated. As one analyst observed, "Webvan invested in infrastructure the way the ill-fated Iridium venture launched satellites, burning through more than $800 million without pausing long enough to test the basic viability of its business model."[27]

In this case, FedEx shows the value of incrementalism. While it could have been argued that FedEx needed to saturate the country with vans and drivers on day one, to freeze out competition, founder Fred Smith took a much more limited approach. He initially built a network involving enough cities to make the service worthwhile, to test his concept and work out the kinks. Only then did he begin his truly massive national rollout. Smith, who first proposed the idea for FedEx in a class paper while studying economics at Yale, got a C for his effort. But we'll give him an A for his intelligently incremental approach.

Tough Questions

Technology is complicated enough that certain problems come with the territory. In *Gödel, Escher, Bach,* Douglas Hofstadter proposed his wonderfully recursive Hofstadter's Law, which is often applied to software development: "It always takes longer than you expect, even when you take Hofstadter's Law into account." That law could be applied to all technology projects. Technology implementation usually takes more time and resources than you think, even when you realize that it will take more time and resources than you think. That law is affecting more and more companies as technology spreads its influence into sectors of the economy it didn't previously touch. All you can really do is try to mitigate the effects of the time and cost problems through smart management.

What shouldn't come with the territory are technology-based strategies that are ill conceived, that will always wind up in a dead end.

To avoid riding the wrong technology curve, start by making sure that you're assessing your options in the right context and over the appropriate time frame. Iridium, for example, was a ten-year development effort, and, once launched, the satellites had a five-year average life span. So Iridium couldn't just be different at the outset of the project. Iridium had to be able to differentiate itself against competitive offerings over at least that fifteen-year period. These offerings included not only other satellite phone offerings but also other telecommunications offerings, such as traditional landlines, cellular offerings, and the Internet.

You need to look at performance trajectories, a concept discussed by Clayton Christensen in his insightful work on disruptive technologies. In numerous articles and books, he provides a valuable framework for assessing the relative positioning of alternative technologies over time. Performance trajectories capture the rate at which the performance of a product has improved, and is expected to improve. Christensen notes that almost every industry has a critical performance trajectory. In mechanical excavators, it is the annual improvement of cubic yards of earth moved per minute. In photocopiers, it is improvement in the number of copies per minute. In disk drives, it is storage capacity. For mobile telephony, it might have been cost per minute, handset size, or some similar measure.

Too often, companies fail to realize that, while their technology might be superior at a point in time, an alternative technology is on a clear trajectory to surpass it. This was certainly true in the case of Iridium. Iridium's satellite technology's design constraints, including the finite capacity of each satellite, the inherent limitations of its low-power signal, and its requirement for line-of-sight connections led to a relatively flat performance trajectory. In contrast, the massive build-out and improvements of the cellular network placed it on a steep performance trajectory.

For digital technologies, there are well-established principles that guide the estimation of future improvements. Moore's Law, for instance, affects almost every aspect of computing, including telecommunications bandwidth, disk storage, memory, and display technology. Never bet against Moore's Law. If you're betting on a technology that doesn't benefit from Moore's Law and hope to compete against a technology that does, you'll lose. Every time.

Another long-established principle is Metcalfe's Law, which says that the value of a network is proportional to the square of the number of users. That's because the number of conversations enabled by a network of n people is roughly n^2. Metcalfe's Law is powerful because, after a certain point, a network achieves critical mass. If someone has a network of one thousand people and another has a network of ten thousand, the larger network has almost surely won. The difference in the value of the networks isn't a factor of ten; it's a factor of one hundred, according to Metcalfe's Law.

With Zapmail, FedEx missed both Moore's Law and Metcalfe's Law. FedEx assumed that physical delivery would maintain an advantage over electronic delivery, even though Moore's Law was constantly making electronic delivery less expensive and was improving the quality, while nothing could do the same for couriers. FedEx also misunderstood how quickly the public network of fax machines would surpass its proprietary network. FedEx built a sizable network of seven thousand fax machines, but, just two years after Zapmail's launch, the public fax network had some five hundred thousand machines attached to it. Given that the two networks couldn't communicate with each other, the public network was five thousand times as valuable as the FedEx network, according to Metcalfe's Law. End of story.

A lesser-known but powerful principle is Reed's Law. Reed's Law, coined by David Reed, a professor at MIT, extends Metcalfe's Law by recognizing that new members increase a network's utility even faster in networks that allow arbitrary group formation. At the risk of introducing a little math, the number of possible groups that can be formed by *n* people is 2 to the *n*th power, which increases exponentially—far, far faster than *n* squared. Reed used his law in 1998 to predict that, of all the Internet start-ups, eBay would be the one with the greatest staying power; eBay drew on the power of group-forming networks by letting people essentially form little subgroups based on their interest in cars, antiques, Pez dispensers, or whatever. Reed's Law also explains why group-forming networks like MySpace and Facebook have become so popular. The law explains why any business strategy that relies on community will have a very hard time if an element of the strategy is to pull people away from a larger, strongly established community. Even eBay found this to be true when it tried to move into some foreign markets where competitors had established online auction sites that had built a big following. eBay's brand name and technical know-how weren't enough to overcome Reed's Law.

With all that as preamble, here are some questions that companies should ask themselves: What will your competition look like by the time you get to market? What if you're six months late? A year? How does your performance trajectory compare with the competition's? Do your projections incorporate Moore's Law, for both yourself and your competition? In other words, is your competition riding Moore's Law while you're more earthbound? Have you allowed for Metcalfe's Law and what it says about the relative value of networks? Is Reed's Law relevant? If so, are you on the right side, with the big network?

Another important aspect of avoiding the wrong technology curve is to get outside of your own biases, to look at potential offerings through the eyes of customers. Take the Chrysler LeBaron convertible. No American automaker had made a convertible since 1976. In 1980, Chrysler Corporation CEO Lee Iacocca sensed that American consumers were ready for an affordable convertible. But his market researchers projected a market for just three thousand cars. Instead of accepting the research, Iacocca had a Chrysler K-Car sent to a custom body shop in California. It was rebuilt into a convertible and secretly shipped back East. That winter, Iacocca personally drove it around Boca Raton, Florida, where his limited but live testing drew such an enthusiastic reception that he decided the market was real. He went ahead, and the car was a hit. It sold twenty-four thousand, eight times what the research predicted.

So the question is: What do customers really think? If Iridium had been able to answer that question through an Iacocca-like test drive, Iridium could have saved itself a lot of time and trouble.

You may have to work hard to figure out what customers think. You not only have to avoid the sorts of leading questions that Iridium asked, you also have to get past the fact that customers sometimes don't know what they want or, for some reason, won't tell you. While we don't have the room to go through a detailed discussion of research methodology—dozens of books have been written on the subject—we'd suggest a look into the work being done at a growing number of companies that have concluded that asking consumers questions is a poor way to find out what they think. Instead, companies like Procter & Gamble Company, Volvo Group, and AB Electrolux have formalized Iacocca's instincts by sending cultural anthropologists out to study consumers in real life, rather than relying on market-research surveys. Electrolux, for example, has switched from using marketing surveys that ask consumers what they want to actually visiting consumers in their homes to see how they use their appliances. "We never ask the consumer what they want," says Johan Hjertonsson, the Swedish appliance maker's head of consumer innovation. "We do anthropology. We study the consumer."[28]

To avoid the lemming syndrome, you have to keep asking yourself questions about the basics of the market and not succumb to the temptation to do something just because the competition has.

The question can't become: Can you beat your competitors to market? It has to be: Is the market real? Oftentimes, your competitors don't know any more than you do. (This applies, by the way, outside of technology issues. When Merck & Company bought Medco Containment Services Incorporated, a pharmacy benefits manager, for $6.6 billion in 1993, other big drug companies decided that Merck must be on to something, that combining drugs with a way to deliver them to customers was the way to go. Several others also bought PBMs. All failed.)

To avoid the "field of dreams" illusion, the question is: Do you have to do it all at once? Or can you try things a bit at a time and learn as you go along?

With some strategies, you have to go whole hog. But plenty of times, as with Webvan, it was eminently possible to proceed a bit at a time.

We're not trying to talk anyone out of pursuing a strategy based on technology. Far from it. We believe that technology can be used to create enormously profitable businesses. In fact, we've spent much of our careers helping businesses understand how to use technology to gain competitive advantage. We'll go further and say that, in a rational world, there would be no start-ups. No start-up should be able to match the industry expertise, customer relationships, brand equity, or other deep competencies of an established competitor. So it makes sense that, when breakthrough opportunities are spotted, CEOs and senior managers at big businesses should pursue them. But in their haste to go after opportunities, companies need to make sure they don't wind up riding the wrong technology curve.

SEVEN

Consolidation Blues

Doubling Down on a Bad Hand

Consolidation is treated as such a natural thing as an industry matures that the term might as well be incorporated into the famous statement from the narrator in Ecclesiastes: "To everything there is a season, and a time to every purpose under the heaven: / A time to be born, and a time to die; a time to plant, and a time to consolidate. . . ."

It makes great sense that, as an industry matures, the number of companies in it will diminish. Some companies thrive, but some die. As production becomes more efficient, overcapacity develops, putting pressure on profits. So there is incentive for those that remain to combine and reduce capacity. Besides, combining offers the prospect of having the best of both companies: You keep the best people, the best manufacturing facilities, the best processes.

When consolidation happens, companies typically want to be the buyers, not the sellers. Buyers are remembered. Sellers are absorbed and forgotten. Executives at the buyers get to expand their domains, probably at even higher compensation.

As an article by consulting firm A.T. Kearney puts it, when an industry reaches the consolidation stage, companies "have reached a crossroads. Either they continue along the path to glory, or they die by the sword."[1]

But it turns out that simply because an industry will consolidate, it doesn't mean you should be the buyer. Sometimes, our failure cases show, it would be better to sit back and let others fumble through the consolidation. Sometimes it would be better to sell, pocketing as much cash as you can before conditions in the industry get worse.

Depending on the conditions of the industry and of your company, buying a company as a consolidation move can amount to doubling down on a bad hand. As consultant and author Gary Hamel puts it pithily, "Putting two drunks together doesn't make a stable person."[2]

A year-long study, sponsored by the Harvard Business School and described in the *Harvard Business Review* in 2001, found that, as bad as the failure rate is for mergers and acquisitions in general, the crummy record for purchases done in the name of consolidation stands out. "Just about anything that can go wrong with integration does," Joseph Bowers writes in the *HBR* article.

Consolidation tends to involve big companies, which have strongly established cultures, making them harder to mesh, Bowers writes. "Years after such mergers, it is common for managers from acquirer Alpha to describe an employee from the acquired company as a Beta company guy," Bowers says. Consolidation plays also fail because, he writes, they're "very much a win-lose situation." The acquiring company's executives usually keep their jobs. Its plants are the ones kept open. So the losers try to make life difficult for the winners by resisting change, and the best of those from the losing company may leave. Everyone, from both the winner and the loser, spends an inordinate amount of time trying to make sure they don't lose any clout in the merger. Bowers says that, while the idea is to just pick the best processes, it's hard to figure out which those are, because there are so many variables. And settling on a single set of processes is disruptive. The processes of a company are at the core of what it is, so a change can drastically reduce productivity, at least for a time. For good measure, there isn't any learning from the merger that will help the combined company down the road; in the early stages of an industry's life, companies may make serial acquisitions, learning from each one and doing the next one better, but the size of acquisitions in the late, consolidation phase of an industry tends to make them one-offs.

Despite the benefits that are claimed for consolidation moves, the article calculates that banks haven't become more efficient even though a wave of consolidation has seen the amount of assets held by the ten largest banks in the United States climb to 51.5 percent as of 2006, up from 19.5 percent ten years earlier. Similarly, the *Economist* wrote in 2000 that, despite decades of merging and cost cutting among airlines, as of 1995 the industry as a whole was still unprofitable over the whole history of flying.

Bowers warns companies to take a hard look at themselves and at the companies they're thinking of buying: "If processes and values aren't similar, back off and reconsider."

The story of the demise of Ames Department Stores Incorporated shows, in stark relief, the potential pitfalls of a consolidation strategy. The company pioneered the concept of discount retailing in rural areas four years before Sam Walton got the itch to give it a try. Ames eventually became the third- or fourth-largest discount retailer in the country, after only Wal-Mart and Kmart Corporation and maybe Target Corporation, depending on who was counting. But Ames got reckless and made a series of bad acquisitions in an attempt to become more productive, so it could compete with Wal-Mart, and to build a national presence, so it could move away from its traditional reliance on the Northeast. The company filed for bankruptcy in 1990 but recovered, only to make the same mistakes again. The company liquidated in 2002.

Ames Department Stores: Success to Excess

In the late 1950s, Milton and Irving Gilman had an idea that they thought would finally get them off the small family farm in South Windsor, Connecticut. The brothers felt that people in rural areas, served by little, cluttered general stores, would flock to a large, well-stocked store. If people came from far enough around, the store could afford to set prices far lower than normal. The brothers resolved to open such a store.

They settled on the small town of Southbridge, just across the border in Massachusetts, because there were no big stores anywhere nearby and because they found inexpensive space in an old textile mill that had been closed after it flooded. The Gilmans' parents tried to take out a mortgage on the farm to finance the boys, but were turned down. The parents transferred the deed for the farm to the boys, who eventually managed to line up a $13,000 loan. That was just enough to outfit a store with used furnishings from a nearby shipyard and to stock the six thousand square feet of space in a corner of the old mill with men's and women's apparel and kitchen goods.

The store, opened on a blustery January day in 1958, was an immediate success. Customers liked having brand-name merchandise in a well-organized, brightly lit environment. They especially liked that the brothers were providing goods at a price 25 percent to 35 percent below what customers would have typically paid elsewhere.

Herbert Gilman, a Yale-trained engineer who had been working for one of the early mainframe computer companies, then joined his brothers. Sam Walton, who became friends with the Gilmans, called Herbert "an astounding and intuitive merchant."[3] Herbert convinced his brothers to add "hardlines," such as hardware and housewares, turning the store into a full-fledged department store.

Together, the brothers settled on an approach so low on frills that they didn't even take down the sign that displayed the old Ames textile mill's name—that's how the Gilman brothers' business came to be named Ames.

The Gilmans soon opened five more stores in former textile mills in Vermont and upstate New York, and those prospered, too. The brothers experimented and learned that their concept was robust. For instance, a rule of thumb said that no chain should have stores within thirty miles of each other because they'd cannibalize each other's sales. But when the Gilmans tried a store within a much closer radius, they found that the stores actually reinforced each other's presence, while letting them save on advertising and other costs. The Gilmans also found that their stores could be profitable in larger towns even though they needed to spend more on décor to meet customers' expectations.

By 1970, they were running two dozen stores, generating $50 million in annual revenue. As other discounters ran into trouble, the Gilmans bought the occasional store and turned it into an Ames. Although the prime rate reached 22 percent in the late 1970s, punishing the economy, by 1981 Ames had grown to 115 stores, covering the area between Maine and Maryland. The company was consistently profitable, and it was still growing by leaps and bounds.

In 1985, Ames made its biggest acquisition yet. It bought G. C. Murphy Company, a chain of discount stores, for $195 million. The acquisition doubled Ames's size, to $1.7 billion in annual sales, and expanded its operations into fourteen additional states.

The acquisition didn't go smoothly. Ames's culture had always focused more on merchandising than on having efficient back-office systems, such as accounting. Under the strain of the doubling in size, the systems collapsed. In 1986, a glitch meant that warm-weather wear was shipped to stores late in the selling season. When little sold, Ames was forced to offer major markdowns. In 1987, Ames seemed to have lost $20 million of merchandise and couldn't tell why. Eventually, it turned out that accounting systems had mispriced many items and lost track of others. In addition, disgruntled or opportunistic G. C. Murphy employees had produced an unusual amount of "shrinkage," the industry euphemism for theft. While goods were en route to G. C. Murphy stores, people would get into a truck, cut open boxes, and remove items. When the boxes arrived at the store, they would be logged in as though they were full, because there was no system in place to check the contents.

"Our accounting systems sprung leaks when the company doubled in size overnight," said Herb Gilman, who was chairman and CEO, following the retirements of his brothers in 1981. "Swallowing Murphy may have turned a small problem into a large one."[4]

Ames also struggled because debt payments soared; after the G. C. Murphy acquisition, debt totaled 80 percent of Ames's market valuation.

Ames shrank considerably, closing or selling 130 stores as it struggled to integrate G. C. Murphy. Gilman said he wanted to get back to the original concept: a no-frills discounter.

He said many companies had "drifted away from the original concept. . . . To build sales, some discounters added excessive advertising, and their competitors had to follow them. Then others started upgrading décor, fixtures, lighting, locations, and so on, and prices became inflated to pay for all of this. Pretty soon, there wasn't as much difference between discounters and other retailers, and a lot of discount chains suffered the predictable consequence: They weren't unique anymore, and their reason for existence had disappeared."[5]

The company soon began humming along again, and Gilman retired as chairman and chief executive in January 1988. In a valedictory interview, Gilman talked about competitors that had gone out of business and said he thought the company's decision to limit its expansion was "the reason we're still around, and they're not." Talking about the company's prospects five years out, Gilman said he still thought Ames "will have at least doubled in size. Our customers are changing, and we'll have to change with them. . . . But one thing will stay the same—they will be looking for a deal, and Ames will continue to build productivity and cut costs to offer the lowest price possible. That's what we've tried to do for 30 years, and I don't see that ever changing."[6]

But trouble was brewing. Despite the problems with the G. C. Murphy acquisition, his successors soon decided to try another takeover, this one far bigger. They reasoned that, with the industry maturing, they needed the additional scale to be able to compete with hyperefficient Wal-Mart. They also felt that they needed to continue to spread westward, with the idea of eventually becoming a national presence. Executives talked about the need for "critical mass."

In late 1988, Ames bought the discount-store division of Zayre Corporation for $800 million. The move doubled Ames's size once again, to 736 stores with annual sales of $5.39 billion. The purchase expanded Ames into Florida, Illinois, and Ohio. As a further benefit, Zayre's stores were mostly urban, so they would complement Ames's rural focus.

Herbert Gilman was livid. Gilman, who had stayed on the board even though he had given up the chairman and CEO posts, felt that buying Zayre's stores would distract Ames from its mission of simple discount retailing. Gilman quit the board in protest. So did another director, John Geisse.

The new CEO, Peter Hollis, pressed on anyway. Hollis had spent thirteen years at Zayre, where he had topped out at the senior vice president level. He went to another discount chain, then joined Ames. Now, he was going to get to run Zayre after all.

It was clear immediately that Ames overpaid. Almost every Zayre store was unprofitable. Zayre's accounting system was in disarray, its inventory was overvalued, and its merchandise was obsolete.[7] Within months, Ames closed seventy-five Zayre stores. The amount of overpayment was so severe that, in a bizarre twist, Ames sued its chairman over the issue, alleging he had a conflict of interest that induced Ames to overpay by hundreds of millions of dollars.

The chairman, James Harmon, had an undergraduate degree from Brown and an MBA from Wharton. He had been on Ames's board for twenty years. He was also—here's the rub—chairman of Wertheim Schroder, an investment bank that advised both Ames and Zayre on the deal. The suit alleged that Harmon assured Ames that Zayre was worth far more than it was—hundreds of millions of dollars more than Wertheim Schroder had told Zayre to expect from a sale. The suit also said that Harmon had helped ensure the deal would be approved by limiting the chances for comment at board meetings by Geisse and Gilman, who was ill with cancer and would die in 1990. The suit said Harmon would have Gilman and Geisse vote last on issues, so their votes wouldn't sway others. In addition, the suit claimed that, when another investment bank performed due diligence, Harmon allowed it just one day and wouldn't let the firm's analysts speak with anyone at Zayre. Harmon and Wertheim Schroder denied the charges, but the firm eventually paid Ames $19 million, essentially refunding the fees it had earned on the transaction.[8]

Trying to make the acquisition work somehow, Ames cut costs by reducing store hours, ending Zayre's practice of having stores open around the clock. Ames also began stocking stores with its own merchandise—basic brand-name goods, versus the inexpensive but fashionable products Zayre had carried—to simplify the handling of inventory and to give Ames more purchasing power. While Zayre had brought customers into stores with periodic sales and carried marked-down items at all times, Ames eliminated deep discounts in favor of steady low prices, to which it hoped customers would adjust. Ames also eliminated the Zayre credit card and stopped the heavy advertising that Zayre had done.

In February 1989, Ames announced it would keep the Zayre name on sixty-one profitable inner-city stores, because Zayre had a long history and customers had an attachment to the name—then went ahead and changed the name anyway in October.

Customers hated the changes. They fled.

To raise cash, Ames sold its G. C. Murphy properties in 1989, but it received only $77 million, about 40 percent of what it had paid for them. In desperation, Ames opened its stores on Thanksgiving Day, but that didn't generate enough business.

The weakness in sales at the Zayre stores, combined with the hefty payments Ames was making on the debt used to finance the acquisition, meant that Ames was unable to pay for its merchandise. Suppliers stopped shipments. Banks refused to lend Ames any more money. In April 1990, Ames filed for bankruptcy.

Ames's board brought on as the new CEO Stephen Pistner, a major figure in the industry because he was a former CEO of Target and was known as a turnaround expert. Pistner closed almost half of Ames's stores, partly to liquidate the merchandise and raise operating funds. Ames laid off 22,500 employees.

To lure customers back, Pistner offered deep discounts on certain items, hoping that people would come to Ames for those items and buy other items while there. Employees got behind the plan in a big way. Showing the folksy enthusiasm that existed at Ames, one wrote a song:

> *Our Ames store is here to stay.*
> *We're here for our customers both night and day.*
> *We call our customers Number One*
> *Because, in sales, we won't be undone!*
>
> *We're here to stay, and that's a fact.*
> *We'll bend over to bring you back.*
> *We open the store when you're in bed.*
> *We're an Ames store; we must stay ahead. . . .*[9]

But the Pistner strategy wasn't any better than the song. "His focus was just on volume, volume, volume, and the more we sold the more we lost," a senior executive said.[10] Customers cherry-picked, buying the deeply discounted items and then leaving without buying anything else. In 1992, Pistner was gone.

At the end of that year, a chastened Ames emerged from Chapter 11. It operated 309 stores, fewer than before Ames bought Zayre.

After an interim CEO, turnaround expert Joseph Ettore was named CEO in 1994 and began to get some traction. He restored the company's focus on its traditional customers, in the lower-middle-income bracket. He also instituted the 55 Gold program, which gave anyone age fifty-five and older a 10 percent discount on all merchandise on Tuesdays. In the process, he added another base of customers: older shoppers. The company returned to profitability.

In 1997, Ettore was named the *Discount Store News* "Discounter of the Year." Writing in *Smart Money* magazine, Gerri Wills lauded Ames in a piece titled, "Taking Ames at Wal-Mart":

"Wal-Mart and its relentless 'everyday low pricing' strategy are clearly responsible for this carnage [among discount retailers]. But that doesn't mean the Bentonville, Ark.–based retailer is unbeatable. . . . Ames stores are smaller than Wal-Mart's and more focused on women. Out go the guns, and in come apparel, jewelry and crafts. Seniors are another target Ames courts. . . . The idea is to provide an easier, more targeted shopping experience than can be had in a cavernous Wal-Mart store. . . . Ettore also keeps costs low with his purchasing patterns. Because his chain is smaller and more regional, he can buy other retailers' closeouts and overruns. He can also buy less of each item, meaning Ames can purchase merchandise closer to when it's needed on the shelves, saving on inventory costs. . . . So far, it's working. Despite razor-thin retailer's margins, Ames's operating profit nearly doubled to $46.2 million last year on $2.16 billion in sales. Analysts expect that number to grow another 20 percent this year, while earnings per share expand at a 15 percent clip. 'A lot of consumers don't want to shop in the big boxes. It's intimidating,' says Steve Richter, an analyst at Tucker Anthony. 'Sometimes, you just want to get in and out.' "

The piece concluded: "Wal-Mart is a force to be reckoned with. But Ames is doing just fine, thank you."[11]

Sounds like a plan. But it didn't last long.

Ames decided, once again, that it needed much more scale to deal with the industry's consolidation. In 1999, Ettore bought Hills Stores Company, a struggling chain of 155 discount stores, for $330 million. The acquisition increased Ames's size by 50 percent, beefing up Ames's presence in New York, Ohio, Pennsylvania, and West Virginia, and adding the states of Indiana, Kentucky, North Carolina, and Tennessee.

Securities analysts initially hailed the move. The press reported that, while the Zayre debacle was still fresh in everyone's minds, this time Ames had a stronger balance sheet, a more digestible partner, and a more reasonable expansion plan. Ames's stock reached almost $50 in 1999. To reward Ettore, the board gave him the additional title of chairman toward the end of 1999. But by late 2000, the stock was trading at 44¢. In 2001, shares hit 6¢ apiece.

The Hills stores, like the G. C. Murphy and Zayre stores, turned out to have more problems than Ames realized. Ames had also picked a fight it couldn't win. While it had stood up to Wal-Mart in a focused area with a focused strategy before the Hills acquisition, moving to a larger area and a broader array of merchandise stretched Ames too thin. A general downturn in the retail market didn't help.

In addition, Ames's systems once more proved too fragile to handle the additional scale. Ames developed a reputation for giving credit cards to anyone who requested one. Sometimes, people had defaulted on their debts to Ames, only to have Ames turn around and give them a new card.

Ames kept closing Hills stores until, in 2001, Ames was operating about the same number of stores that were open before the Hills takeover, but Ames couldn't get out in front of its problems. Soon, Ames was again closing stores so it could cannibalize the merchandise and sell it to raise cash to keep operating. Ames also sold the real estate beneath many of its stores to raise $25 million. But it wasn't enough. In 2002, Ames announced that it was liquidating. It closed its remaining 327 stores and laid off its final 21,500 employees.

RED FLAGS

Ames shows the four kinds of issues that can beset a consolidation play:

- You may not just be buying the assets you think you're buying; you may also be buying problems.
- While the focus is generally on getting bigger to generate economies of scale, there may also be *diseconomies* of scale because of increased complexity.
- Although companies typically assume that they can hold on to customers of a company they buy, that's often not the case.
- If you're just thinking about being the industry's consolidator, you may not be considering all your options.

We've already seen all these themes in other chapters, so we won't belabor the points here. We'll just offer a few examples to show how these problems manifest themselves in the context of consolidation.

Buying Problems

With the purchases of Murphy, Zayre, and Hills, Ames focused on the stores it was buying that would move it into new markets. What Ames somehow repeatedly overlooked is that many of those stores were damaged goods. Once Ames got a chance to inspect those stores up close, it wound up closing so many of them that Ames repeatedly shrank back to about the number of stores it operated before the acquisitions. Ames was running remarkably hard just to stay in place—and, of course, with the bankruptcies and then liquidation, Ames wound up disappearing from the race altogether.

DaimlerChrysler Corporation is Exhibit A when it comes to buying problems. With enormous overcapacity in the auto industry, Daimler AG bought Chrysler in 1998 for $38 billion, hoping that combining the companies would save $3 billion in annual costs. Daimler hoped to save by increasing its purchasing power, by closing some plants, and by, in general, using the combined manufacturing facilities more efficiently. While focusing on the opportunities, Daimler ignored a slew of problems at Chrysler. Like all U.S. auto companies, Chrysler operated with a union contract that included health and pension benefits that, by some estimates, added almost $2,000 more to the cost of each car than Toyota paid for those benefits. Chrysler was also obliged to pay wages that far exceeded what its principal competitors paid. Although some new models had done well shortly before the Daimler takeover, historically Chrysler had been losing market share.

The problems hit Daimler hard. Costs stayed high as U.S. car companies struggled to get out from under the union contract, and heightened competition in the U.S. market, coupled with tepid product introductions by Chrysler, cut into Chrysler's sales.

In the meantime, because of the sorts of problems we covered in chapter 1, on synergy, the plans for cost savings didn't materialize. For instance, plans for technology transfer didn't occur. Mercedes' elite engineers didn't want to share with what they saw as Chrysler's plebeian engineering group. Top management, in fact, didn't even want the transfer to occur because they worried that talking too much about the Mercedes influence on Chrysler cars would dilute the Mercedes brand. Management had seen the problem occur at Ford, which bought Jaguar PLC in 1989 and bragged about how many parts were shared between the two lines, only to see Jaguar lose cachet and have sales fall.

So Daimler had the worst of both worlds. It didn't get the benefits envisioned, yet suffered from all the problems it had conveniently ignored while laying out the rationale for the merger. Daimler ended up *paying Cerberus $650 million* to take Chrysler off its hands. And Daimler may have been lucky the transaction occurred when it did, because, as of this writing, Chrysler's situation has deteriorated significantly since Cerberus's takeover.

Imperial Sugar Company bought a whole series of problems. The company, whose roots go back to 1843 in the aptly named Sugar Land, Texas, bought Holly Sugar Corporation in 1988, Spreckels Sugar Company in 1996, Savannah Foods & Industries Incorporated in 1997, and Wholesome Foods L.L.C. and Daisy Crystals Specialty Foods Incorporated in 1998. The hope was that the scale would give Imperial the sort of efficiency that would let it compete in a commodity market where prices were under severe pressure. But the math was never going to work.

Imperial was paying the government-supported price of 22.5¢ a pound for domestic sugar. After spending 4¢ a pound on operating costs, Imperial was selling the sugar for 27¢ a pound. While those numbers allowed for a sliver of profit, the whole market was moving against Imperial, so increasing in size just compounded the extent of the problem it would have to solve.

While the amount of sweetener consumed per person in the United States was staying steady at 124 pounds per year, the share accounted for by sugar was dropping precipitously—between 1973 and 1983, for instance, sugar consumption dropped from 107 pounds per person per year to 71. Even worse, various trade agreements meant that the United States was going to allow far more sugar from other countries into the domestic market, and the international price for sugar was about half what it was in the United States.

Although Imperial's expansion let it approach $2 billion in annual sales, the company filed for bankruptcy in January 2001, blaming low prices and high energy costs. Imperial emerged from bankruptcy in August 2001 and spent the next year and a half unwinding its acquisitions. These days, a far smaller Imperial is profitable. Rather than try to grow, the company has been returning its cash to shareholders—in the past three years, special dividends have totaled almost $80 million.

Diseconomies of Scale

As Ames learned the hard way—more than once—systems that work well for a business of a certain size may break if the size of the business is increased greatly. Ames first learned the lesson with the accounting problems it had following the G. C. Murphy acquisition, then had similar trouble following the Hills acquisition, when controls on issuing credit cards turned out to be too lax. As Ames shows, in the search for economies of scale, companies often find diseconomies, as well.

US Airways had many of Ames's problems with systems when, in the name of consolidation, it bought Pacific Southwest Airlines for $400 million in 1986 to expand into the West and then bought archrival Piedmont

Aviation Incorporated for $1.6 billion in 1987 to become more powerful and efficient in US Air's core markets in the East.

US Air began life in 1939 as a regional mail carrier founded by the du Pont family. Originally called All American Aviation, the company renamed itself Allegheny Airlines in 1953. (Not known for its stellar customer service, it was later dubbed "Agony Air" by disgruntled passengers.) After a series of small acquisitions broadened its reach, in 1979 the company took the name US Air (quickly getting itself labeled "Useless Air"). No matter what passengers may have thought, investors loved the airline. US Air, along with Southwest Airlines Company and Piedmont, were the only three major airlines in the mid-1980s that had been profitable every year since the industry was deregulated in 1978.

When US Air bought the two other airlines and almost tripled in size in a bit more than a year, its information systems couldn't handle the load. More than once, the computer systems broke down on payday, and armies of secretaries had to type paychecks manually.[12] US Air's archaic scheduling system was also taxed to the limit. Most airlines required that a crew member find a replacement if he wanted not to be on a particular flight that he'd been scheduled to fly, but US Air took that responsibility. The result was that the scheduling of six thousand pilots wasn't completed until 4:00 p.m. the day before they flew. Scheduling was also complicated because the three airlines' combined route system was a rat's nest of small hubs and spokes.

A conference report by the National Bureau of Economic Research found that, in general, US Air didn't have the structure to handle its new size. National airlines had large groups to handle marketing and pricing, general management, and information technology. But US Air had small groups, in keeping with its stature as a mostly regional carrier before the mergers.

In addition, US Air's rigid hierarchy limited the decision making that could occur in the ranks—a sometime-problem that could be tolerated in a modest-sized organization, without too many layers of managers, but that was amplified in the complex business that US Air had become. The hierarchy also created morale problems. Pacific Southwest had an informal culture—flight attendants going through their preflight announcements said things such as, "For those of you who haven't been in a car since 1962, this is a seat belt"—so employees chafed under the US Air culture. Many Piedmont employees recall reacting angrily when US Air CEO Ed Colodny introduced himself at crew bases by saying, "Warm Southern hospitality is going to be replaced by cool Northern efficiency."[13]

While US Air sought efficiencies by having all its operations adopt a standard set of processes, many of the processes made operations less productive at Piedmont and Pacific Southwest, which were versed in different approaches. Baggage handling among former Piedmont employees slowed markedly. Piedmont flights, which had been above average in on-time performance, dropped to twelfth among the thirteen major airlines.

The newly expanded US Air had one more problem, too: wages. US Air's employees were paid more than their counterparts at Pacific Southwest and Piedmont, so US Air felt obliged to rationalize its pay structure by raising the wages of those at the acquired businesses.

The litany of diseconomies clobbered US Air's economics. The report by the National Bureau of Economic Research calculates that the three airlines that made up US Air earned $522 million from 1984 through 1986. As a combined entity, the three airlines had more than $3 billion of losses from 1989 through 1994. (The report didn't calculate results for 1987 or 1988 because they were transition years.) The average cost per seat mile, a key industry measure, rose from 9.1¢ before the merger to 10.5¢ afterward. Before the merger, US Air and Piedmont had operating profits that were six to seven percentage points higher than the industry average. After the merger, operating profits were 2.6 points below the industry average. So much for economies of scale.

Trouble Converting Customers

As Ames found, companies tend to be more loyal to their customers than customers are to the companies that sell them things. Just because a store had been a Zayre, for instance, didn't mean that a customer would keep going there once the store hours, pricing, and product mix had all changed.

That may seem obvious, but companies have repeatedly missed the fact that customers have options. In the midst of a major transition, such as the move from the Zayre format to the Ames format, customers may well defect.

Albertsons Incorporated committed this oversight when it bought American Stores Company for $11.7 billion in 1999. Among the brands acquired was Lucky, a chain with a strong presence in northern and southern California and with a strong brand and devoted customer base. Albertsons changed the name of these stores to Albertsons and got rid of the popular store-card program that offered discounts on many items. Albertsons also applied its no-frills approach, even though Lucky had catered to local tastes and had spent heavily on marketing. Albertsons also made the mistake of dropping the recognized "low-price leader" philosophy of Lucky. Customers, many of whom ranted online about the loss of their Lucky store, took their business elsewhere. Albertsons briefly reintroduced the Lucky name in select markets and reintroduced store cards in the early 2000s, but it was too late.

Albertsons, which was also guilty of ignoring the threat posed by Wal-Mart's rapidly growing grocery business, took $400 million of write-offs associated with the American Stores acquisition. Albertsons sold itself in 2006 to private-equity investors and two grocery chains and was broken up into three pieces. The price, $17.4 billion, suggests that Albertsons's losses were actually in the billions of dollars. If Albertsons had been worth just the same amount as American Stores at the time of the acquisition—and, of course, acquirers tend to have a higher valuation than their targets—the value of Albertsons and American Stores would have been $23.4 billion, meaning Albertsons had frittered away $6 billion of value in the seven years it owned American Stores.

As technology companies, telecommunications giants Lucent Technologies Incorporated and Alcatel SA actually had a strong hold on customers when Alcatel acquired Lucent for $13 billion in late 2006. Any customers who defected were likely to face higher costs. The customers would have to train their people to use equipment from a new manufacturer—not a trivial task, given the complexity of telecommunications gear. Support and maintenance costs would rise, because the customer would have to maintain two sets of equipment, rather than just the equipment it had already purchased from Lucent or Alcatel. The customer would also have to wrestle with the incompatibilities that typically mean one manufacturer's gear doesn't share information perfectly with another's.

Yet competitors still used the occasion of the merger to attack the Lucent and Alcatel customer bases. While the merged company did a reasonable job of fending off competitors, the victory came at huge cost. Alcatel-Lucent had to engage in a price war that clobbered profitability. The company has taken more than $4 billion of write-offs since the merger. The market value of the company has fallen 60 percent since the merger.

Not Considering All Options

Ames somehow got it into its head that it needed to go toe-to-toe with Wal-Mart, operating as a hyperefficient national retailer, even though Ames was doing nicely as a regional retailer with a far more limited product line. As far as we can tell, Ames never seriously considered just maintaining its position, extracting cash while holding on to the niche that seemed to offer protection from Wal-Mart, and never thought about being a seller rather than a buyer. Yet withdrawing cash or selling would have been far more profitable strategies.

Likewise, Hospital Corporation of America decided it should be the one buying up competitors and consolidating the industry, so it merged with Columbia Healthcare Corporation in 1994 in a $10.25 billion deal. HCA intended to close acquired hospitals in markets where it already operated, so HCA's existing hospitals could charge higher rates. Following the acquisition, the combined company continued this strategy of buying and closing. But HCA couldn't buy every hospital, and those that remained undercut it on prices. In fact, as HCA became their prime competitor, they studied its efficient practices and improved enough that they could undercut HCA significantly. For good measure, as hospitals around the country saw that HCA was closing the hospitals it bought, hospitals refused to sell to the company. So the company didn't even come close to removing as much capacity as its strategy called for.

With its strategy in tatters, HCA systematically overbilled government agencies such as Medicare and Medicaid for its services. After a sprawling series of civil and criminal investigations, HCA paid $1.7 billion in fines and settlements to resolve the issues raised by the fraud investigations.

Rather than merge with Columbia, HCA would have been much better off selling to another consolidator, waiting for someone else to remove capacity, or even just maintaining the status quo. HCA eventually changed its thinking: The company sold itself to private-equity investors for $21 billion in 2006.

Tough Questions

It makes sense in a mature industry that is ripe for consolidation that companies would be under pressure. That's the whole point: Competition is depressing profitability, and companies are looking for ways to relieve the pressure. So the odds are high in a consolidation strategy that any company you buy is going to be damaged goods.

To avoid pursuing a flawed consolidation strategy, the place to start is to list all the problems that an acquisition target may have. For Daimler-Benz, for instance, this approach would have meant acknowledging the legacy costs from health care and pensions for retirees, the generally tough state of the U.S. car market, the fact that Chrysler (like other U.S. car companies) has too many dealerships, that Chrysler's market share had generally been declining, and on and on. Once identified, problems can be debated and, to some extent, quantified, rather than just being swept aside in the name of a strategic vision about consolidation and synergy.

Because consolidation targets are more likely than most to have hidden problems, it's especially important to have thorough, independent due diligence—not the one-day approach that Ames took with Zayre.

It's also crucial to project out a few years. The tendency is to take a snapshot of a business, usually as part of a situation analysis, and assume that the business will perform at roughly that level for years to come. If anything, the tendency is to assume that the performance will improve because of efficiencies that should result from consolidation. In fact, because profitability for the whole industry is in decline, the likelihood is that the acquired business will continue to decline, too. So a prudent acquirer should list all the ways that the target's business might deteriorate.

Similarly, those considering acquisitions in the name of consolidation should list all the potential diseconomies of scale. What systems might fail under the weight of the increased size? How much would it cost to fix them? How long would it take? What revenue might be lost in the interim? What relationships might be harmed? What departments are too small, or are for some other reason not up to the task of handling the new size? Which people aren't up to the task? What else might go wrong, such as the need to increase wages at Piedmont and Pacific Southwest that somehow snuck up on Wall Street analysts who welcomed the acquisitions by US Air?

Companies should also, as always, look at what will prevent them from obtaining the promised economies of scale. How much will be lost as people jockey for position in the new organization? How much drag will develop as you try to find efficiencies by standardizing processes? Who will resist change? How effective will they be?

We realize that it's common to bring in "change management" teams to ensure that economies are realized, but, as our consolidation cases show, those teams aren't always effective. In any case, there is a cost—in time, money, and attention span—that needs to be considered ahead of time to be sure a consolidation strategy makes economic sense.

Companies need to also consider all the reasons why customers might defect. This is a significant problem in many consolidation strategies. Although companies tend to tell themselves that their increased size will benefit customers because they'll be dealing with a more stable business, with broader reach, better customer service, and so on, many consolidation takeovers are, in fact, driven by a desire to increase pricing power. In other words, the acquirer wants to raise prices. How does that benefit customers?

In the face of attempts to wring more profits out of them, customers are inclined to go elsewhere. That may mean going to competitors. Or, as in the case of an airline merger, that may mean taking the train, driving a car, using a videoconferencing system, or just staying at home rather than traveling.

In any case, it's important not to assume that customers will stick around. Certainly, you try to find ways to keep them all. But, before deciding to proceed with a merger, you need to assign a number to the percentage that you think may leave. You also need to assign a number to the costs you will probably have to incur to entice uncertain customers to stick around. Only once you've addressed the likely loss of revenue and the likely increase in costs can you fairly evaluate whether an acquisition is a good idea.

Even when an industry is consolidating, it's crucial to consider all options: Analyze carefully the prospects of selling or doing nothing, rather than assuming that the right answer is to buy. This process should begin with the sort of framework, provided by Michael Porter, that we described in chapter 4. If it seems that an industry will wind up with a profitable cost structure, such as the steel industry has, and you can be a market leader, then by all means proceed (carefully) as the industry consolidator. If the industry has a good cost structure but you're not likely to be the industry leader, then sell pieces of the business selectively and try to get as much cash as possible out of the business as you wind it down. If you're a leader in an industry with a bad cost structure, like photography, move into profitable niches while getting out of the rest of the business. If you face a double whammy—you aren't a leader, and you're in a business with a bad cost structure—then Porter says to head for the hills. Sell as fast as possible.

Sometimes, those that don't consolidate an industry can even get lucky. When Seagate Technology LLC, the leader in the disk-drive industry, bought the number three company, Maxtor Corporation, for $1.9 billion in 2005, it was a pure consolidation strategy. Seagate kept Maxtor's brand but almost none of its technology or employees. Seagate moved all manufacturing into Seagate plants. Seagate reckons the takeover a success: While it lost half of Maxtor's market share, the market share it kept, combined with the higher pricing for the industry as a whole, left Seagate better off than it was before the merger, according to Charles Pope, Seagate's chief financial officer. But how much better to be Western Digital Corporation, the number two disk-drive maker? It picked up most of the Maxtor market share that Seagate lost. It benefited from the stronger prices that disk-drive companies can now charge. And it didn't have to pay $1.9 billion for the privilege.

"Western Digital got a real freebie out of this deal," Pope says.[14]

Coda

Okay, we realize we just threw a lot of information at you. The sheer volume of failures may feel overwhelming and may make you feel as if we're telling you to just sit inside all day, for fear that if you venture anywhere you'll get run over by a semi. Some of the information may also feel like it overlaps—because it does. Strategies that pursued synergies sometimes failed for the same reasons that moves into adjacent markets did, and adjacent-market strategies sometimes failed for the same reasons that consolidation strategies did. There's no getting around it.

Before moving into part 2, which holds the real payoff, we want to make two points. One is about whether you should avoid any bold strategy for fear of failure. The other is about the overlap.

First, we aren't at all suggesting that aggressive strategies for growth are doomed to failure. It'd be stupid to suggest that, because there are so many counterexamples, offered by healthy, growing companies. We've tried in many cases to cite examples of companies that succeeded by pursuing one of the seven strategies that we've found are most often associated with major failure. We even note that one of the seven types of suspect strategies is doing nothing, like those companies mentioned in chapter 4, "Staying the (Misguided) Course."

Rather, we beat you over the head with all the stories about failure because they're so often ignored. Everyone wants to read about those healthy, growing companies and about how to emulate them. So, to get everyone focused on the flip side of going from good to great, we felt we had to offer lots of evidence about the breadth and depth of the failures that have occurred in corporate America. We want you to take us seriously in part 2 when we lay out ways to double-check yourselves, to make sure you don't join our list of failures.

We're well aware that many people feel that any attempt at double-checking opens the way to second-guessing and can paralyze a business. But we think you'll agree, after reading part 2, that the methods we lay out require modest time, effort, and expense. Good ideas should continue to sail through and be implemented as successful strategies.

Second, concerning overlap, we'll suggest that some reasons for failure are more equal than others. If you want to look across all our failure cases and boil them down to the most common, the main problems to watch out for are these:

- Underestimating the complexity that comes with scale. Companies begin with a simple, perfectly reasonable argument that goes something like this: We have a certain amount of fixed costs for running our business; expanding will let us spread those costs over more revenue, meaning that overhead expenses will drop as a percentage of the total business. We'll be more efficient. What companies often don't allow for is that when they double in size, they aren't just doing precisely the same thing, twice as many times. They may be dealing in different markets, with different customers, different sales channels, and so on. Car companies and computer makers are famous for saying they'll share parts across product lines, then "optimize" those parts for a particular car or computer—once you tinker even a bit with a part you've lost almost all the benefit that would come from having a truly common part.

- Overstating the increased purchasing power or pricing power or other types of power that come from growing in size. That's the sort of claim that looks reasonable on a PowerPoint slide but that doesn't hold up to scrutiny, because it is based too much on an internal perspective. Doubling or tripling in size feels like a real achievement to those inside the company, but the outside world may not notice. If the company remains a small part of the industry, it still isn't going to get much purchasing, pricing, or other power.

The term "critical mass" sets off alarm bells in our heads. Anytime we hear a company claim that it's going to get critical mass, we worry it has overestimated the power that size will give it.

- Overestimating your hold on customers. Certainly, customers can be creatures of habit. Absent some reason to change, they'll probably keep shopping where they always have. They'll have loyalties to certain brands, certain products. But, as many retailers have learned, customers don't like change. You may think you aren't doing much, but if you put a new name on the door, change the pricing strategy, and alter the product mix, customers may well head next door. And, as some of our failure cases show, companies sometimes talk themselves into truly strange ideas about their tight relations with customers—think of the utility that decided people would buy its insurance just because they bought its electricity.

- Playing semantic games. It may be true that you have a "culture of caring," as Avon claimed, but that isn't enough to help a cosmetics sales staff figure out how to run nursing homes. Any strategy that relies on a turn of phrase—such as saying that railroads were really in the transportation business, not the railroad business—is open to challenge.

- Not considering all the options. We all live under this imperative to grow. We all understand that the survivors are the ones who are remembered. So we try to grow and survive—even though our fiduciary duties dictate that, at times, we should forgo certain attempts at growth because they'd just be a waste of money. Even harder, we should sometimes consider selling the business; that way we'll collect a high valuation, while if we try to hang on, we'll just fritter away the value of the business.

- Overpaying for acquisitions. But you didn't need us to tell you that. There's already a wealth of information about the fact that businesses often overpay when buying other companies.

Now, on to the meatiest and most satisfying part of the book: principles that build on our research into failure and offer you a greater chance of succeeding—by diminishing your chance of failing.

PART TWO

Avoiding the Same Mistakes

EIGHT

Why Bad Strategies Happen to Good People

Awareness Is Not Enough

Battles should be fought in the marketplace. So why are so many lost before a strategy even gets off the drawing board?

The short answer is this:

Humans are far from rational in their planning and decision making. Psychological studies going back decades consistently demonstrate that humans face huge impediments when making complicated decisions, such as those involved in setting strategy.

Anthropological studies underscore the difficulties, as shown by Donald E. Brown in his book *Human Universals.* Rather than looking at the differences between cultures, Brown looked at what all cultures have in common. He reasoned that those common features are part of the fabric of being human. He found that oral language is universal, while writing is not. Basic reasoning is universal, but the sort of abstract reasoning used in mathematics is not. Unfortunately, the more than two hundred universals that Brown found include many of the psychological characteristics that interfere with complex decisions.

In other words, humans are hardwired to come up with bad strategies.

The really aware executives (the sort who read books like ours) realize the limitations they face. So they redouble their efforts, insisting on greater vigilance and deeper analysis.

The problem is that that isn't enough. As our first seven chapters show, vigilant and analytical executives can still come up with demonstrably bad strategies.

Our suggestion is not to be more careful. We believe that decision makers must accept that the tendency toward errors is deeply ingrained and adopt explicit mechanisms to counter those tendencies.

If our short answer convinces you, feel free to skip ahead to chapter 9, where we explore the organizational impediments to good decisions, or even to chapters 10 and 11, where we lay out the mechanisms that can catch errors. If you still have doubts whether you need to add a process to stress-test your strategy, then please stick with us for a few more minutes in this chapter. We will lay out what we believe to be an overwhelming body of research and insight that refutes the belief that extra vigilance and analysis will suffice.

Our long answer goes something like this:

It is obvious that those formulating strategies should gather all relevant information. They should process that information objectively. They should consider a wide array of possible strategies. They should evaluate all possibilities thoroughly, considering both the negatives and the positives. They should hone their skills by learning from experience—their own, their company's, and other companies'.

Problems and unexpected roadblocks always pop up during implementation, but avoiding major conceptual mistakes should take no more than a tight focus on Michael Porter's "Five Forces," or some other rigorous approach to strategy setting. In fact, psychology and anthropology show that taking a rigorous approach is extremely difficult because of these natural tendencies:

- People home in on an answer prematurely, long before they evaluate all information.
- People have trouble being objective about many kinds of information because they aren't set up very well to deal with abstractions.
- Once people start moving toward an answer, they look to confirm that their answer is right, rather than hold open the possibility that they're wrong.

- People conform to the wishes of a group, especially if there is a strong person in the leadership role, rather than raise objections that test ideas.
- People also don't learn as much as they could from their mistakes, because we humans typically suffer from overconfidence and have elaborate defense mechanisms to explain away our failings; sharp people (the kind entrusted with setting corporate strategies, or so we hope) appear to be even less likely to learn from mistakes or to acknowledge their errors.

That's a lot to overcome.

We'll look at each of the five types of problems in turn.

Premature Closure

Psychological studies show that it's hard—physically hard—for people to avoid reaching conclusions before evaluating all the evidence. We get a first impression of an idea in much the same way we get a first impression of a person. Even when people are trained to withhold judgment, they find themselves evaluating information as they go along, forming a tentative conclusion early in the process. They then test additional information against that conclusion, but that's not the same as giving all the information the same weight and keeping an open mind until all evidence is viewed. Conclusions, like first impressions, are hard to reverse.

A study of analysts in the intelligence community, for instance, found that, despite their extensive training, analysts tended to come to a conclusion very quickly and then "fit the facts" to that conclusion.[1] A study of clinical psychologists found that they formed diagnoses relatively rapidly and that additional information didn't improve those diagnoses.[2]

In fact, it's hard to change a conclusion even when we're told that the information it's based on is erroneous. In one study, people were given a false sense of success. They were asked a series of questions and told they were right almost all the time—even though they weren't. The participants in the study were asked to rate their capability and, not surprisingly, felt pretty good about themselves. Participants were then told their real results, which were typically far worse than they had initially been told. Yet, when asked to rerate their capabilities, the participants still concluded that they were almost as good as when they were asked the first time, under false pretenses.[3]

Part of the reason we don't consider all possible information stems from what psychologists call "the availability bias." The bias means that we typically recall information or ideas that are "available," either because we came across them recently or because they are particularly vivid. Someone who is asked whether more words in the English language start with the letter *r* or have *r* as the third letter is likely to say more words start with *r*, because those words are more vivid, more available.

Irving Janis, in his classic book *Groupthink*, blames the availability bias for the early U.S. involvement in Vietnam in the 1950s and 1960s. He says U.S. presidents and generals could remember vividly that an appeasement policy hadn't worked with Hitler before World War II and that intervention had succeeded in the Korean War, so it was easy to conclude that the United States needed to intervene aggressively to contain Communism.

The availability bias basically means that it isn't just generals and politicians who fight the last war. We all do—sometimes disastrously. It seems that Robert Galvin pursued Motorola's disastrous Iridium project because Motorola's previous successes with grand engineering projects were so available to him that he spent little time considering the downside.

The availability bias also means that we respond to narratives and analogies more than we do to statistical information, even though the raw data typically provides a more accurate picture of reality. Random facts are hard to remember, but those same facts become more "available" once we weave them into a story or decide they are analogous to other situations with which we're familiar. Studies involving chess masters and grandmasters have found that they're no better than the rest of us at memorizing where pieces are on a chessboard if the pieces are placed randomly. Everyone remembers roughly half a dozen. But if a board is set up based on an actual game, the masters and grandmasters quickly memorize the entire board, while mere mortals still remember only where half a dozen pieces are.[4] The reason: The pieces are now connected through a sort of narrative for the masters and grandmasters.

Narratives and analogies aren't necessarily bad, as long as they are used properly and recognized for what they are—and what they aren't. At Walt Disney Company, executives know they need a story if they are to sell management on investing in a major project. When Joe Rohde wanted to build an amusement park with wild animals in a natural setting, he went through all the PowerPoint presentations and the other rigmarole associated with trying to prove the economic viability of an idea, but he wasn't quite carrying the day. At the final meeting to decide whether the park was a "go," then-CEO Michael Eisner said, "I still don't quite get what the thrill is with live animals." Rohde walked to the door of the conference room and opened it. In walked a Bengal tiger, tethered with the lightest of lines and restrained only by a young woman. Eisner understood the thrill, and Rohde got his money.[5] By all accounts, Animal Kingdom, which opened in 1999, has been a success for Disney. Lots of people get the thrill of exotic wild animals in the flesh.

The problem is that anecdotes can be used to support either side of any argument. Haste makes waste . . . but the early bird gets the worm. Make hay while the sun shines . . . but save for a rainy day. Birds of a feather flock together . . . but opposites attract.

Narratives can also be dangerous because they can tie facts up in too neat a package or make causal links that aren't really there. Analogies can also fool us because they're never perfect, as Galvin learned so painfully. Iridium was analogous to earlier projects in many ways, just not enough. (Now Iridium serves as a vivid analogy for those trying to figure out how *not* to evaluate the potential of new technologies, but that's cold comfort to Galvin and Motorola.)

Brown's anthropological treatise *Human Universals* lists myths as one of his universals, meaning that the tendency to use stories rather than statistics is deeply ingrained in all of us. So, feel free to use the power of myth—but make sure you aren't manipulated by it.

Difficulty with Abstraction

Even Albert Einstein didn't like certain abstractions. Sure, he did just fine with abstraction, as his elegant thought experiments show. But until the end of his life he resisted the interpretation of quantum mechanics—now generally accepted—that described the world in probabilities. Even though Einstein was one of the pioneers of quantum mechanics, it just didn't feel right to talk about an electron as being 81 percent in one orbit, 5 percent in another, and so on, based on the likelihood of where that electron would be at any given instant.

So, how comfortable are the rest of us with abstraction? Not very. When it comes to processing all the complex relationships and messy data out there in the real world, our minds play all kinds of tricks on us.

One problem is what psychologists call the anchoring bias. If you ask someone to estimate anything whose amount is between, say, one and one hundred units, but first tell them a randomly chosen number, that number will greatly influence the estimate. Even though the random number and the estimate have nothing to do with each other, a low random number will produce low estimates. A high random number will produce high estimates.[6]

The anchoring bias poses particular problems in setting strategy because we subconsciously tend to work from whatever spreadsheet or other document we're presented with. We tend to tinker rather than question whether the ideas behind the document are even worth considering.

When making forecasts, the anchoring bias means we tend to assume that trends will continue pretty much as they always have. This causes particular problems in evaluating how technological progress will unfold. People see an explosion of interest in something and assume the pace of change will continue indefinitely. So we typically overestimate the effect of something like the Internet in the short run. Remember all those stories about how stores would disappear, and all our purchases would be delivered into special, locked boxes that we'd put in front of our houses? But we also have a general comfort level with our lives and assume they'll change about as fast as they always have, so we underestimate the long-term effects of something like cell phones. Did anybody guess twenty years ago that doctors would now be treating a problem known as cell phone thumb, common among those who bang away too hard on their BlackBerries?

Brown's anthropological studies in *Human Universals* underscore the depth of the anchoring bias. He lists a universal "interpolation," which is the tendency to take a linear approach to estimating future results. Interpolation may make sense in many situations but doesn't serve us well in volatile environments, where a product may be about to take off or die suddenly, or where businesses face forces that change exponentially rather than linearly. Even when we know a situation requires more sophisticated analysis, it's hard for us to get our heads around the concept, because we just aren't built for it.

What psychologists call the bias toward survivorship means that we remember what happened; we don't remember what didn't happen.

Well, duh, right? But the fact that we don't remember what didn't happen is actually a profound problem in how we think. The faithful troop to Lourdes every year to pray for miracle cures, even though a study by astronomer and TV personality Carl Sagan found that the rate of cure is actually somewhat lower for those who make the trek than for those who stay away.[7] We may read about those who pray to Mary and survive, not those who pray to Mary and die.

Similarly, we are encouraged to take risks in business, because we read about those who made "bet the company" decisions and reaped fortunes—and don't read about those that never quite made the big time because they made "bet the company" decisions and lost. Or we read *The Millionaire Next Door* and think about concentrating our investing in just one or two assets, to emulate the millionaires, because we don't read about those individuals who invested big-time in some disastrous company and lost all their savings. We read about Pierre Omidyar, who founded eBay and made a fortune off online auctions. We don't read about Jerry Kaplan, who *almost* had the idea for eBay. Kaplan is actually the better model. Omidyar lucked into eBay while trying to find a way for his girlfriend (now wife) to trade Pez dispensers. Kaplan, after a long and distinguished history in the personal-computer software world, made a well-reasoned guess about the auction potential of the Internet and founded an auction site, called OnSale, before eBay came along. Sure, Kaplan got the model slightly wrong. He auctioned off things that his company bought, such as refurbished electronics, rather than set up a site where anyone could auction anything to anyone. But it would be a lot easier to duplicate his thinking and reasonable success than to duplicate the bolt of lightning that hit Omidyar. Yet Omidyar will show up in the history books as a shining example of the entrepreneurial spirit, while Kaplan will not.

Medical journals have recently faced up to the survivorship problem. They found that they were running articles about, say, a correlation between a genetic defect and the onset of a particular disease, but weren't writing about studies that didn't find a correlation between the defect and the disease. Sometimes, taking all studies as a whole would indicate there was no correlation, but, because only correlations were typically highlighted, researchers spent time and resources pursuing false leads.

What is sometimes called the "house money" effect means that people are more likely to take risks with "house money" than with their own. For instance, some people were given $30, then asked whether they'd risk $9 on a coin flip. Some 75 percent said they would. Another group was given the identical choice, but phrased differently. This group was told that it had two choices. Members could take $30, or they could have a coin flip decide whether they would receive $21 or $39. In this group, which made its choice before receiving its "house money," only 43 percent said they'd take the chance.[8]

Let's face it, at some level almost all business is done with what Silicon Valley types call OPM—which stands for "other people's money" and which, yes, is pronounced like "opium." While executives generally respect their fiduciary duties and understand that taking excessive risks can cause them to lose their jobs, the tendency is still to take more risks than people would if they were wagering their own money.

In his books *The Black Swan* and *Fooled by Randomness*, Nassim Nicholas Taleb coins a term, "platonizing," that helps explain why people overlook problems. The term refers to Plato and his explanations of ideals. Taleb says ideals actually corrupt our thinking. We see something that is sort of in the shape of a triangle and process the shape mentally as a triangle. We ignore the data that don't fit the ideal.

That's no doubt an efficient way to process impressions, but the result is that we tend not to see small problems that can create frictions and keep us from achieving our goals. The technology world is full of grand plans that fell by the wayside because of the most mundane of reasons; as Jim Barksdale said when he was CEO of Netscape, "The problem with Silicon Valley is that we tend to confuse a clear view with a short distance."[9] Webvan, for instance, didn't take into account the difficulties its vans would have finding parking spots in cities or with double-parking. Webvan's strategy didn't allow for the time and effort that would be required to carry groceries up elevators or, worse, flights of stairs in apartment buildings. Webvan didn't pay enough attention to the troubles it would have when a customer wasn't home on a hot day and there was ice cream in the order. Webvan didn't realize that all its working customers would want groceries delivered at pretty much the same time, in the evening. All sorts of little things got ignored. They weren't, individually, enough to derail the plan to reinvent the world of groceries. But, given the thin margins in the food business, the frictions as a whole helped Webvan burn through hundreds of millions of dollars.

Psychologists also say we have problems processing new ideas because of mental ruts. People develop neuron-firing sequences in their brains that become so well-defined they are, almost literally, ruts. Certain things will always be perceived the same way.[10]

In *Groupthink*, Janis says mental ruts explain the U.S. decision to fight in Vietnam. Americans had developed certain ways of thinking about Communists, based on the expansionistic behavior of the Soviet Union following World War II. The North Vietnamese government was Communist, so U.S. officials couldn't imagine that their primary goal might be to merely unify their country under a Communist government. Instead, the unquestioned assumption was that the Vietnamese wanted to work in concert with the Soviet Union and China to make all of Southeast Asia Communist.

The tricky thing about such mental ruts is that you can't get rid of them just by being aware of them.

Studies of cognition show that we judge how far away an object is partly by how clearly the object appears to us. Makes sense. But what about days when visibility is especially good or especially bad? We're going to guess wrong. On a clear day, we think objects are closer than they really are. On a hazy day, we think objects are farther away. The errors of judgment persist even when people in studies are told that a day is especially clear or hazy.[11]

It's possible to correct for the problem. Pilots, who need to be able to judge distances accurately in many situations, go through special training to adjust for visibility. Golfers have yardage books, markers in fairways, and, these days, perhaps a laser range finder so they don't get fooled by appearances on a foggy Sunday morning.

Still, correcting for a mental rut is hard and requires special training or tools. Just ask any golfer who's stood there in a fairway and said, "It sure looks farther than that," and then, while trying to trust the yardage marker on the sprinkler head, still pumps the ball over the green into some deep rough.

Confirmation Bias

Way back in our psychology classes in college, one of the odder concepts was "cognitive dissonance." It makes sense that you read a lot about cars before deciding which one to buy, but you'd think that you'd pretty much stop reading after you bought one. You already own the car. What's left to decide? In fact, people keep reading. Some even step up their reading. They try to reduce their dissonance by assuring themselves they made the right choice. So they don't read just anything. They read things that support their decision while assiduously avoiding anything that challenges it. If you bought a Corvair in 1967, it's unlikely you then read Ralph Nader's *Unsafe at Any Speed.*

The same sort of issue shows up in decision making, as part of what psychologists have more recently labeled "confirmation bias." Once people start to head to a conclusion, they look for information that confirms their decision and ignore anything that contradicts it. A simple experiment shows how this works, and how it can lead to errant conclusions. P. C. Wason had people try to figure out a rule that generated a number sequence. He told participants that the sequence 2-4-6 fit the rule. Participants could get additional information by asking whether some other sequence also fit the rule. They could ask about as many other sequences as they wanted. Once they felt they knew the rule, they offered a guess. In one version of the experiment, only six of twenty-nine people were right on the first guess. In a later version, fifty-one out of fifty-one were wrong. The problem: Once participants felt they had a reasonable guess at the rule, they asked about sequences that would confirm that they were correct. If someone decided the rule was "ascending, consecutive even numbers," he'd ask if 8-10-12 satisfied the rule. If someone decided the rule was "ascending even numbers," he'd ask if 10-22-30 satisfied the rule. In fact, the rule was simply "ascending numbers," but very few got to that conclusion because they didn't ask about sequences that would contradict their ideas. If participants wanted to be sure that "ascending, consecutive even numbers" was the rule, they needed to come up with a sequence of ascending even numbers that weren't consecutive, or ascending odd numbers, or descending even numbers. Just asking about multiple sequences that they thought were correct wasn't going to get them to the right conclusion. They had to ask about sequences that they thought were wrong, but the confirmation bias prevented them from doing so.[12]

The confirmation bias is so strong that people often won't admit they're wrong even when it's clear to the rest of the world that they made a knuckleheaded choice. A classic example is a question asked by Mickey Schulhof, former president of Sony USA, following a write-off on Sony's acquisition of Columbia Pictures. (An acquisition made, as it happens, based on a flawed analogy. Sony looked at the computer industry and saw the tight coupling of hardware and software, so it decided that it needed movies—a sort of software—to run on its consumer-electronics hardware.) Pressed about the write-off, Schulhof said, "What makes you think the Sony acquisition of Columbia Pictures was a corporate blunder?"[13]

Um, because you wrote off $3.2 billion, almost the total value of the purchase of Columbia?

Although science is supposed to be the most rational of endeavors, it constantly demonstrates confirmation bias. Thomas Kuhn's classic book, *The Structure of Scientific Revolutions*, details how scientists routinely ignore uncomfortable facts. Ian Mitroff's *The Subjective Side of Science* shows at great length how scientists who had formulated theories about the origins of the moon refused to capitulate when the moon rocks brought back by Apollo 11 disproved their theories; the scientists merely tinkered with their theories to try to skirt the new evidence. Max Planck, the eminent physicist, said scientists never do give up their biases, even when they are discredited. The scientists just slowly die off, making room for younger scientists, who didn't grow up with the errant biases.[14] (Of course, the younger scientists have biases of their own that will eventually be proved wrong but won't be relinquished.)

An interesting book by Charles Perrow, *Normal Accidents*, has numerous examples of disasters caused by confirmation bias. Take, for example, a dam that was planned for the Snake River. The plans were approved and funded, when geologists found a problem. The area experienced earthquakes, and building a dam would make earthquakes more likely. The geologists issued shrill warnings—at least, shrill in scientists' terms—but the warnings got toned down as they passed up through channels, to the point where they could eventually be ignored. Other red flags were raised and ignored. In fact, the dam's operator got permission to fill the dam at several times normal speed, even though that increased the stress on the dam. When the dam started falling apart, the problems were trivialized; earthmoving equipment was simply dispatched to patch the cracks that were appearing in the dam. Eventually, the earthmoving equipment got sucked into a whirlpool. The dam burst on June 5, 1976, killing eleven people and doing more than $1 billion in property damage.

In *Human Universals* Donald Brown suggests that the confirmation bias is wired into us. He says "mental maps" are universal, meaning we take new information and fit it into the map that already exists in our heads. We don't typically use the new information to challenge the validity of what's already in there.

Conformity

Normal Accidents blames conformity for a truly odd nautical phenomenon that bureaucrats refer to delicately as "non-collision-course collisions." Stripped of the delicacy, the term means this: A captain took a vessel that was in no danger and deliberately changed his course in a way that caused him to collide with another vessel.

Why would he do this? No, drinking wasn't involved. Nor was great fatigue or time pressure. Instead, the captain simply misjudged the relative movements of his vessel and the other vessel. Of the twenty-six collisions investigated in the book, nineteen to twenty-four would not have occurred except for a last-minute course change by a captain. Others on board read the situation correctly, but they either assumed the captain knew what he was doing or were afraid to contradict him—until it was too late. Perrow writes, "It is not unusual for a deck officer to remain aghast and silent while his captain grounds the ship or collides with another."

In 1955, Solomon Asch published results from a series of experiments that demonstrated wonderfully the pressures to conform.

Asch's experiments put a subject in with a group of seven to nine people he hadn't met. Unknown to the subject, the others were all cooperating with the experimenters. An experimenter announced that the group would be part of a psychological test of visual judgment. The experimenter then held up a card with a single line on it, followed by a card with three lines of different lengths. Group members were asked, in turn, which line on the second card matched the line on the first. The unsuspecting subject was asked toward the end of the group. The differences in length were obvious, and everyone answered the question correctly for the first three sets of cards. After that, however, everyone in the group who was in on the experiment had been instructed to give a unanimous, incorrect answer. They continued to agree on a wrong answer from that point on, except for the occasional time when they'd been instructed to give the correct answer, to keep the subject from getting suspicious. As Asch put it, subjects were being tested to see what mattered more to them, their eyes or their peers.

The eyes had it, but not by much. Asch said that, in 128 runnings of the experiment, subjects gave the wrong answer 37 percent of the time. Many subjects looked befuddled. Some openly expressed their feeling that the rest of the group was wrong. But they went along.

Interestingly, Asch found that all it took was one voice of dissent, and the subject gave the correct answer far more frequently. If just one other person in the room gave the correct answer, the subject went along with the majority just 14 percent of the time—still high, but not nearly so bad.

Asch wrote: "That we have found the tendency to conformity in our society so strong that reasonably intelligent and well-meaning young people are willing to call white black is a matter of concern. It raises questions about our ways of education and about the values that guide our conduct."[15]

Following in Asch's footsteps, Stanley Milgram conducted a disturbing experiment into the influence of authority figures. It was 1961, and Adolf Eichmann had just gone on trial for war crimes committed as a senior member of Hitler's staff during World War II. Milgram wondered why so many Germans had gone along with the atrocities and decided to test to see if we might all react to superiors the way many Germans did. He brought in people who had been paid $4.50 to participate in what was billed as a test of how feedback can improve learning. Each subject was paired with an actor who was in on the experiment. The subject was always the "teacher" and was given a series of words to teach the "learner," played by the actor, who was positioned on the other side of a wall. The subject was told that, when the "learner" was prompted for a word and gave the wrong answer, the subject was to turn a dial, which would give the "learner" an electric shock. The subject was then given a 45-volt jolt to get a sense of the shocks he'd be administering.

During the testing, the dial was actually connected to prerecorded sounds of people acting as though they'd been jolted; no shock was being administered to the "learner." When the "learner" began making his scripted mistakes, an experimenter ordered the "teacher" to administer a shock. When the mistakes continued, the experimenter told the "teacher" to increase the voltage, then increase it again and again and again. The "teacher" heard moans, yelps, and sounds of protest. As the voltage continued to increase, the "learner" would pound on the wall and say he was afraid he was going to have a heart attack. In the face of all this, "teachers" often complained to the experimenter about having to continue. Some got up and paced around. Some offered to return the money they'd been paid, if they could just stop the jolts. But the experimenter ordered them to continue, and they did. No one stopped before reaching the 300-volt level on the dial. And 65 percent went all the way to the 450-volt level, which they'd been told at the start of the experiment was potentially a fatal shock.[16]

We draw two conclusions from these and related experiments:

- First, never trust a social scientist. Whatever he tells you he's testing surely isn't what's really going on.
- Second, our psyches lead us to go along with our peers and to conform, in particular, to the wishes of authority figures. In the Asch experiment, the test was simple, the answers were obvious, and the subject had no prior ties to the rest of the

> group—yet subjects went along with the group to a surprising degree. Imagine how much greater the pressures are in a business setting, when the subject is complicated, when the answers aren't clear, and when there are social and economic bonds that tie a group together.

Again, Brown says in *Human Universals* that the tendency to conform is built into us, based on his findings that "in-group/out-group," "socialization," and "status" appear in all cultures. "In-group/out-group" means that people form groups with those they feel close to, and avoid those outside the groups. "Socialization" and "status" mean people also focus heavily on their interactions with others and their status within their groups. From a business standpoint, these three universals suggest that even senior executives, as bright and decisive as they typically are, may value their standing with their peers and bosses so highly that they'll conform to the group's wishes. Executives may not raise objections even when they see a strategy is flawed. (Some scientists have recently argued that conformity is built into us through evolution—people with a "conformity gene" were more likely to band together and dominate those who chose to go it alone.)

Brown also says every culture reveres leaders. This high esteem can, obviously, be great for a company. You can't go anywhere very quickly if the troops won't follow the generals. But the reliance on leaders can contribute to conformity and let bad ideas go unchallenged.

Peter Drucker once cautioned against trying too hard to find strong leaders, noting, "The three greatest leaders of the twentieth century were Hitler, Stalin and Mao."[17]

Overconfidence and Defense Mechanisms

Call it the Lake Wobegon effect. Just as Garrison Keillor's fictional town is a place "where all the women are strong, all the men are good-looking, and all the children are above average," our psyches make us overly confident of our abilities and resist attempts to teach us otherwise.

For example, a simple experiment, repeated many times, has shown how bad we are at estimating. People are asked to think about any of a variety of quantifiable things—how many manhole covers there are in the United States, how many physical books are in the Library of Congress, whatever. Then people are asked to provide a range of estimates in which they believe they have a 98 percent chance that the right answer falls within their range. The first time the experiment was done, instead of having 2 percent of the ranges not include the right answer, it lay outside the ranges set by 45 percent of the participants. More typically, 15 percent to 30 percent are wrong.[18] (The subjects of the initial experiment were Harvard Business School students. Make of that whatever you like.)

Yet we don't seem to realize our inadequacies. In Sweden, 94 percent of the population believe that they are above average for Swedish drivers.[19] In France, 84 percent of the men say they are above average as lovers.[20]

Perhaps because it's more fun to twit experts than to go after Swedish drivers or even French lovers, many studies have focused on experts. The findings: Even experts aren't terribly good in their fields—and don't know it. As far as we can tell, no one has done a systematic study of overconfidence among executives, but plenty of studies have been done in technical fields, because of the real-world consequences of miscalculations. For instance, some MIT engineers took advantage of an abandoned roadway project and tested some road-construction experts. The engineers chose a straightforward question: How much landfill can be piled on top of a clay foundation in a marshy area as the base for a road? In this situation, the engineers had the luxury of being able to get a definite answer. They piled on the landfill until the clay foundation collapsed. The answer was that 18.7 feet of landfill was the maximum the foundation could support. The engineers provided all the relevant information about the clay foundation to the experts and asked for estimates. None of the experts was close. The MIT engineers then asked for a range, so that the experts felt they had at least a 50 percent chance of having the right answer within their range. None of the ranges included the correct answer. In other words, all the experts had confidence in their guesses, and all were wrong.[21]

In *The Wisdom of Crowds*, James Surowiecki writes: "The between-expert agreement in a host of fields, including stock picking, livestock judging, and clinical psychology, is below 50 percent, meaning that experts are as likely to disagree as to agree. More disconcertingly, one study found that the internal consistency of medical pathologists' judgments was just 0.5, meaning that a pathologist presented with the same evidence would, half the time, offer a different opinion. Experts are also surprisingly bad at what social scientists call 'calibrating' their judgments. If your judgments are well-calibrated, then you have a sense of how likely it is that your judgment is correct. But experts are much like normal people: They routinely overestimate the likelihood that they're right."

Studies show that experts are actually more likely to suffer from overconfidence than the rest of the world. After all, they're experts.[22]

In the business world, this overconfidence shows up all over the place. For instance, *The Three Tensions: Winning the Struggle to Perform Without Compromise* cites a Bain study in which 80 percent of companies thought their products were superior to their competitors'—even though only 8 percent of customers agreed.

Human Universals says every society shows what the book calls "overestimating objectivity of thought." We humans aren't as rational as we think we are. The study also says every culture demonstrates "risk-taking." It seems that teenage boys aren't the only ones who think they're invincible. In every culture, taking risks is seen as bold and admirable. It's so much more fun to go all in and bully an opponent off a hand in no-limit hold 'em than it is to fold a hand because you're surely beaten. It's hard to get people to back away from bad risks.

Brown's study also found that "self-image" and "psychological defense mechanism" are universal. By those terms, he means that people think highly of themselves even if they shouldn't and that people blame problems on bad luck rather than taking responsibility and learning from their failures. Our rivals may succeed through good luck, but not us. We earn our way to the top.

In the business world, a long-term study of Exxon Corporation executives found that "cognitive maps that explain poor performance contain significantly more assumptions about the environment while those that explain good performance contain more assumptions dealing with the effects of executives' actions."[23] To translate that to English: If something went wrong, the executives blamed the business climate; if something went right, they took credit.

Look at how most of us think about our golf games. According to the

USGA, American male golfers say they hit their drivers an average of 236 yards. The reality: 191 yards. When a man hits a good drive, he thinks that's the real him; he dismisses bad drives as aberrations.

Or look at the business press. When someone fails, he's crucified, even if he's a bright guy who had a sound strategy. When someone succeeds, he's lionized. Michael Dell, for instance, is credited with having a grand vision way back in the 1980s about selling people made-to-order computers. His was a great business model for a long time and may yet be again. But here's a secret: He was lucky.

In 1986, when one of us—Paul—first started covering the computer beat for the *Wall Street Journal*, he went to the huge Comdex trade show in Las Vegas and, being new, was willing to meet with almost anyone. That's how he spent an hour with a twenty-one-year-old college dropout who had started selling computers out of his dorm room at the University of Texas—in other words, the young Michael Dell. Dell was shooting for publicity because PC retailers were stocking only the major brands, and Dell was desperate to get shelf space in stores. Sure, he sold computers through mail order, which eventually morphed into his make-to-order, Internet-based sales machine. But he'd have happily dumped mail order if he could just get the big chains to carry his goods. He deserves tons of credit for taking advantage of his luck, developing a respected mail-order brand name just in time for the Internet, but it is revisionist history to say he always intended to pursue his current model.

The tendency to take credit, fairly or not, is reinforced by what psychologists call the "narrative fallacy." That is the tendency to construct stories to explain events, even when no story exists. If we succeed, it must be because we're talented, right?

One study took teams of MBAs and had them predict companies' financial results based on the prior year's annual report. Ten of the teams were told that their results had been exceptionally good. Ten were told that their results were substandard. In fact, the results for each group of ten were almost identical. (Remember, don't believe what social scientists tell you when they're conducting a study.) But the groups that were told they did well rated themselves much more highly on interaction, leadership, and several other factors than did the teams that were told they were below average. The "success" needed explanation.

We make up stories about our pasts, too—stories that may contradict the facts but that justify our opinions of ourselves. Example: While it's been widely found that some 70 percent of corporate takeovers hurt the stock-market value of the acquiring company, studies find that roughly three-quarters of executives report that takeovers *they were involved in* had been successes.[24]

Those executives were, no doubt, sincere. We're all simply wired to think highly of ourselves and our efforts, so we don't dwell on possible failings—and don't learn from them.

NINE

Why Bad Strategies Happen to Good Companies

Awareness Is Still Not Enough

Theoretically, businesses are set up in ways that acknowledge individuals' failings, that learn from people's flaws and that overcome them. Many people get involved in major decisions, to bring in all kinds of expertise and to ensure that a single person can't lead the business astray. Due diligence is done to ensure that all information has been considered and that strategies have been determined objectively. Business schools and executive-training courses offer frameworks to help sort through the complexities of business.

But as our failure cases show—and as anyone who has ever worked in business knows from personal experience—the organizational structures of business can hurt decision making as well as help it. After all, businesses are social structures. They function much like any of the other social structures that Donald Brown investigated in *Human Universals.* Actually, they're more complicated than many social structures because of the money involved.

In other words, while organizational structures and disciplines can sometimes filter out errors, they are far from perfect. In fact, they sometimes introduce problems.

Organizational complications show up in four areas: the peculiarities of the CEO's position; the interpersonal dynamics at the top of a company; organizational structures; and the tools companies use for determining strategy.

The CEO

When someone is named CEO, it's usually after two or three decades of scratching and clawing, of outwitting the other guys, of surviving some final, nail-biting contest to see who gets the top job. Now's the time to shine. Now's the time for some fun.

That fun typically comes in two flavors: money and legacy.

In and of itself, the money isn't a problem. If a basketball player can leave college after his freshman year and get $100 million in contracts with an NBA team and apparel manufacturers, then why shouldn't a CEO be entitled to big bucks, too? The problem is that CEO money tends to push them toward extremes, encouraging them to either take on excessive risk or exercise excessive caution.

The excessive risk comes because the CEO may have incentive to go for the home run. He has a bazillion options that would be worth serious buckaroos if he can pull off a breakout move into a new market or somehow redefine the industry. Then he could retire and fly around in his private Gulfstream 550 (not just the Gulfstream 450) or become a philanthropist through a foundation with his name on the door. If he fails, well, the options can't be worth less than nothing. The size of the failure doesn't matter to the CEO personally in the same way it matters to investors.

The CEO of Iridium, for instance, had options that would have made him a very rich man if the business was even a moderate success but that would be worth nothing if he pulled the plug.

Even if the CEO doesn't swing for the fences, he still has reason to do whatever he can to increase the size of his business—the bigger the business, the higher the CEO's compensation, in general. That often means acquisitions. This is true even in a maturing business, where it might be better to cash out by selling the business; takeovers usually end with the members of the acquiring management team keeping their jobs while those at the acquired company lose out, so management teams have strong incentives to be the buyers, not the sellers.

Excessive caution can appear if a CEO decides he's in it for the long haul. He gets his initial, big chunk of options when he ascends to the top job, and he counts on having the stock price rise 5 percent to 10 percent a year, just by coasting. After a decade in the job, his options are at twice the strike price, and he's looking mighty good.

CEOs also may have incentives to defer painful actions. If they're anywhere near retirement and they see a major threat to their market, they have reason to wait, keep collecting their bonuses, and let the next guy deal with the earnings-wrecking write-offs from plant closings or layoffs.

In any case, compensation has a way of distorting results. To no one's surprise, a study by Flora Guidry, Andrew Leone, and Steven Rock in 1999 found that senior management manipulates earnings based on bonuses. If (happy day!) bonuses max out for a year, management tends to find ways to defer to the next year any earnings above what is needed to generate that maximum bonus. If results are so weak that there won't be any bonuses, management tends to take charges or find other ways to pull extra expenses into the crummy year to make future years look better.[1]

The desire to leave a legacy can also distort decisions. The typical CEO didn't do all that work to get the top job just so he could be a caretaker and turn the job over to the next guy (even if he could make good money in the caretaker role). CEOs are typically men and women of action. They have some vision they want to pursue. They want to be Lou Gerstner, not Frank Cary (who managed IBM brilliantly as CEO in the late 1970s and early 1980s but didn't have to make the dramatic changes that Gerstner did).

CEOs and former CEOs who read this manuscript for us said this issue is the big one, the one that, beyond all others, can cloud judgment. It's hard to be a great CEO except in times of great change. And if that change isn't happening of its own accord, CEOs are tempted to manufacture change through some big acquisition or bold venture.

Sometimes the bold charge works. But sometimes it doesn't.

Even when a CEO doesn't try the equivalent of Napoléon's invasion of Russia, the stock market is a demanding master. Every CEO knows that the big gains go to those companies that outperform the competition, and he can argue that the stock market will have a real effect on the business, not just on his personal portfolio. Companies with rapidly rising stock prices can attract the best talent, make the biggest acquisitions, and raise capital at the lowest costs. So, in this era where the mantra for many

CEOs is "maximizing shareholder return," many CEOs start from the stock price and work backward. They decide what rate of stock appreciation they "need," then decide what growth rate would justify those rises. They then formulate strategy to generate that sort of growth—even though it may not be possible. Often, companies promise double-digit growth in earnings, yet a recent McKinsey study of one thousand companies found that only 15 percent generated such growth for five consecutive years. Less than 1 percent sustained such growth for a decade.

Then there are those pesky quarterly conference calls with securities analysts. While CEOs would prefer to deliberate carefully behind closed doors, they (or the CFOs, who often have the calls delegated to them) have to deal with a cacophony of questions from young MBA know-it-alls. If earnings are anything less than great, there will be a bunch of squawking (and downgrades) unless senior management can promise a strategy that will soon make earnings great. You'd be amazed how many cost-cutting decisions are made in the days or hours leading up to one of these conference calls. Or maybe you wouldn't.

Our CEO readers say these conference calls are number two on the list of things that can distort thinking.

Hedge funds add to the pressure. Although the credit crunch may eventually diminish their war chests, funds have raised hundreds of billions of dollars and have declared that all companies are in play, no matter their size. If a company slips up, a hedge fund may pounce, buying the company and replacing management. Even generally well-managed companies like McDonald's Corporation spent much of 2006 and 2007 fending off hedge funds. Sometimes it's clear to management that the strategy a hedge fund is proposing will provide a short-term boost to the stock (so the fund can sell out at a profit) but cause problems in the long run, yet management still finds it hard to resist. The hedge fund is surely creating a stink in the press, and it's threatening management's jobs. As one CEO put it, "Sometimes it's safer to follow the strategy that seems rational than the strategy that is rational."

For good measure, every CEO is told these days that he needs to be a strong leader. That doesn't just mean being tall, with chiseled features and a commanding presence in front of large groups. It also means having some vision and being consistently right. But how does the CEO formulate that mistake-free vision? He may find it hard to seek too much counsel from subordinates, at the risk of seeming weak. He may likewise find it hard to talk too much to outside board members, who, in any case, surely draw their experience from different industries. The CEO can bounce ideas off friends, but only within the bounds of confidentiality. It wouldn't do to have a major initiative leak because of a conversation at the bar at the country club. The CEO has hired advisers, such as investment bankers, but they come with an agenda. Investment bankers get paid to do deals, and they make their money whether or not the ideas are any good.

We hasten to add that we're not saying CEOs are venal people, looking out only for their wallets or their reputations, or so weak that they can't stand up to pressure or criticism. We like CEOs. Honest. We have lots of friends who are current or former CEOs.

We're just being realistic. Even when people try to do the right thing, they're driven at least partly by personal interest. They wouldn't be human otherwise.

In theory, boards are supposed to be a check on CEOs, but boards are a fairly blunt instrument. CEOs certainly keep their boards informed but don't always have to ask for approval, even for major initiatives. Marvin Zonis, a professor at the University of Chicago business school, who has been on several boards, described an insurance CEO who decided he would buy numerous employee-leasing firms as a way of lining up more customers for the company's insurance. Zonis and other board members protested. The insurance company didn't know anything about employee leasing. (Employee leasing is a complicated arrangement in which Company X becomes the employer of large groups of people and leases them to Companies A, B, and C, where they have long done their work. The idea is that Company X will achieve economies of scale and manage the employees more effectively than Companies A, B, and C would individually.) The CEO said he was going ahead with the plan anyway. The board wasn't ready to fire him, so it acquiesced initially. Eventually, the board did fire the CEO. The problem is that the board had been denied an advisory role that would have headed off a series of ill-fated purchases. The board had been limited to being an on/off switch. Either it went with the CEO, or it didn't.[2]

Interpersonal Dynamics

When Hitler was planning his invasion of Poland, his foreign minister, Joachim von Ribbentrop, asserted that Britain wouldn't declare war on Germany as a result and vowed to personally shoot anyone who contradicted him.[3] Zonis, who is also an expert on the Middle East, says Saddam Hussein did personally shoot a senior minister in his government when that minister suggested, quite mildly, that Iraq might want to consider looking for a peaceful settlement of its 1980s war with Iran.[4]

While less dramatic, senior managers often communicate that they don't want to be contradicted—whether or not they intend to send that message. In addition, some corporate cultures and the camaraderie among a management team can keep valid challenges from being made.

Ed Schwinn, CEO of the business that bears his family name, was up front about not wanting to be contradicted. When a Schwinn team looked into the possibilities of mountain bikes in the 1980s, he felt that they were a passing fad and argued against major investment in them. Schwinn was the dominant maker of bikes in the United States, and he didn't see any reason that would change. A senior executive felt otherwise and argued his position vociferously. Ed Schwinn adjourned the meeting and said the group would reconvene on the issue in two weeks. They did—after Schwinn fired the contrarian.[5] Do you think anyone else spoke up, to try to head off what turned out to be a catastrophic misjudgment?

Even when managers aren't that harsh, dissent is often withheld, whether for fear of offending the top guy or of being wrong. According to one Samsung executive, all members of the board doubted the chairman's plan to enter the car business in 1997, because the Korean market was already saturated. Local carmakers churned out 2.4 million cars a year, while consumers were only buying 1.6 million. But he was the chairman, and the son of the founder, so no one dared challenge him. Samsung sold just 50,000 cars, mostly to employees, despite pouring $5 billion into a venture that had the capacity to build more than 240,000 cars a year. By early 1999, the venture was in receivership. In 2000, Samsung sold 70 percent of the venture for $560 million.[6]

Just relaying bad news can be hazardous to your career health. A study found that those who delivered bad news in corporations were tainted, even if they had nothing to do with causing the problem and even if their bosses said they knew the messenger wasn't at fault. Executives aren't stupid. Whenever possible, they delay delivering bad tidings.[7]

Some companies have cultures that make it even harder to talk about bad news. At IBM in the pre-Gerstner days, for instance, executives were culturally forbidden from talking about problems; they could only talk about solutions. Obviously, saying that something needed a solution implied that there was a problem, but the IBM approach changed the conversation in crucial—and sometimes costly—ways.

OS/2 is a good example. It may be hard to remember OS/2 at this remove, but it was IBM's alternative to Microsoft's Windows in the late 1980s and early 1990s. IBM pushed OS/2 as hard as it knew how, because it was desperate for all kinds of strategic reasons to retrieve the near-monopoly it had created for Microsoft in personal-computer operating systems. The problem was, the market had rejected OS/2. Once Microsoft came out with a vastly improved version of Windows, in May 1990, the battle was over. Microsoft won. IBM lost. But IBM executives couldn't admit that to themselves. They kept talking about ways to reposition OS/2, about ways to improve it. They couldn't say, "This OS/2 thing is a disaster. Let's shoot it in the head and move on." As a result, IBM spent roughly $1 billion on OS/2 work after the rest of the world knew the fight was over. In all, IBM lost some $2 billion on OS/2 before pulling the plug in 2005.[8]

Even after Gerstner arrived on the scene as CEO in 1993, facing up to bad news turned out to be hard. The IBM PC business was bleeding red ink. PCs had become commodities in all but a few niches, such as laptops. Many analysts argued that IBM was culturally incapable of running a commodity business profitably and should sell its PC operations. But Gerstner and his team decided they could fix the problem, remaining determined even as they tallied up losses of hundreds of millions of dollars a year, losses that peaked at $1 billion in 1998. It wasn't until 2005 that they realized their problem didn't have a solution and sold the business to Lenovo.

The current emphasis on teamwork can create problems, too. NBA coaches, mountaineers, and other leaders of elite teams explain how to foster strong teams, and, in good conditions, those teams can function with impressive efficiency. But the bonds of teamwork can make it hard to deliver tough news. Teams tend to be formed of people who resemble each other in many ways, and they become friends. You don't want to tell your friend he's messed up.

James Kilts, the former CEO of Gillette, documents in his book, *Doing What Matters*, what a disaster Gillette was when he took over in 2001. The company was losing market share. Sales and earnings were flat. The company had missed its earnings estimates for fifteen straight quarters. The stock was getting creamed. Yet criticism was so lacking that two-thirds of the company's executives were getting top ratings and, thus, maximum compensation.

Rather than create friction, many companies completely forgo important types of feedback. Franz Reither did a study that found what he called "ballistic behavior"—companies launched a project, much as they'd fire a cannon, but never checked to see where the cannonball ended up.[9] Robert E. Mittelstaedt Jr., in his book, *Will Your Next Mistake Be Fatal?*, says he canvassed five hundred executives in the course of teaching management courses over the years and found fewer than ten who had any sort of process for reviewing the quality of past decisions.

Even when feedback is provided, it is often soft-pedaled. One of us—Chunka—was once brought into a company to do an after-action review when an error in a spreadsheet caused a consulting team to exaggerate by a factor of one hundred the savings that could come from a project. The potential savings were so great that they were communicated to top management and to the board. When the error was found, it was acknowledged, but the communication wasn't very good. Some senior partners at the consulting firm and senior executives at the client felt blindsided. Chunka spent a couple of days interviewing those involved, checking the e-mail traffic, and writing a report—which disappeared without a trace. The consulting firm's CEO, who had commissioned the report, just shrugged and said he guessed those involved had decided it was better to ignore the report than to sort out the blame. (The client apparently had no problem sorting out the blame. It has yet to reengage that consulting firm.)

In *Groupthink*, Irving Janis says cohesive teams don't just emphasize collegiality in ways that suppress dissent. He also says cohesive teams:

- Dehumanize the enemy and think it is incompetent. (A Bain study seconds his notion. The consulting firm found that 80 percent of companies think their offerings are superior to competitors'. Lake Wobegon, anyone?)
- Limit the number of alternatives they will consider.
- Show even more overconfidence than members would as individuals. ("When a group of people who respect each other's opinions arrive at a unanimous view, each member is likely to feel that the belief must be true," writes Janis.)
- Create "mind guards," who stomp out dissent. (Janis, who dissected planning disasters by the U.S. government, says Bobby Kennedy appointed himself to that role in the ill-fated Bay of Pigs invasion. His brother, the president, had initially approved the invasion only if the United States' involvement could be hidden. That meant secret training of the Cuban refugees who would invade the island. That meant no American military equipment could be used in the attack. That meant the Cuban refugees needed to be able to avoid capture if the plan failed. As planning progressed, all those conditions went out the window. The training was so public that many newspapers wrote about it. Planes with clear U.S. markings bombed Cuba in the assault. The Cuban refugees couldn't flee to the hills because the point of attack had been changed; instead of being near the hills, the attack occurred miles away, with treacherous marshes blocking the route to those hills. Yet Bobby Kennedy—a bright guy who showed willingness to stand up to anyone—got himself so worked up about the invasion that he headed off any attempt to get to the president to tell him that the planning had gone awry and that the United States was about to be embarrassed throughout the world.)

Janis adds that it's hard to avoid these groupthink problems just by being aware of them. He says Kennedy learned from his mistakes and made changes that ensured that all alternatives were aired and that encouraged dissent on all important decisions. As a result, the same group that mishandled the Bay of Pigs handled the subsequent Cuban missile crisis brilliantly. But the lessons only sort of made their way to Lyndon Johnson's administration. Johnson said he welcomed dissent and even formed a council to challenge his decisions on Vietnam. But he clearly didn't welcome dissent. In fact, he became his own mind guard. If someone challenged him, he'd welcome the person loudly at the next meeting, saying something like, "Well, here comes Mr. Stop-the-Bombing."

In practice, the tendency to withhold bad news and to be nice to each other can look something like this:

If a CEO (or boss at any level, for that matter) decides to try to find the flaws in a plan, he might circulate it among some trusted advisers. But these are people who like and probably admire him, even if they don't report to him. If they have objections, they're likely to hide them. They'll say, "I like this a lot. I like this. I like that. I like this other thing. You might want to consider X, Y, and Z. But, on balance, I like this a lot." What the advisers are saying is, "Boy, are you in trouble. X will kill you. Even if it doesn't, Y will, and so will Z." What the CEO hears is, "Boy, you've done it again." He'll even congratulate himself for having the intestinal fortitude to look for objections.

Organizational Structures

Those of us who have wives have learned the hard way not to touch that most toxic of questions: "Does this make me look fat?" But our wives aren't stupid, either. They may make inferences based on how long it takes us husbands to respond, our tone of voice, or whatever. In other words, at some level, we all are accustomed to dealing with the sorts of interpersonal dynamics that complicate discussions within companies, and we can make at least some allowances. What *really* complicates decision making inside companies—what we aren't at all prepared for based on daily life—are organizational structures.

Different operating units have different priorities, so it's hard to produce a unified view of the world. A CEO can certainly try to impose a strategy from the top down, but even he typically needs to get many of his aides to agree. It's hard to tell the marketing group to go sell some glitzy new product if the manufacturing folks say they can't make it.

A result of having to get agreement from so many diverse parties is what is sometimes called "satisficing." This is akin to what happens in government when a leader tries to pull together a coalition in support of an idea. While businesses rarely produce a Bridge to Nowhere (the $250 million Alaskan bridge project that Congress approved to connect an island of fifty people to the mainland), there still can be plenty of horse trading at the top levels of businesses and, as a result, weak strategies. In the early days of the PC business, for instance, IBM's mainframe business tried to prevent the PC business from using the most powerful processor available from Intel, for fear it would cut into mainframe sales. A compromise was reached: The PC business could use the chip but not until a few months after its introduction. This was, of course, naïve. Competitors such as Compaq used the chip right away and became perceived as technology leaders. They soon rendered IBM's PC business profoundly unprofitable. IBM still faced whatever decline in mainframe sales it was going to suffer because of increasingly powerful PCs.

The negotiations that go on as part of the "satisficing" also make it hard to derail a strategy once it has reached a certain point. It's just too painful to go back and start over. People wind up betting their careers on a strategy once they've lined up significant support, so they can't let go. Even if something comes up that makes it seem that the strategy is mistaken, that will usually get ignored. Whether something will actually work is another issue for another day. The important thing is to keep the coalition together.

Layers of bureaucracy can cause problems by filtering out important information, turning organizations into a game of telephone. What's said initially can get distorted each time it is relayed and can be completely different by the time it reaches its destination. "She sells seashells by the seashore" can quickly become "Cecil says he snores." Or, if you're Ford, an engineer's strong recommendation for buffering fuel tanks in the Pinto can disappear entirely, on cost grounds, by the time the management committee approves the final specs for the car. Because of the possibility that the Pinto would catch fire after a crash, the car became known as "the barbecue that seats four."[10] Ford faced numerous lawsuits over the Pinto, which *Forbes* put on its list of fifty worst cars of all time.

In addition, the tenor of an organization can have a major effect on the likelihood that a strategy will work, even though strategists often don't think that way; they do their thinking based on opportunities in the marketplace. Cisco, for instance, has a history of integrating acquisitions effectively, so a strategy based on acquisition will likely work better there than for a company that is new to the takeover game. Organizations often miss that point. They assume they can quickly build what some consultants call an "acquisition engine" or just be more diligent and avoid major mistakes.

Tools for Planning Strategy

Niels Bohr, the eminent Danish physicist, said, "Predictions are hard, especially about the future."[11] (Yes, Yogi Berra said the same thing, but Bohr beat him to the line by decades.) Bohr was right, and the corporate approach to forecasting sometimes makes predictions harder, not easier.

At Diamond, the firm where we were partners for eight years, any sales forecast at a partners' meeting drew guffaws. The CEO often ribbed the forecaster as "the greatest sandbagger of all time." The tone was light, but there was a serious game of cat and mouse going on, as there is with most any forecast at most any firm. Those making the forecasts want to set the bar as low as possible for sales or earnings, so they can look like heroes when they beat the numbers.

The cat-and-mouse game is almost impossible to end because, while businesses don't like to admit it, standard planning methods are highly susceptible to manipulation.

In many cases, there just isn't much to go on. How do you really know whether you're going to sell ten thousand copies of a book or one million until you release the book and see the reaction? You can do some research and make an educated guess, but you'll still miss the mark, maybe by a lot.

Yet businesses are built on numbers, spreadsheet by spreadsheet, so forecasts still get made, even though everyone knows they're suspect. It's like the military group that was asked to make weather forecasts three months out. After a while, the group said it was going to stop making the long-range forecasts because the guesses were no better than chance. Makes sense: Weather forecasts can be pretty good a week out and maybe shed some light on the week after that, but, after two weeks, who knows?

The message came back from headquarters: "Yes, the general knows the forecasts are useless, but he wants them anyway for planning purposes."

In most business settings, decision makers can be steered to a particular business plan through the use of worst-case and best-case scenarios. Someone advocating a plan simply cherry-picks the data to provide a worst-case plan that doesn't seem too awful and a best-case plan that shows considerable upside potential. Even though decision makers may know, at some level, that they're being manipulated, they often still approve the plan.

In laying out plans, analysts generally don't acknowledge the probabilities of their assumptions. A plan may depend on, say, having three things happen. All three may seem probable, so the assumptions may be accepted. But if all three have a 70 percent chance of occurring, the chance that all three will happen is only about one in three. Even if assumptions have a 95 percent chance of being right, if you have to make ten of those assumptions you'll have a less than 60 percent chance that all will occur. Yet, because the probabilities usually aren't quantified, nobody does the math to figure out the overall probability.

Analysts also don't acknowledge the sensitivities of their assumptions. For example, a small change in interest rates might radically affect the demand for new houses, but analysts tend not to acknowledge that their best estimates could be wildly off.

While worst-case scenarios are supposed to be just that—worst imaginable cases—they often aren't. They're likely to be kinda-bad scenarios. Brave companies may prepare really-pretty-bad scenarios. Analysts rarely fully explore the catastrophic consequences of seemingly low-probability scenarios. These analysts are like the person who learns that a river is relatively calm and, on average, four feet deep—without allowing for the fact that the river has a nasty set of rapids and is fifteen feet deep for stretches. Companies can be left exposed if the market turns against them.

In addition, companies often think they're diversifying their risks when they aren't. They're merely making multiple bets on the same assumption. Several of the failures that we investigated for this book occurred because of a misunderstanding of risk. The companies thought they had diversified by adding a financial-services business—credit cards or other types of lending to customers—to their core retailing business. But the financial-services business and retailing business were really the same bet. If customers turned out to be bad credit risks, they would have to stop buying the retailer's goods. Likewise, if customers got access to other credit, they'd take much of their business elsewhere. A decline in one part of the business would lead to a decline in the other.

Even straightforward financial tools such as net present value can distort analysis, as Clay Christensen, Stephen P. Kaufman, and Willy Shih point out in a *Harvard Business Review* article. The idea makes great sense theoretically. You figure out what the earnings will be from a business down the road, then do a calculation to see if it's worth investing a certain amount of money now to generate that earnings stream. There are two problems. The first is that the most important part of the calculation concerns what the earnings will be five to ten years down the road, yet that's the part of the calculation that is least certain. It may be relatively easy to know about the first few years, but the more distant future is inherently murkier. The more insidious problem with net present value is that by presenting a precise number about the current value of future earnings, it hides the uncertainty about the number. In fact, the analysis is wide open for manipulation. If an analyst wants to make an idea look good, he assigns a favorable number for five to ten years out. If he wants to make the idea look bad, he assigns a meager number.

We're not saying that business structures are hopeless. There are organizations out there that learn from mistakes and institute processes to head off repeats. The military conducts after-action reviews to learn what went right and what went wrong in combat and does a pretty good job of adjusting. Hospitals often conduct reviews after patients die to see if mistakes can be identified and averted in the future. Airlines and federal transportation officials hold intricately detailed investigations after a plane crash. The result: an extraordinary record for safety.

We're just saying that learning from mistakes is hard. Few organizations even try if they aren't involved in the sorts of life-and-death situations that confront the military, hospitals, and airlines. And even those guys are subject to pressures that distort the results. Witness the Pat Tillman case. When the NFL-safety-turned-army-ranger was killed by friendly fire in Afghanistan, the army worried about the potential for a public-relations debacle. So the investigation into his death became a cover-up. So did the investigation into the investigation. As did the investigation into the investigation into the investigation, and the investigation into the investigation into the investigation into the investigation. (We'll stop now.) Similarly, fear of malpractice cases limits hospitals' willingness to delve too deeply into some cases—and a widely quoted study from 2004 estimated that nearly two hundred thousand people die in U.S. hospitals every year because of errors by doctors and nurses.[12] Even airlines aren't as good as they might be. They do an admirable job of preventing crashes, which are a PR nightmare that causes potential passengers to eschew flying. But airlines don't make upgrades, such as anchoring seats more firmly to the floor, that are known to limit deaths and injuries when a crash does somehow happen. From a business standpoint, a crash is a crash is a crash. Whether fifteen die or thirty doesn't matter nearly as much as whether the crash happened in the first place (unless, of course, you're one of the extra fifteen to die).

It's interesting to note two things about the fact that the airlines have been the best about learning from their failures. First, if the commanding officer of an army unit makes a mistake, his troops die; he probably doesn't. If a doctor makes a mistake, the patient dies; the doctor doesn't. If an airline pilot makes a catastrophic mistake or if his equipment fails, *he dies* along with his crew. There's rather more incentive for the pilot to insist that everyone avoid mistakes. Second, the pilots had to fight to have their safety be paramount. In the early days of flying, transporting mail became a huge business. But it was dangerous in those flimsy little planes that were used right after World War I. Of the first forty pilots with the U.S. Mail service, thirty-one died carrying the mail. The life expectancy of a pilot was four years. Finally, in 1922, the pilots worked out a deal. If the manager of a field told a pilot he had to take off to deliver the mail even though the pilot thought the weather was too dangerous, the manager had to be willing to sit in the plane's second seat and fly once around the field. That year, U.S. Mail pilots had zero fatalities.[13]

In other words, if we're to learn from failures, the incentives have to be just right.

TEN

The Devil's Advocate

Unleashing the Power of Conflict and Deliberation

Alfred P. Sloan, the legendary builder of General Motors, once said to a meeting of one of his top committees, "Gentlemen, I take it we are all in complete agreement on the decision here?" Everyone around the table nodded. "Then," Sloan continued, "I propose we postpone further discussion of this matter until our next meeting to give ourselves time to develop disagreement and perhaps gain some understanding of what the decision is all about."[1]

Our research suggests that too many companies got to the point of complete agreement and proceeded. We believe some disagreement is in order.

The research for this book, combined with others' research and our experience advising companies, argues for finding ways to institutionalize dissent. We'll lay out nine ways for increasing the level of disagreement during the ordinary course of business. These methods are designed to tease out and harness the knowledge and insight already accessible to the organization. Utilized well, these safeguards encourage dialogue and go a long way to raising important questions that need to be considered during strategy development. Because each of those methods has limitations and because some can be corrupted over time, we'll then lay out a formal method that should be used to test any major strategy that a company intends to pursue.

All of these methods can be applied, to one degree or another, to the sorts of strategic decisions made at every level of an organization, whether that's reorganizing marketing teams, changing incentives for the sales force, expanding a product's capabilities to appeal to a new set of customers, or whatever.

Our approach to dissent borrows its name from an error-correcting practice the Catholic Church used for centuries: the "devil's advocate." Traditionally, before the church declared someone a saint, it appointed a devil's advocate. That person's role was to take a skeptical view. He worked in concert with other investigators, but his role was to critically assess all evidence and presumptions and to lay out all reasonable arguments for why the prospective saint should be denied recognition. (Pope John Paul II abolished the office in 1983, after it had been in place for nearly four hundred years. Since then, five hundred saints have been canonized, a yearly rate about twenty times faster than in the earlier part of the twentieth century.)

Applied to business situations, the devil's advocate would "argue the 'no' side," to use the phrasing of Bill Smithburg, the former CEO of Quaker Oats, who lost his job because he failed to have someone do just that. As Smithburg reflected several years after his failed acquisition of Snapple, "There was so much excitement about bringing in a new brand, a brand with legs. We should have had a couple of people arguing the 'no' side of the equation."[2]

Dissension can work wonders. IBM, under Tom Watson Jr., used a form of dissension to produce one of the most spectacular runs of success in the millennia during which humans have been trying to scratch out a profit.

When Watson took over the helm of IBM from his father in 1956, he inherited a very centralized organization. As part of decentralizing authority, Watson Jr. devised what he referred to as a "check and balance arrangement" that became known as the IBM contention system. Operating executives were authorized to solve problems quickly but with the proviso that staff experts could challenge their decisions and force them to explain their reasoning. As Watson wrote in *Fortune*, "No decision was final without a staff man's concurrence—and if he signed, his job was just as much at stake as the executive who made the decision. When an executive and a staff man couldn't agree, the problem got kicked upstairs to senior management, which didn't suffer indecisiveness gladly."

With his contention system, Watson found a workable balance between inaction and ill-considered decisions. He described this balance in his *Fortune* article: "I never varied from the managerial rule that the worst possible thing we could do would be to lie dead in the water with any problem. Solve it, solve it quickly, solve it right or wrong. If you solved it wrong, it would come back and slap you in the face, and then you could solve it right. Lying dead in the water and doing nothing is a comfortable alternative because it is without immediate risk, but it is an absolutely fatal way to manage a business."

Note the emphasis on quick decisions. Executives sometimes quash dissent because they feel that it will keep them from moving quickly. Some argue that allowing disagreement can halt action entirely. Tom Kelley, the renowned innovation expert at the design firm IDEO, wrote in his book *The Ten Faces of Innovation:* "Every day, thousands of great ideas, concepts, and plans are nipped in the bud by devil's advocates." But, as Watson showed, done right, disagreement can sharpen ideas while not slowing down the business—his fifteen years at the top of IBM prompted *Fortune* to label him on its cover "The Greatest Capitalist in History." Indeed, the formal name for the office in the Catholic Church that was known as the devil's advocate was *promotor fidel*, which translates as "promoter of the faith."

Drawing on IBM and others, prominent management theorists agree about disagreement.

Peter Drucker wrote in *The Effective Executive* that "decisions of the kind the executive has to make are not made well by acclamation. They are made well only if based on conflicting views, the dialogue between different points of view, the choice between different judgments. The first rule of decision-making is that one does not make a decision unless there is a disagreement." Drucker says airing disagreement safeguards decision makers from special interests and preconceived notions within the organization, where, as Drucker says, "everybody is a special pleader, trying—often in good faith—to obtain the decision he favors." More important, only disagreement can provoke imagination and alternatives. "A decision without an alternative is a desperate gambler's throw, no matter how carefully thought out it might be," Drucker observes.

Edward de Bono, the originator of "lateral thinking," proposes what he calls "black hat" thinking.[3] In de Bono's scheme, black hat thinking is applied once an idea and its claimed benefits have been spelled out. Black hat thinking points out what is incorrect, how something does not fit experience or accepted knowledge, why something may not work, where the risks lie, what the faults in design are.

In *The Essence of Strategic Decision Making*, Charles Schwenk reports that numerous field and laboratory research studies support the effectiveness of devil's advocacy in improving organizational decision making. It improves analysis of data, understanding of a problem, and quality of solutions. In particular, devil's advocacy seems most effective when tackling complex and ill-structured problems. It increases the quality of assumptions, increases the number of strategic alternatives examined, and improves decision makers' use of ambiguous information to make predictions.

The question isn't whether devil's advocacy improves decisions. The question is how to introduce devil's advocacy in a way that organizations can tolerate. As one executive warned us, "Devil's advocates, if occasionally right, will get hunted down and killed by the antibodies in a company. Remember, they just won an argument. That means that someone else lost."

With the antibodies in mind, here are the nine ways that we've found companies can introduce acceptable levels of useful disagreement—at least for a time:

1. Grant license to the devil's advocate.
2. Smooth out management ruts.
3. First, decide how to decide.
4. Find history that fits.
5. Bet on it.
6. Stare into the abyss.
7. Construct alarm systems.
8. Always have escalation mechanisms.
9. Hold second-chance meetings.

Remember, these are not meant as alternative methods for setting strategy. There are already many different ways to develop strategy, captured in numerous books and translated into volumes of detailed methodological instructions. Each has its strengths, which depend partly on the industrial, organizational, and competitive context. In each case, we suspect that the methods' proponents would argue that, if used systematically and as designed, many of the mistakes that we've discussed would have been avoided. Perhaps so, but both research and experience demonstrate that even the best methodologies are not immune to weaknesses and decision-making traps of the sort we cover in the first seven chapters of this book.

In any case, our approach is to work in concert with existing methodologies. Our nine methods are process safeguards that serve as overlays on whatever strategy development process is currently used.

1. Grant license to the devil's advocate

In our experience, it is common to find someone playing an informal devil's advocate role inside most organizations. Sometimes this is a normal part of how conversations happen. Someone may be pessimistic about an idea and take it on himself to air tough questions. Or, perhaps, a conscientious group might assign someone to play that role to explore multiple sides of an issue.

These informal devil's advocates can be useful. President Kennedy showed as much when he asked his brother Bobby to fill that role during the Cuban missile crisis—actually, "useful" is far too tepid a word to describe Bobby's contribution, which did a lot to head off a nuclear holocaust. While Bobby had served as a "mind guard," shielding his brother from information that might challenge his thinking during the planning for the Bay of Pigs, he challenged everyone's thinking relentlessly and ruthlessly during the Cuban missile crisis. For instance, General Curtis LeMay argued that the United States could bomb the missile sites in Cuba without fear of retaliation by the Soviet Union. In the Bay of Pigs planning, the civilian leaders deferred to the military as experts in many areas. In the Cuban missile crisis, however, Bobby challenged LeMay's statement and got the group of advisers to imagine themselves in the Soviets' shoes. The group realized that the Soviets couldn't afford to lose too much face and would have to retaliate if the United States bombed the missile sites.

Leaders should foster their devil's advocates, publicly encouraging them and privately protecting them. IBM's Watson came up with an affectionate nickname for his devil's advocates: He called them "wild ducks" because they didn't fly in formation. He also frequently proclaimed that he liked "harsh, scratchy people" who challenged him. Gavin Rawl, when he was CEO of Exxon, encouraged a policy of "healthy disrespect." Under Jack Welch, GE was known for confrontation and argument. Frank Doyle, Welch's senior vice president for corporate relations, said, "I told Jack that what passes for conversation around here would be seen as a mugging" elsewhere.

One straightforward approach is to assign someone to the task, much as President Kennedy publicly gave his brother the responsibility and authority to play the devil's advocate. There are two schools of thought on how to do this. One approach is to have one person play the role on a continuing basis, therefore learning over time how to be more effective. The other approach is to rotate the role among a group, perhaps based on the topic in question, so that no one person becomes tarred as a naysayer. We lean toward rotating, to deter those dreaded antibodies as long as possible.

Even better is if a company can build an organization or culture that includes devil's advocacy, as Watson did at IBM. At the heart of this trait is the license to speak truth to power, where anyone in the organization can voice his or her deepest concerns to those higher in the organization. Doing so requires deep commitment and a deft touch, as the rank and file quickly discerns sincerity from platitude. Sometimes this can be done with humor, as demonstrated by our former colleague, Mel Bergstein, who we've seen cultivate candor in multiple organizations, and in teams numbering from tens of people to thousands of people. Bergstein, who, among other things, founded Diamond, used to have a regular rumor contest. At "all hands" company meetings, Bergstein would invite anyone to submit rumors, which he would then address. He would pay cash prizes for the best ones. With playful prodding, and a consistent record of candidly addressing any question, Bergstein cultivated cultures where all thoughtful questions were fair game. Another of his techniques was an open-door policy, where anybody in the organization could walk in and raise any issue. The rumor contest and the open-door policy assured employees that they could speak truth to power. It also sent a powerful message to all layers of management that all employee questions were to be taken seriously because, as with Watson at IBM, if they weren't, they could be kicked upstairs.

The informal approach to devil's advocacy does have its limits, especially in high-stakes situations such as the major strategies we've explored in this book. If left to chance, a devil's advocate may not appear. If one is appointed, informal questioning might not be particularly comprehensive or insightful, and neither might the response. Besides, one against everybody isn't a fair fight. Even when vested with resources, responsibility, and authority, that person will be up against the rest of the organization, itself armed with ample resources, enthusiasm, and, sometimes, hopeless optimism. Everyone now knows who has to be beaten to win their argument, and whom to blame if they lose. In addition, informal devil's advocates inevitably pick their shots, in terms of when to raise questions and whom to challenge. They self-censor because they know they act at their own risk. And, because the big failures we studied typically had champions at the highest levels, the risky moves where devil's advocates are the most needed are the very places that most self-appointed devil's advocates will least likely go.

Informal devil's advocacy can also be used to avoid the need for real challenge. In the heat of one major acquisition, for example, we saw one CEO convene his senior management to address persistent pockets of dissent. He promised to hear all concerns and to put the matter up for a vote. But he had one condition—once the vote was taken, all of the participants had to publicly support the outcome, and if they failed to do so they had to offer their resignation. He then proceeded to hear objections without much comment. At the end, he strongly reaffirmed his support for the acquisition. He then took an open vote, which, not surprisingly, supported his position. Few of the concerns were addressed, but the opposition was effectively squashed. (The combination was eventually dismantled, after much distraction and cost, with most of the acquisition resold for less than 10 percent of the purchase price.)

David Pottruck, the former CEO of Charles Schwab, says he wishes he'd had the foresight to look for a devil's advocate when the Internet bubble burst and Schwab's stock-trading volumes plummeted. Pottruck, who had a long and successful career at Schwab, became an absolute star when he reacted quickly to the Internet and repositioned Schwab for low-fee trading, in ways that traditional brokers did not—for a stretch, Schwab's market capitalization far exceeded that of Merrill Lynch. But, Pottruck says, when trading volumes plunged, he couldn't take an objective look at his strategy. He had become part of what he calls "the orthodoxy." He cut costs in ways that were too limited and too slow. Finally, the board took the objective look that Pottruck hadn't—and showed him the door. Pottruck says he has since recommended devil's advocacy to many other CEOs.[4]

2. Smooth out management ruts

We've had the occasion to sit in on many management meetings. While each one is different, some dynamics are common. The leader tends to sit in the same chair each time, and the others tend to stay in the same position relative to that leader. Agendas tend to follow the same format each time and are usually carefully orchestrated. Discussions follow familiar protocols, whether focused on operational or strategic issues, with most participants paying careful attention to the boundaries set by the leader. These process ruts perpetuate mental ruts.

When critical issues arise, familiar roles and protocols need to be cast aside to ensure all perspectives can emerge. Otherwise, groups that have been together for a while tend to fall into these traps, as Janis describes in *Groupthink:*

- Incomplete survey of alternatives
- Incomplete survey of objectives
- Failure to examine risks of preferred choice
- Failure to reappraise initially rejected alternatives
- Poor information search
- Selective bias in processing information at hand
- Failure to work out contingency plans

One of the first things that Lou Gerstner did when he became CEO of IBM in 1993 was to make a small change that did a lot to get the company out of its mental ruts: He banned "foils," or overhead transparencies. As IBM had atrophied over the years, becoming a caricature of the organization that Watson had designed, the company had developed an extraordinary reliance on foils. One CEO, in the 1970s, even had an overhead projector built into his mahogany desk. People preparing for big meetings would produce a dozen or so main foils, then do ten backups for each of the foils and ten backups for each backup. When Gerstner banned foils, executives at first thought he was kidding. It didn't seem possible to think at IBM without foils. When Gerstner persisted, however, he got a different, less scripted, more probing type of interaction with his executive team.[5]

À la Gerstner, it can be valuable to keep the spreadsheets out of a meeting. We've seen more than one management team hold meetings where each participant has the relevant spreadsheets opened on his own computer in front of him. (One CEO playfully convened such meetings by saying, "Gentlemen, start your spreadsheets.") This causes the tendency to anchor the conversation to what is on the computer, including the assumptions built into the model. Participants focus on the budgetary consequences of various decisions, especially in terms of how it affects them or their fiefdoms, rather than discussing the assumptions or opening the conversation to more possibilities.

Other kinds of technology can also inhibit group processes, but a flip of a switch can sometimes dispel the distractions. Observing a group of senior managers listen to presentations preceding one he was about to make, Chunka noticed that most presentations were greeted with silence, with no more than a few perfunctory questions. The fifty or so line managers occasionally glanced up when a new slide was shown but were generally disengaged and not really making much eye contact with presenters. Chunka realized that this behavior was not rudeness; it was normal protocol. Welcome to the multitasking world. The managers were all armed to the teeth with numerous communication devices. Group protocol kept mobile phones in vibrate mode, but each person in the room was actively communicating with many others via e-mail, instant messaging, BlackBerries, and the like. Back-channel conversations between the participants via computer were also happening at a furious pace. But, measured in terms of open dialogue, the group process was broken. As he set up for his own presentation in the day-long session addressing the future of that organization,

Chunka saw that the wireless network for the room was plugged into the same power strip as that provided for his computer. With the seniormost client's approval and the on-site technical support person warned (though he turned ashen), Chunka flipped off the power strip a few minutes into his presentation. He kept a straight face as the various participants checked their cords, glanced at others' screens, and cast deadly stares at the tech support person. Yet, as hoped, they slowly drifted out of their multitasking fog and started engaging in the conversation. Eventually, one of the most spirited conversations on the future of the organization that anyone could remember ensued.

Our favorite example—the contrast between the Bay of Pigs and the Cuban missile crisis—also suggests ways to change the dynamics of a group and possibly improve communication profoundly. After the Bay of Pigs, President Kennedy occasionally didn't attend meetings where a range of alternatives was being discussed for the first time. Bobby Kennedy commented, "I felt there was less true give and take with the president in the room. There was the danger that, by indicating his own view and leanings, he would cause others to fall in line." In another move to break things up, President Kennedy would occasionally devote whole sessions to frank, freewheeling discussions. No agenda was imposed. The usual rules of protocol were suspended.

To broaden the information available, outside experts were regularly invited to give their views and actively drawn into meeting discussions. President Kennedy also periodically augmented his team with new advisers to ensure fresh perspectives and take advantage of particularly relevant experience.

Finally, as a special device to facilitate critical thinking, Kennedy would sometimes break his executive committee into two subgroups. Each would work independently on a policy decision and reconvene for debate and cross-examination.

Kennedy also changed the rules of engagement. In addition to naming Bobby as his devil's advocate, Kennedy decided that everyone in the room should feel free to voice any concern, even if it wasn't in their particular area of expertise. This is important, because the tendency to defer to the expert is often the excuse people use for censoring themselves about obvious flaws in a strategy. At Iridium, there were plenty of people who realized the satellite phones would perform poorly in cities, where the core market of business travelers would need to use them, but it was hard for a nontechnologist to voice those concerns in a meeting of technologists—unless the leader specifically invited questions from nonexperts.

3. First, decide how to decide

We've seen this pattern play out many times: The CEO or some other senior executive perceives a strategic problem that the rest of the organization does not yet acknowledge. In one case, it's an eroding customer perception of value. In another case, it's the long-term consequences of not forcefully responding to an emerging competitor. A third case is an overresponse to short-term problems, where investors push for cuts that threaten the company's long-term viability. The CEO has a strong sense of the looming problem but knows that he has to sell his board of directors, other senior managers, and, ultimately, the rest of the organization. He works feverishly to rally the organization, expending tremendous amounts of time and political capital. At the same time that he's convincing everyone of the importance of the problem, he also has to demonstrate that he has a solution, so he commissions trusted lieutenants to develop a plan of attack. He bundles the problem definition and solution and sells them together. In almost every case, the CEO manages to motivate his organization and pursue his strategy. Strategic success, however, is spotty.

That's because the process of developing the right strategy gets tangled up with mobilizing the organization to face the problem. The desire to create consensus to act is confused with the need to immediately adopt a course of action to take. Scenarios are subtly shaped, and estimates are massaged, to make the proposed strategy attractive. Alternatives are explored in cursory fashion, often only so far as needed to discredit them, because any ambiguity about the right course of action is viewed as a distraction. All this weakens the exploration and design of the ultimate course of action.

One way to forestall this danger is to decide how you're going to decide before there is something to decide. Agree ahead of time to lay out problems in detail before starting to form responses. Then agree on the decision criteria for new strategic moves before those strategies are needed. By making it clear that the two steps must be treated separately, you allow the question of "what to do" to be deferred until the question of "what is the problem?" is addressed.

This process safeguard helps to avoid the tendency toward confirmation bias, which shapes decision-making processes to support some desired outcome. It also opens the space for comprehensive questioning of proposed strategies, forestalling the rush to act under flimsy strategic rationales such as Avon's justification of its move into health care because it fit into the company's "culture of caring."

There are many methods for considering opportunities, once problems are diagnosed. Two we like come from Andrew Campbell and Robert Park and from our colleague George Day.

In their book *Growth Gamble*, Campbell and Park offer questions on four criteria by which they judge business diversification strategies:

- Differentiation: Does the strategy offer enough potential differentiation to warrant the cost and risk of entering the new market, where "enough" is at least 30 percent better profit margins than the competition?
- Profit pool: Rather than looking at the size of a market in terms of revenue, look at the total profit pool for the new market. Is there sufficient profit to be won, or does competition or commoditization destroy profitability for all participants?
- Leadership: Are the leaders of your potential new business and the sponsors within your existing business superior to, similar to, or weaker than competitors?
- Impact on existing business: Will the new business have a significantly positive, uncertain, or significantly negative effect on the existing business?

The consultants call these tests "traffic lights," where a strong response is a green light, a marginal response is a yellow light, and a negative response is a red light. Campbell and Park argue that one green light is enough to make an opportunity worth considering, while one red light should be enough to stop the effort.

Day offers another comprehensive screen in a *Harvard Business Review* article titled "Is It Real? Can We Win? Is It Worth Doing?: Managing Risk and Reward in an Innovation Portfolio." The screen guides evaluators to dig deeply for the answers to six fundamental questions: Is the market real? Is the product real? Can the product be competitive? Can our company be competitive? Will the product be profitable at an acceptable risk? Does launching the product make strategic sense?

The development team answers these queries by exploring an even deeper set of supporting questions. A definite no to any of the first five fundamental questions typically leads to termination of the project, for obvious reasons. Only when a project has passed all other tests in the screen should the company consider the sixth question: Does launching the product make strategic sense?

The prior adoption of these or other decision criteria is no guarantee of strategic success, because all the irrational tendencies and organizational encumbrances that we've discussed might influence objective application. Yet, our experience is that having clear criteria establishes the grounds for deliberation and helps to deflate sweeping generalizations like synergy, consolidation, adjacency, and the rest that too often suffice as strategic justification for flawed strategies.

Another way to enhance discipline is to link decisions to future reviews and compensation. Clear Channel, for example, requires line managers to commit to the cash flows that their sponsored acquisitions are forecast to deliver. This is done by explicitly linking compensation to meeting their division's cash flow projections, including results from acquisitions. The compensation for the acquisition teams is also tied to the actual contribution of their acquisitions to overall company performance. Annual reviews are conducted of all acquisitions over the previous three years to assess their performance against forecasts, and to review the compensation of those involved in the deals. As Randall Mays, the Clear Channel CFO, puts it, the deals that the line managers and acquisition teams make "are tied to them forever."

4. Find history that fits

As we've said, we understand that looking at history can be dangerous. Think about "Been there, done that." Those four words are among the most frustrating responses that CEOs can hear to their strategic initiatives. The phrase conveys apathy and disdain and implies that a proposal doesn't even merit consideration, much less support. One client that we've worked with, for example, experienced a very high-profile failure because of an ill-conceived joint venture. For almost a decade afterward, most managers immediately dismissed any potential partnership or joint venture, before any discussion of merits.

Despite the dangers, we think history is underutilized. Strategies would be better served with a richer use of history, both internal history and lessons to be learned from others, as long as proper safeguards ensure that the history fits and is fully considered.

There are two key elements to using history. The first is to use history to illuminate the context in which a decision is being made. In other words, to forestall the tendency to launch into action too quickly, use history to get a better understanding of "How did we get here?" before plunging into "What are we going to do?" Too often, historical data points are lined up to support a decision about what should be done, rather than being considered, in all their messy complexity, before a decision is made.

Our friend Alan Kay likes to say, "Context is worth 80 IQ points." That concept has certainly worked for Kay, who is often described as the father of the personal computer and who has generated some fascinating innovations through his work at Xerox, Apple, Disney, and elsewhere. At a lunch the three of us once had with Peter Drucker, Kay told Drucker that Drucker's context had had "quite an influence" on the invention of the personal computer. Drucker had never heard that one before, so he expressed surprise. Kay said he had read Drucker's early work on the knowledge worker and, believing it wholeheartedly, used the concept to help guide his decisions on developing electronic tools, such as the personal computer.

In *Thinking in Time*, Harvard professors Richard Neustadt and Ernest May lay out a way for executives to use history to understand better the context for their strategic decisions. Neustadt and May talk about the importance of "issue history" in public-policy decisions, but we've found that it's just as important in corporate strategy.

Rather than relying on situational analysis, which typically takes a snapshot in time, issue history calls for following the present back in time, understanding trends, events, and, especially, key changes relevant to the present situation. Issue history calls for tracking the relevant history of key people and organizations, to better understand their motivations and potential issues. The goal is to develop as rich a story as possible, rather than to rely on sketchy outlines drawn to suit particular viewpoints.

For example, Neustadt and May tell the story about how a Soviet military brigade was discovered in Cuba in the late 1970s around the time of the U.S. Senate's debate about whether to ratify the SALT II arms reduction treaty. The treaty's opponents seized upon the existence of the brigade as an illustration of the Soviet threat. President Jimmy Carter, a treaty supporter, was caught off guard and promised to respond strongly to the Soviet escalation. Further research showed that the Soviet brigade had actually been stationed in Cuba since the early 1960s and that prior administrations had known about it. By the time this was remembered and the crisis had dissipated, the treaty was dead. Had the Carter administration understood the issue history, the presence of the brigade would have been a nonevent.

Undertaking an exploration of issue history would have been valuable in a number of the failures that we explored. Unum, for example, had exited the very line of business that Provident brought to them in their failed merger. What were the issues in that prior experience? What were the lessons to be drawn about the ability to cross-sell between individual and group disability customers? What attempts had been made toward overlapping products, such as those a Unum-Provident merger might enable? The Revco LBO was another failure that would have benefited from better historical context. The structure of the LBO depended on an assumption that Revco's performance just before the transaction was a temporary setback, and the buyers forecast that Revco would return to historical numbers (or better). Following the issue history for Revco, and for key competitors, would have shed better light on this assumption.

Exploring issue history is an opportunity to engage various sources of institutional knowledge within the organization, including those who might be the strongest purveyors of the "been there, done that" attitude. You can reach out to the principals involved, including retired employees or those who have moved to other organizations, but don't limit the interviews to this group. In one organization we worked with, the deepest institutional memory resided in the financial analysts and other staff who often had a bird's-eye view of executive deliberations. External perspectives are important, as well. Journalists and industry analysts have valuable insight into prior strategic moves and industry trends. Some, of course, might have axes to grind. The key is to get a broad range of input.

Note that it's crucial to focus the investigation on the historical events, rather than their application to today or to future options. Those issues must be separate. Get the history right, then figure out what it says about possible strategies.

Charting the history of an organization is especially informative for new management or potential acquirers. The concept of organizational culture or DNA is still poorly understood. We know that it exists. We know that it is important. We know that organizations seem to have certain tendencies, to be able to do certain things well and unable to do others. But there's not any strong theory that explains why, or how to manipulate the organization beyond its tendencies. So it's all the more important to understand where the organization has been; that speaks volumes about where the organization will—and *won't*—go. Warren Buffett talks of the "institutional imperative" and says "rationality frequently wilts when the institutional imperative comes into play. . . . As if governed by Newton's First Law of Motion, an institution will resist any change in its current direction."[6]

The second key element to using history effectively is to learn from previous successes *and* failures.

While many executives are willing to take risk, few want to blaze completely new paths. Thus, in our experience, whenever a strategic option is explored, the CEO inevitably asks, "Who else has done this before?" The implicit coda to this question is "and succeeded?" Yet, learning from successes is easy. Corporate strategists, management consultants, and writers of business books provide legions of examples of successes and best practices for inspiration. But, as we've said throughout this book, it's crucial to also look at failures if you want a true history, one that fits. Think of failures as lessons in "worst practices." (When Thomas Edison was asked whether it was frustrating to have failed so many times in trying to make an incandescent bulb work, he famously responded with the defiant: "I have learned a thousand ways not to make a lightbulb."[7] Contrast his approach with Joseph Wilson Swan, who chose not to learn from his mistakes. Swan, who developed the theory for making a lightbulb, tried three times to make one, then gave up.)[8]

One straightforward way to ensure deeper learning is to require both examples and counterexamples. When asking about who else has done something before, explicitly add, "and tell me about both successes and failures."

The key to using historical analogies, whether about successes or failures, is to ask about both the similarities and the differences. Understanding similarities and differences helps to distinguish valuable from misleading analogies. It also defines issues or concerns that might not be well understood in the current situation, or risks and secondary effects not adequately explored in future options. In our experience, many executives are diligent about looking at the similarities in analogies but don't focus nearly enough on the differences.

5. Bet on it

In *Bay of Pigs: The Untold Story*, Peter Wyden reveals that when asked by President Kennedy to assess the CIA invasion plan, the U.S. Joint Chiefs of Staff responded that it had a "fair chance" of success. Kennedy took that as a positive assessment. Instead, they meant that they judged the chances of success as "three to one against." But this was never clarified at the time.

Unfortunately, Kennedy's misinterpretation of the Joint Chiefs' assessment is not uncommon. For whatever reason, they gave a qualitative answer. Perhaps "fair chance" was well-understood terminology at the Pentagon. Kennedy certainly didn't get its intended meaning.

A straightforward method to dispel such confusion comes from our friend Gordon Bell. Gordon is a pioneer in the computer industry, having developed the first minicomputer at Digital Equipment and having managed that company's four thousand engineers. After leaving Digital, Gordon headed computer science research at the National Science Foundation, where he was instrumental in the commercialization of the Internet. After that, he became an active "angel" investor in start-ups.

Gordon has a wonderful bluntness about him. At Digital, he was known for saying things such as, "The most reliable parts of a computer are the ones you leave out." As an investor, he used that bluntness and found one remarkably simple way to see at least whether technology and management forecasters had the courage of their convictions. For example, when someone made a presentation laying out predictions for company performance, Gordon would zero in on one number and ask the CEO, "Wanna bet? A side bet, you and me, for $1,000. I'm saying you won't reach that number." If the CEO gulped, Gordon knew that in his heart he had doubts. At least once, when an underperforming CEO didn't take the bet, Gordon decided that was the last straw and had him fired.

Even though executives clearly take the issues seriously when they are making corporate commitments of billions of dollars, there's something about betting your own money that makes you think twice.

More generally, framing forecasts as personal bets forces those involved to be very clear. Also, the use of odds in bets forces everyone to be precise about probabilities. Had John Kennedy, for example, forced the Joint Chiefs to quantify their estimate, he would have realized that their "fair chance of success" estimate really translated to a "one-in-four" chance.

Structuring bets clarifies time estimates, as well. For example, senior managers at a large trade group that we worked with generally held the assumption that an important revenue stream from information was going to go away as the information became available from public sources online. The assumption was so widely held that no one thought to get more specific, until we asked everyone to write down how long they thought it would be before the revenue fell below a certain level. Some thought the group was six months away from that level. Some thought six years. Getting the assumptions on the table led to a valuable discussion that produced a sharper strategy.

In addition to simple one-on-one bets, it can be useful to engage in a sort of large-scale betting known as prediction markets. As we've seen, experts can not only be wrong but be overwhelmingly forceful about their misguided idea—an expert colleague of ours once described his operating philosophy as "sometimes right, sometimes wrong, but never in doubt."

We're not suggesting that expert opinion should be ignored, but rather that a process safeguard is to have other formal mechanisms for gathering information and forecasting.

Try this experiment: Fill a big jar full of jelly beans (count them first) and turn a group of people on to the task of guessing the number of beans in the jar. If your experience is like most, the guesses will be all over the map. You'll also find that the average of all those guesses will be closer to the correct answer than most, if not all, of the individual guesses. This is the effect that James Surowiecki dubbed "the wisdom of crowds" in his book of the same name. All the various guesses have a way of canceling out the errors that each person makes, and the collective sense of the group zeros in on the right answer.

The wisdom of crowds applies not only to jelly beans, but to forecasting and estimation of all sorts. Take sales forecasts. As we've discussed, official forecasts are rife with sandbagging and fudge factors, as estimates are rolled up over multiple people and departments, and all parties involved try to game the system to their own advantage. Such gamesmanship often leads to faulty estimates, causing organizations to misallocate resources and mismanage inventory.

As an alternative, prediction markets try to harness the wisdom of crowds by opening up the forecasting problem to a larger group of participants inside and outside the organization. Many people beyond traditional forecasters also have a sense of market demand, like frontline salespeople, customer service representatives, and the customers themselves. A crowd approach tries to integrate all those various perspectives into a single forecast. Typically set up like a stock market, prediction markets have participants buy and sell shares for contracts for which the payoff depends on some future event. For example, a contract might pay $1 if a product is ready for introduction by a certain date. As people who think they have some insight into this issue buy and sell these contracts, the price will reflect the probability that the event will happen. If the price of the contract is 20¢, it means that the crowd collectively estimates that there is a 20 percent chance of its happening. Numerous applications have shown that, when structured properly, prediction markets tend to be much more accurate than traditional forecasting methods. Hewlett-Packard, for one, found that a prediction market was more accurate at predicting printer sales than HP's traditional process.

Surowiecki gives four conditions for wise crowds: diversity of opinion, meaning that each person should have some private information, even if it's just an eccentric interpretation of the known facts; independence, meaning that people's opinions are not determined by the opinions of those around them; decentralization, meaning that people are able to specialize and draw on local knowledge; and aggregation, meaning that some mechanism exists for turning private judgments into a collective decision.

Researchers at Intel, which also had success with prediction markets, named three factors that led to strong performance: anonymity and incentives, which encourage honest, unbiased information; the averaging of multiple opinions, which produces smooth, accurate signals; and feedback, which enables participants to evaluate past performance and learn how to weigh information and produce better results.[9]

Few would argue that prediction markets should replace the use of experts altogether. For one thing, there may not be enough time to assemble a market if a decision on strategy needs to be made quickly. For another, it's hard to maintain confidentiality with a market, so it isn't appropriate when thinking about some hush-hush merger prospect. Finally, there are issues where experts have specialized information that "the crowd" doesn't. It's instructive to look at the "ask the audience" lifeline available to contestants on *Who Wants to Be a Millionaire,* often cited by advocates of prediction markets. While the audience's accuracy can seem uncanny, contestants tend to call on them for help early in the game, on questions where the ordinary person has a chance of knowing the answer—for example, who played Matthew Broderick's sister in *Ferris Bueller's Day Off*? If confronted with a technical question—what is the tenth digit of pi?—contestants invariably called an expert friend.

Still, prediction markets can be used in many cases as a check and balance against traditional forecasts. If prediction-market results run counter to what the experts are saying, it's important to figure out why.

6. Stare into the abyss

On December 2, 1941, Admiral Husband E. Kimmel, commander of the Pacific Fleet, was told by his chief of naval intelligence that the U.S. Navy had lost radio contact with the Japanese aircraft carriers. Kimmel jokingly replied, "Do you mean to say that they could be rounding Diamond Head and you wouldn't know it?"[10] Unfortunately, the carriers were almost doing just that. Diamond Head was on the approach to Pearl Harbor, where the Japanese fleet carried out its devastating surprise attack just a few days later.

Much as the U.S. Navy never seriously considered the possibility of a surprise attack on Pearl Harbor, companies rarely take a hard look at the chance that something truly significant could go wrong.

One process safeguard is to force the organization to collectively stare into the abyss and have a clear view of the worst-case scenario. The organization then must do all it can to assess the probability of such calamity, decide if the risk is tolerable, and make whatever adjustments to a strategy are necessary.

In our work with clients, we often use an exercise we've dubbed "Be Your Own Worst Competitor." In it, we divide managers into small groups and give them a simple charge: Imagine you know everything you already know about your company and industry. You get a call from an investor with plenty of capital who offers to fund a competitive venture to your current business. Assuming no "noncompete" restrictions, how could you destroy your current employer and other competition and dominate the industry? We then send them off to develop business plans to do just this. Each team returns to pitch its venture to the entire group, which then debates and votes on the best plan. Basically, we're asking the group to stare into the abyss and report what they see.

Freeing the participants from explicit and implicit organizational encumbrances often has a cathartic effect. Dangerous weaknesses, untapped opportunities, competitive challenges, and crisp interpretations of market trends often fall out of the discussion. That happens because few know a market as well as the leaders of businesses competing for dominance in that market. The issue is finding ways to navigate past individual tendencies and the larger group process to let people articulate what they know.

One abyss that often needs more contemplation has to do with leverage, and whether organizations appreciate the risks associated with debt used to finance strategic moves. Leverage is usually measured by snapshots such as the debt-to-equity ratio. This gives a relative sense of the debt load but doesn't give much information about how changes in a company's circumstances might limit its ability to make debt payments. Companies should compare likely cash flows against fixed debt-payment schedules and try to imagine scenarios in which they couldn't make the payments.

More generally, we think that simulation is a valuable technique for prompting deeper discussions of assumptions and risks. Using simulation methods forces the odds of key assumptions to be quantified. And they force the organization to actually do the math about the overall probability of success. From high school math class, we know that if a plan depends on three things happening, the odds of the plan working are just the multiplication of the odds of each thing. So, if each has a 70 percent chance of happening, the odds of the whole plan working are just $0.7 \times 0.7 \times 0.7$, or 0.34. In other words, just about one in three. While 70 percent sounds reasonable, one in three starts feeling dicey. But planners rarely make that kind of calculation.

Our experience is that the value of simulation doesn't come so much from the final numbers. Executives rarely accept such calculations, especially if they run counter to their intuitions or desired actions. Instead, the value comes from engaging decision makers in the model itself. Forcing the conversation about the key assumptions and how they interact is where the real value lies.

Facing stiff competition, one large telecommunications client was contemplating a major overhaul of its customer service and network provisioning functions. The proposed changes would have involved thousands of workers in multiple centers reporting to different parts of the organization. Turf wars and sincere concerns about the viability of the strategy bogged the organization down for months. In response, we helped the leaders of the various functions design a simulation model of the proposed design. Running simulations of historical demand against alternative designs allowed the leaders to understand how the new system might work, including the potential advantages, savings, and bottlenecks. The process of coming to an in-depth, shared understanding allowed issues to be identified and resolved (or at least arbitrated). And it gave the CEO enough confidence to proceed, though with significant modifications from the original design.

7. Construct alarm systems

Failed strategies sometimes fly like cannonballs. Kodak decided in 1981 that it was safe from the threat of digital technology, for a host of reasons. Digital cameras were too expensive. Printers weren't of high enough quality. It was too hard to display a digital image on a computer or TV screen. All those impediments largely disappeared during the 1980s, but Kodak had launched its strategy like a cannonball. Rather than revisit its strategy every time a core assumption changed, Kodak just let it fly.

Rather than cannonballs, strategies should be more like cruise missiles. Once strategies are launched, there should be mechanisms to gather feedback and continuously adapt the flight path to the terrain and strike the intended target.

One useful approach is to construct alarm systems around key conditions that must continue to hold for a plan to remain viable. An alarm system is a simple warning device that detects when a condition has changed and warrants attention. Applied to strategies, it might be nothing more than a list of critical success factors that are continuously monitored, to make sure that changes in the plan, key forecasts, or market conditions do not overtake previous calculations.

Companies can construct alarm systems in numerous ways, perhaps using the sorts of key screening factors we describe in this chapter, in the section on first deciding how to decide. If those screening questions are periodically reassessed, new evidence and elaborated options become a natural part of the strategy development process.

The construction of alarm systems has some important secondary benefits as well. Merely legitimizing the discussion about alarm systems opens up group conversations about key factors and the assumptions and conditions upon which they depend. Why do we believe this? On what evidence does this depend? What new evidence would change our minds? All these are natural questions when designing alarm systems but don't otherwise naturally flow into many deliberations.

8. Always have escalation mechanisms

The tendency for employees to remain silent, even in matters of criminal activity, is well documented. For example, the collapse of Barings Bank has been blamed on the fact that Singapore-based Nick Leeson hid his trading losses in a secret account. Account #88888 was not, in fact, so secret—many people, from junior staff in Singapore to managers in London, knew about it. Yet that information never reached someone who had the clear responsibility to act on it.

An important process safeguard is to have formal escalation systems in place that enable vital information and divergent viewpoints about strategic moves to reach decision makers, even when that information doesn't fit into normal communication channels or, more critically, when the regular channels might otherwise squash that information.

In *Why Smart Executives Fail*, Sydney Finkelstein cites the inability to act on vital information as a key cause of failure. Finkelstein gives a number of reasons for this failure. First, vital information is not recognized as such. Second, there are no clear communications channels for it to move from those who have it to those who can act on it. Third, even if there is a communications channel, there is no motivation for the holder to move it along or for the recipient to act on it. Fourth, there is no oversight to ensure that the process is working.

It won't always be possible to know that information is vital. But it should be possible to address the other three problems—making it possible to send information to the top, providing motivation for people to do so, and ensuring that the process is working. One method is to use anonymous surveys, such as those Microsoft routinely conducts. Rather than relying on a group leader's promise about when a product will be delivered, Microsoft surveys members of the team and asks for their predictions. The group leader knows that such surveys can happen at any time, which tends to keep him honest, and, if he's overly optimistic, senior management will probably know. (He could, of course, also be too pessimistic, but that rarely happens.) The surveys don't help Microsoft avoid product delays, but they at least give management an accurate picture, which it can then use for planning and communicate to investors. Other methods include open-door policies and rumor contests, as we described earlier.

In our research, it was common for someone in the organization to know something that meant a strategy was doomed to fail—the information just didn't get communicated to the right person at the right level. The Sarbanes-Oxley Act of 2002 already requires publicly traded companies to have confidential, anonymous reporting mechanisms for questionable accounting and for criminal activities. The U.S. False Claims Act shows that such whistle-blower mechanisms can work, especially if there are incentives. The act, which provides an incentive for reporting fraudulent charges against the federal government by giving informants a share of recovered funds, has to date been responsible for the levying of more than $6 billion in fines, with more than $1 billion of that going to informants.

The challenge, then, is to design incentives for reporting information that is short of fraud but that is relevant to impending strategic errors and other potential missteps that might well have equally devastating consequences for the organization.

9. Hold second-chance meetings

Herodotus, the Greek historian, reported that the ancient Persians tended to deliberate on important matters while they were drunk. They then reconsidered their decisions the following day when they were sober. If it happened that their first deliberation took place when they were sober, they would always reconsider the matter under the influence of wine. If a decision was approved both drunk and sober, the decision held; if not, the Persians set it aside.[11] It's hard to argue with the Persians' success. They ruled much of western and central Asia for almost three hundred years.

This story always draws a chuckle when we tell it to management audiences and tends to elicit joking proposals to adopt the practice regarding the wine. The funny thing is that many already do make decisions in a state like intoxication.

The emotion that goes along with a big takeover or some other event that accompanies a major shift in strategy often produces what Dan Ariely calls in *Predictably Irrational* a "hot" state. He vividly explains that people in hot, or emotionally aroused, states will make decisions that they would not otherwise make when in a dispassionate, or cold, emotional state. Ariely details a number of experiments where subjects in a cold state were asked to predict their sexual and moral responses to a number of scenarios. The same questions were asked while the subjects were in a state of sexual arousal. As Ariely observed, "the conclusions were consistent and clear—overwhelmingly clear, frighteningly clear." In every case, the subjects responded very differently when in hot versus cold states. The subjects' propensity toward odd sexual activities, immoral actions, and unsafe sex were not only substantially higher, but the participants in Ariely's studies were unable to predict the degree to which passion would change them.

Behavioral economists have demonstrated the dangers of hot versus cold decision making in numerous aspects of business, as well. Take the concept of competitive arousal, also known as auction fever, where participants in auctions or other competitive situations adopt a "win at any cost" posture, in which winning becomes not just about the outcome but also about beating the competition. Skilled negotiators know how to manipulate this tendency, such as when Green Tree's CEO, Lawrence Coss, convinced Conseco's Steve Hilbert that he was bidding against unnamed rivals under a tight deadline, when neither the rivals nor the deadline existed.

The Persians, in a sense, were just acknowledging reality when they mandated a wine-induced hot-state analysis of their decisions. Their real innovation was to mandate a subsequent cold-state deliberation. This "second-chance meeting" was, in essence, what Alfred P. Sloan mandated when, as we recounted earlier, he adjourned a management meeting "to give ourselves time to develop disagreement."

In *Groupthink*, Irving Janis also proposes second-chance meetings as a technique for countering unexamined assumptions. He suggests that such meetings be held just before the group commits itself to a policy. The role of everyone at the meeting should be to present any objections that have not been adequately addressed—especially challenging his or her own favorite arguments. The meeting should also explore the riskiest scenarios and most dreaded outcomes, to ensure that decisions are made with negative potential consequences fully explored.

One way to increase the odds that challenging questions will be asked is to include fresh perspectives in second-chance meetings. For example, Bridgepoint, a European private-equity firm, assembles a six-person team to establish a "walk-away" price on every acquisition. This team includes one manager explicitly assigned to be the devil's advocate and another senior director who no longer has any operational role and therefore is less susceptible to corporate politics.[12] Pitney Bowes Incorporated, the mail-management company that has acquired more than fifty companies since 2000, has an acquisition process that includes two reviews by people who were not personally involved in earlier stages of planning. Bruce Nolop, the company's chief financial officer, refers to this as "a last line of defense" to ensure that the proper analytical tools have been applied correctly and to avoid "deal fever."[13]

ELEVEN

The Last Chance Meeting

An Independent Devil's Advocate Review

"More often than not, failure in innovation is rooted in not having asked an important question, rather than having arrived at an incorrect answer," observed Clay Christensen. Unfortunately, the internal process safeguards that we proposed in chapter 10 are no guarantee that the important questions will be asked about unfounded assumptions, unattainable forecasts, untreated deal fever, or any one of the many other individual and organizational tendencies that can lead to ill-conceived strategies. In the heat of the moment, even the most experienced executives and the strongest safeguards can fail.

Steve Hilbert, the CEO of Conseco who acquired Green Tree Financial, is a testament to this hazard. Hilbert had successfully built Conseco through dozens of acquisitions. He had a rigorous acquisition process and a crack team, both honed through almost two decades of deals. Yet, in Conseco's biggest deal, Hilbert's experience failed him. His vision of taking Conseco "to the next level," to create a broader financial services company—a financial services Wal-Mart for middle America—led him to pay an exorbitant premium for a company that was clearly in trouble. He was willing to gamble more than $6 billion based on his vision and just seven days of due diligence. Given that the investor and analyst skepticism was immediate and overwhelming, he surely faced internal skepticism as well. But that skepticism was muted. It is well nigh impossible for someone inside an organization to tell the CEO that his rousing vision is flawed and that he has fallen victim to deal fever.

Better to be like Lou Gerstner, who says his success at IBM in the 1990s came not only because of what he did but what he didn't do. Gerstner says he was offered all sorts of opportunities to buy major telecommunications companies, apparently on the theory that there would be synergy between telephone systems and computers. But he subjected the synergy claims to the kind of informed skepticism that we've called for throughout this book. Among other things, he could draw on IBM's own history, its acquisition of telecommunications equipment maker Rolm in the 1980s. IBM found no synergies. Instead, it found complications, partly because of major cultural differences between the "Rolmans" and IBMers. After several frustrating years, IBM sold Rolm to Siemens at a substantial loss. So, Gerstner passed on the acquisition proposals. And it's a good thing—any kind of major acquisition in telecom would have overwhelmed all the good work he did in other areas, and his legacy would be far different than it is.

Many businesses rely on what one Fortune 50 CEO recently told us he thinks of as the genius model—you hire a genius and get out of his way. He says companies reason that if you're making a long-term bet like Hewlett-Packard did with the printer business in the 1980s, you have to trust your leader and see what happens. If you fail, you fail. That's capitalism. But, as we've seen throughout this book and as the recent financial crisis has underlined, a high percentage of failures can be foreseen and avoided. The rule of thumb is that about two-thirds of M&A deals fail, but if you eliminate half of the failures—as our research suggests is possible—you flip the odds and give yourself a two in three chance of success and make it far more likely you'll be remembered as a Lou Gerstner, not a Steve Hilbert. So, to quote something Ronald Reagan said in a very different context, we think that when it comes to leaders the right idea is to "trust, but verify."

To that end, on major strategic decisions we call for a final, quick review—a series of rigorous "last-chance" hearings by an independent devil's advocate.

Whenever an organization is embarking on a high-stakes strategy, it should subject that strategy to a final devil's advocate review by a fresh set of eyes. Ideally, as we described in chapter 10, this is a formal part of the strategy development process. It is one of our "first, decide how to decide" process safeguards; it should be well understood by all involved before the strategy itself emerges. Just the anticipation of the review will lead to better outcomes. In addition, strategy developers would benefit from the questions raised by the devil's advocate throughout the process, rather than see them as attacks on their hard-earned positions. The CEO would also get feedback and challenges along the way, before making any sort of public commitment and risking embarrassment if he later backed away from the strategy. This independent devil's advocate review would culminate in a final "last-chance" review, which should be done toward the end of the strategy-formulation process but before it's too late, before the momentum is so great that almost nothing could stop the strategy—as one executive put it, "Once the lawyers enter the room, it's too late to turn back." In the event that, for whatever reason, the devil's advocate review is not initiated during the planning process, CEOs should still commission a formal review at the end of the strategy-setting process.

We find that a devil's advocate review can build consensus among a management team and convince a board that it doesn't need to probe too deeply into a strategy; if a formal review from an independent viewpoint can't find a problem with a strategy, then it's hard for the board or executive team to object. Some CEOs have commissioned reviews even after a strategy is set to identify the problems that might surface and let everyone be better prepared if they do. We still believe the review should happen before the big bet is placed, but we won't argue with success.

Before diving into the details, it's worth noting a distinction made by one former CEO who read early drafts of this book. This ex-CEO, who retired a few years ago after a long run at the top of a business with more than $20 billion of annual revenue, noted that CEOs are loath to do anything that would cede any authority, but he said he'd accept a formal devil's advocate review as long as we maintain a key distinction: that between governance and management. He said he'd resist any attempt to take over the management of the business from him. But he accepted that, in the interests of good corporate governance, the board had every right to understand and react to his decisions.

This is what we've been saying all along: that we're not trying to take decision-making authority from the CEO or anyone at another level of the business who has earned the right to decide about a strategy. But we thought it might be worth putting the issue in a CEO's terms: The devil's advocate review is about governance, not about usurping management authority.

Now for the details: The exact design of the independent devil's advocate review will depend on the context and particulars of the strategy in question. But, based on our research and experience, the review generally should begin with three screens designed to spot potential problems. The review should then move to a meeting or series of interviews. The review should end with a report and discussions with senior management that provide closure, while laying out a map that will allow for continued monitoring of issues that are key to a strategy's success. Ideally, the three parts of the process occur over the course of several weeks or even months, but the process can be condensed into a single weekend if urgency is required, such as often happens with an M&A possibility.

We'll go through each of the three stages, then end with some general principles that should underlie the whole process.

The Three Screens

The first screen draws on the material in part 1 of this book. Based on the strategy being pursued, the reviewers would use our red flags and "tough questions" to look for problems. If a company is pursuing a synergy strategy, the reviewers would look, for instance, for signs that the synergy might exist only in the minds of the strategists and not matter to customers.

The second screen draws on the material in the Coda to part 1, which looks at the most common mistakes, regardless of strategy. The reviewers would look at a strategy to see whether the company pursuing it was, say, overestimating the benefits of scale while underestimating the complexity that comes with increased size.

In the third screen, the reviewers would find examples of similar strategies that were pursued by the company itself in the past, by others in the same industry, and by others in different industries. The reviewers would then do a deep dive into the examples to look for areas where problems occurred.

Armed with the data from these screens, the reviewers would then compile a list of questions that need to be addressed. To show how this looks in practice, we'll describe what happened at a company that was considering buying AOL's dial-up business in 2008.

The first screen turned up some reasons for potential caution about a consolidating industry. For instance, competitors might use the acquisition of AOL to make a major pitch for its customers—if you've been hanging on, thinking of switching from AOL, what better time to do so than when you're going through a change of ownership? The second screen turned up some more general concerns. In particular, the expected efficiencies from increased scale might not all show up. At the least, getting all the efficiencies would require expenditures of cash in a mature business where conserving cash is paramount. The third screen was a mixed bag. On the plus side, it found examples of situations where technologies, such as dial-up, had stayed profitable longer than conventional wisdom would have suggested—many people still use pagers, for instance, for specialized purposes. On the minus side, the screen found combinations in the telecom world where, among other problems, merging back-office systems proved to be more difficult than expected.

In the end, the potential acquirer decided to wait—and is very happy it did. It picked off many AOL customers without having to shell out big bucks to buy the whole business. Talks were later revived, based on a far lower price and a far simpler deal structure, but those, too, fell apart, and Time Warner announced it was spinning off AOL.

The Last-Chance Meeting

This meeting begins with the insights drawn from the three screens, then draws on the expertise embedded in a business to quickly bring to the surface all the assumptions that underlie a strategy and all the possible issues with them. Organizations that tell themselves, "Well, we have to do *something*" are especially likely to benefit because they've probably glossed over potential problems in the strategy-setting process.

If a strategy is important enough, it generally makes sense to bring the leaders of the business together for a day for the last-chance meeting. But, in many cases, the meeting can be delegated down a level or two. The "meeting" can also consist of a series of interviews with individuals. The crucial points are to have representation from all parts of a business, so marketing can't drive an idea that manufacturing can't stomach, or vice versa, and to make sure interactions are blunt.

One technique that we've found effective for this purpose is the Strategic Assumptions Surfacing and Testing (SAST) process designed by Ian Mitroff, Richard Mason, and Jim Emshoff (and taught to us by Vince Barabba). SAST is typically used at the beginning of a strategy-development process. We've adapted it for our devil's advocate review, which happens nearer to the end of the planning process.

In our version, we organize divergent groups to examine and debate the assumptions that underlie the proposed strategy. Each group is chosen so there is commonality within the group but so members represent divergent experiences and perspectives relative to the other groups. There might be three groups, for example. One group could consist of key developers of the proposed strategy. Another group could be the review panel, which would represent an informed but objective group. A third group might be a group of high-performing middle managers, drawn from diverse parts of the organization.

Each group works independently through a facilitated process to identify key assumptions of the strategy. What must hold for it to succeed? Do we know enough to know whether these assumptions will actually hold if we proceed with the strategy? The result is a prioritized list of several kinds of assumptions: assumptions that are, in fact, strategic premises, and we are certain are true; assumptions that are strategic premises, but we are uncertain whether they are true, and thus require monitoring and research; other assumptions that might be explored if time and resources allow; and irrelevant assumptions.

Next, the groups come together to compare notes and debate differences. They do so based on role-playing. While this may sound hokey, groups find role-playing liberating because individuals can say whatever they want without fear that they're making a career-ending move. We've found it especially effective to get the leaders of a group to argue against what others assume their position to be.

From this debate comes a prioritized list of the most critical issues and a collective sense of which ones are well-understood, and which ones need more exploration. We call these issues the pivot points of the strategy. They might involve key forecasts, risk assessments, possible scenarios, assessments of customer behavior, probabilities, etc. In some cases, work will be needed to verify them. In other cases, it might be easier to try to disprove a key pivot point. In either case, some of the techniques that we described earlier might be deployed. Prediction markets could be set up to test key forecasts. Management bets could be used to crystallize odds and time predictions.

Another technique for making critical assumptions explicit is the reverse income statement, introduced by Rita Gunther McGrath and Ian MacMillan. The reverse income statement is part of McGrath and MacMillan's Discovery Driven Planning, a systematic method for planning that all companies should consider. In the context of the independent devil's advocate review, we use the reverse income statement to organize and verify the basic economics of the proposed strategy.

Ordinarily, a group determining a strategy starts with some knowledge and some assumptions about the world, then sees if it can construct a plan that would surpass some minimally acceptable level of profitability. The McGrath-MacMillan approach does the reverse. It starts with an income statement that states what the minimally acceptable profit is, what revenue would need to be and what major components of allowable cost are. The approach then asks what assumptions must be true for the numbers to hold true. This approach can focus attention on the right issue: the assumptions that go into a strategy. Without this sort of approach, there can be too much attention on the numbers in a proposed business plan—but anybody can massage a business plan to make the numbers look good enough to pass a standard corporate screen; the question is whether the numbers are believable.

Once the main assumptions behind a strategy are on the table, the last-chance review looks at the question: How might the future confound our plans? No battle plan survives first contact with the enemy. So a discussion needs to occur about two aspects of the future. The first aspect is tactical. What new evidence might change important current assumptions? And, as a result, what trip wires should be designed around issues that might drift over time, both to monitor changes and to facilitate adaptation? The second aspect is more hypothetical. Can the review panel envision future scenarios that would thwart the proposed strategy? The reviewers probe a number of potential scenarios: What if a key supplier goes out of business? What if a major customer goes away? And so on, to see whether some event might favor one strategy over another.

Another key element to explore is strategic fit. Is the proposed strategy within the operational reach of the organization? Because strategy is not organizationally neutral, the review team should explore the unvarnished truth about the fitness of the organization to implement the proposed strategy. What are the key strengths upon which this strategy will build, and what are the barriers that need to be removed to implement this strategy?

To see how this might look, consider our recent experience with a large organization in the health-care world. The organization had a strategy that made a great deal of sense in the abstract. But once we facilitated a session that had executives push on the strategy for a day, they realized that they were undertaking a software project far larger than they'd ever attempted. In fact, their history with smaller software projects was awful, so they had every reason to believe they'd fail with the large one. The organization outsourced the software work, greatly reducing its risk.

Closure

More than once we've seen leaders exercise the equivalent of a "pocket veto" of a review team's findings by thanking the team for its findings and disassembling the panel without formally addressing the findings. At some point, of course, management needs to make the final call and, as we've discussed, choose from the finite alternatives in front of it. That said, the work of the review team should not end with the delivery of a report. At the very least, some type of formal response to the team should be built into the process. Ideally, the review team should work with management and the board of directors until a final decision is made on the strategy.

After all, it does no good to know a strategy is bad and not be able to head it off. Covisint learned this the hard way. In the late 1990s and early 2000s, our friends at Diamond were doing some work at Covisint, which was expected to become the electronic exchange to end all exchanges. GM, Ford, and Chrysler, along with Nissan and Renault, had hoped to funnel tens of billions of dollars of component and supply business to Covisint. Covisint would post the companies' needs electronically, so suppliers could bid on the work. The car companies hoped the increased competition would drive down the prices they paid. In addition, the companies hoped that Covisint, which they owned jointly, would be able to collect fees for acting as the middleman. When some of our then-partners at Diamond conducted a version of a devil's advocate review, however, they found all sorts of problems. For instance, governance was lacking, so the jockeying for position among the car companies made even routine decisions slow and painful; often, those decisions were formally revisited several times. This fact raised all sorts of questions about whether Covisint could work as efficiently as the strategy called for. In addition, there was no historical precedent for the sorts of fees Covisint hoped to collect, so revenue projections were dubious. When Covisint took no action on the problems, Diamond resigned. The problems never did get fixed. Covisint did get launched and now offers some reasonable capabilities, but, when it was sold in two pieces in 2004, it was generating just $60 million in annual revenue—a tiny fraction of what some had projected. Covisint wasn't yet profitable.

Principles

The closest analogies to what we're prescribing are probably formal due diligence efforts conducted in the course of acquisitions and joint ventures. In particular, our reviews conceptually overlap with "strategic due diligence," the stage that probes the logic of the transaction to ensure that it is aligned with the strategy of the acquirer.

Strategic due diligence is very important but often gets short-changed. This happens, in part, because once the due diligence stage is reached, the corporate strategy motivating the transaction is pretty much assumed, and not an open topic of discussion. The due diligence team is assembled to assess the quality of the target and to assign the right price to it, not to assess the motivating strategy or the target's fit with that strategy. Even if the motivating strategy were subject to inspection, due diligence teams are usually not equipped to address it. Due diligence requires extensive investigation into every aspect of the target, including legal, financial, accounting, tax, operational, human resources, technology, and organizational issues, just to name a few. Team members are chosen for their expertise and doggedness at ferreting out the details and skeletons in one or a few of those areas. They rarely have the context, skills, or time to relate the findings back to the original strategy. As a result, flawed strategies, and even the lack of a strategy, are usually not flagged in the due diligence process. For example, a study by Bain of 250 senior executives involved in major acquisitions found that more than 40 percent had no clear strategy of how the acquisition would boost profits and market value. Of those who claimed that they did, half admitted that they discovered that their approach was wrong.

If the strategic due diligence does go well, all the better. It will ease the devil's advocate's efforts. But, in general, the review that we will describe is designed to highlight the issues that should have otherwise been raised in the strategic due diligence.

To make sure all the issues are hit, it's important to follow four principles:

1. Establish a clear and limited charter

The license and charter of the devil's advocate review should be open and widely communicated. This allows the individuals or panel to conduct its review effectively, especially as it pursues sensitive information and explores uncomfortable questions. The charter also establishes a transparent social contract about the scope, conduct, and ultimate use of the findings. This keeps the review panel from ranging too far, addresses potential concerns about ulterior motives, and lessens the chances that uncomfortable findings will be buried.

The scope of the review should be clearly limited to the strategy being reviewed. Depending on the strategy itself, this might well open up a wide range of questions relevant to the context and history around the strategy. But the review team should resist straying further than it needs to in order to do the review. This constraint is intended to ease organizational concerns that the panel is some sort of parallel management team or that it was set up to evaluate people rather than the strategy. Ranging into these domains would undermine the effectiveness of the panel in carrying out its core function.

The conduct of the review should be restrained. The charter to "argue the no side" is not a charter for indulgence. The devil's advocate is not an inquisition. Instead, explorations should be based on facts, not feelings, intuition, or emotion. The review should focus on pivotal aspects of the strategy on which success or failure will ultimately depend, not on minor defects. It is important that all understand the purpose of the review is to uncover important questions about the strategy, not to suggest alternative approaches. This is so that those who formulated the strategy won't feel any more challenged than they already do and so that the panel will not enter the review with its own agenda. Panelists must separate themselves from their own preconceptions of the "right" answer.

Panelists also need to stay in the real world, which is one of alternatives. Panelists can't merely compare strategies against some model of perfection, because they'd dismiss all strategies as not measuring up. The review panel needs to focus on whether a strategy is the best one possible, even if it has warts and a boil or two, not whether the strategy is perfect. The panel also needs to remember that, as we've shown, doing nothing can be a bad strategy, too.

2. Organize for success

In general, the credibility and effectiveness of the devil's advocate review hinges on the credibility and position of the review's leader. Our experience is that this leader should be outside the management hierarchy directly affected by the proposed strategy. A corporate executive or executive from a different business unit might lead a business-unit-level devil's advocate review. An independent board member or some other seasoned outsider familiar with the organization, such as a retired executive, might lead a corporate-level devil's advocate review. Ideally, the review leader should not have been involved in the strategy development and, without doubt, should have no strong conflict of interest in the outcome of the review. The review leader should also not be the chairman, chief executive officer, or the lead outside director. Those leaders must grant license to the devil's advocate review and orchestrate the proper use of its findings. Therefore, they should not be conducting the review themselves.

Beyond the leader, there are two other important components of the review team: staff support and the other reviewers. The staff team will help gather information, organize the review process, and explore issues raised by the panel. The staff team should be experienced in the range of issues surrounding the proposed strategy, including business, operational, financial, organizational, technology, and human resources issues. The team mirrors in some ways the skills that would be found on a due diligence support team, though the level of resources should be much less as the review staff team should be able to leverage prior work. (Our experience is that one warning sign that a strategy may fail is when the devil's advocate staff team needs to do significant primary analysis—in other words, that the normal process hasn't already done the work.) It is actually a plus if the staff team members were involved in the planning and analysis of the strategy. They should not, however, have had leadership roles. They also need to understand and accept the important change in point of view that the review team members must adopt. Given these provisos, devil's advocate reviews are wonderful learning opportunities for young managers and analysts.

The rest of the review panel is probably the most difficult organizational task and is a key determinant to success or failure. One important aspect to keep in mind is that the review should provide a different point of view, not merely replicate existing expertise. The strategy development process probably already engaged a range of operational and strategic experts. The review team is not intended to be smarter versions of those experts. Instead, the team should collectively offer a divergent perspective, assembled to surface and test critical issues associated with the proposed strategy. But it would be a mistake to see the devil's advocate panel as merely a panel of experts. Our experience is that expertise is necessary but far from sufficient. More important is the ability of the participants to step back, listen, ask questions, be contemplative, and take a broad, systems-oriented approach.

To give you a flavor of the kind of person we think should be on a review panel, we'll mention two of our favorites. One is Vince Barabba.

Vince has held senior strategy and market research positions at General Motors, Kodak, and Xerox. He was twice director of the U.S. census. He has written a number of books based on his experience. Thus, Vince always brings deep, practical experience in market research and strategic development. But Vince is not just an advocate for ideas and positions shaped by his immense experience. He has a natural tendency to search for the connected parts of any business problem and to ask questions that tease out the systems-level assumptions, issues, and consequences of any design. David Reed is another person we often call to participate in reviews. David was the chief scientist at Lotus Development Corp. and at various times a professor in computer science at MIT and the famed MIT Media Lab. He has conducted advanced research at various world-class laboratories including Interval Research and HP Labs and is credited as one of the original architects of the Internet. David clearly brings immense technological expertise, a key underpinning to many strategies. (Mike Hammer, the late consultant and author, taught a legendarily difficult graduate class in computer science and said he was stunned to find a freshman in his class. The next semester, he had that freshman teach the class. As you've guessed, that freshman was David.) David also brings a propensity for looking at the broad consequences of designs, in particular how otherwise attractive solutions might or might not work at scale.

By contrast, we've found that panelists with deep subject matter expertise fail miserably if they tend to come to quick conclusions and spend the rest of the review looking for confirming data and advocating their viewpoints to other panelists. Readers might recognize that this profile, unfortunately, fits most experts. Actually, the more expert they are, the greater the tendency to fit the profile.

In general, all members of the devil's advocate team must understand and accept the charter of the review.

3. Focus on the strategy, not the process

Too often, quality-assurance reviews focus on process rather than content. Reviewers check that all required steps were taken, that proper analyses were conducted, and that all the right forms and documents were constructed. If all items on the checklist are crossed off, the reasoning goes, then the strategy is ready to go. While checklists are valuable, we don't think that you need to convene an independent devil's advocate review just to verify that appropriate steps were taken to develop the strategy. Nor would that be enough. At the end of the day, the strategy will stand on its own or not. The review should focus on the strategy itself.

One process point: As the review team immerses itself in the strategy, it should decline any opportunity to have a senior executive present the plan, because that executive can sway the reviewers through force of personality. Instead, reviewers should start by asking for a detailed written description of the strategy. And we don't mean slides and spreadsheets, at least as the principle documentation; they allow too much hand waving and leave much to reader interpretation. As Bruce Nolop, Pitney Bowes' CFO, observed, "I've been amazed at how many elements of a deal that seemed clear in PowerPoint can fall apart when they're subjected to prose. In bullet-point format, the rationale for a deal might be summed up in a phrase, such as 'cross-selling.' But a memorandum demands clarity about exactly who is cross-selling to whom—and how and why."

4. Deliver questions, not answers

Perhaps the hardest aspect of the devil's advocate review for many to accept is that the goal is to deliver questions, not answers. Many corporate cultures espouse the attitude that one should not point to problems without also having answers. In general, planning processes try to produce the best answers. The devil's advocate review will focus on generating the most illuminating questions. This helps to ensure that members of the review team do not push their own agenda or preconceived answers but, instead, focus on examining the strategy as presented. In this vein, the review team might well leave the patient chopped up on the table, if that is warranted. It shouldn't try to sew it back up or even make it presentable. While this might sound harsh, it is important to head off any attempt to replicate the strategy process to provide "better" answers. That's just not possible in the short window of the review. At the same time, good questions should lead to better answers.

When everything goes right, a devil's advocate review looks something like what happened at an insurance company, which had a large consulting firm help it formulate a strategy that would have a division double revenue to almost $6 billion in five years, beginning in 2006. Our friends at Diamond reviewed the strategy and found numerous assumptions that were, at best, dubious. For instance, the strategy required that the division win 50 percent of all new business that came to market over the five years, even though the company's best-performing products had never managed that high a share. In fact, a historical analysis of the competition revealed that no offering from any company had ever achieved the growth targets that the strategy required in the unit's target markets.

The CEO of the insurance company wasn't interested in having his assumptions challenged. He was ready to move on the strategy. But senior executives at the division supported the review because they didn't want to sign off on growth targets that couldn't be achieved. They eventually won a hearing with the CEO, who scaled back his expectations for the strategy. Rather than assume 17 percent growth annually, the company settled for a stretch goal of 13 percent. The CEO set up a "White Space" project to look for new ideas that would provide the additional $1 billion of annual revenue by 2010 that he was acknowledging would not come from the original strategy.

As it happens, one major piece of the division's revenue grew 12.5 percent in 2006 and 5.5 percent in 2007. The other major piece saw revenue rise 5.6 percent over the two years. If the original strategy had been implemented unquestioned, the division would have overinvested in search of growth and would have crushed earnings. Because targets were scaled back to more realistic levels, earnings rose along with revenue: Net income increased 12 percent in 2006 and 5.7 percent in 2007. That steady performance left the company far better prepared for the onslaught of the financial crisis that hit in 2008.

Even though the CEO didn't initially like the idea of a review, his willingness to listen made him come out looking like a hero, and everyone else involved was happy, too.

A devil's advocate review costs so little and takes so little time, while potentially delivering such major benefits, that it's hard to see why you wouldn't be happy, as well, if you make them a regular practice.

Epilogue

Two Revolutions

Robert A. Lovett, President Harry S. Truman's defense secretary during much of the Korean War, observed, "Good judgment is usually the result of experience. And experience is frequently the result of bad judgment."[1]

Throughout this book, we've strived to help shorten the normal managerial learning cycle by reporting on the bad judgment of otherwise talented executives at good, and sometimes great, companies. Our hope is that awareness of common mistakes can help managers avoid them, without having to live them firsthand.

Unfortunately, telling someone to be more aware of a potential problem is not much of a remedy. Thus we also offer methods for changing how organizations assess big strategic moves, primarily by instituting safeguards against process failures that make even the best organizations susceptible to bad strategies.

In doing so, we try to be both pragmatic and revolutionary.

We try to be pragmatic by suggesting techniques that don't depend on fundamental rewiring of how individuals think or how organizations make strategy. That's not to say that some fundamental rewiring might not be appropriate in some cases, but we don't depend on it because, quite frankly, it probably won't happen. Our suggestions are, instead, designed to be overlaid on current processes.

At the same time, we hope our pragmatic techniques will spark several revolutionary changes. First, we hope to revolutionize the decision-making process at the very top. Rather than driving for consensus, we hope to provoke chief executives, senior managers, and board members to expect, accept, and even demand frank discussion and robust analysis whenever "bet the company" moves are on the table. To help this happen, and to safeguard the organization when it doesn't, we believe an independent devil's advocate review of such strategic moves should always be conducted before adoption. We think that such a review can be a powerful tool for clearheaded assessment, and that its mere presence in the planning process will serve to make the prior planning sharper.

We also hope to foment and legitimize a revolution in middle management. We're willing to bet that in every failure that we studied, there were critical thinkers in the heart of the organization who saw the dangers of the proposed strategy. We hope to legitimize their voices to question and, when appropriate, to quash doomed strategies while they are still on the drawing board.

Acknowledgments

We take the approach that nobody is as smart as everybody, and, fortunately, we have a lot of smart friends and colleagues. We imposed shamelessly on them all in the service of this book, and they responded like champs. This book wouldn't be nearly as good without their ideas and support. We thank and acknowledge them.

The place to start is with our former partners at Diamond Management & Technology Consultants—in particular, Adam Gutstein, the CEO; Mel Bergstein, the chairman; and John Sviokla, the vice chairman. They didn't just offer freely of their thoughts and relationships. They also employ many, many smart folks and made nearly twenty of them available to us over the course of more than a year, to pound our data into submission and make it yield up its secrets. The members of the research team were: Teji Abraham, Ken Archer, Anitha Chalam, Michael Czyz, Devin Henkel, Vivek Khati, Prakash Natarajan, Ritesh Patel, Chris Rzymski, Paul Singh, Andrew Sofield, Ariel Soiffer, Lance Thomas, Sarah Warning, and Sara Xi. We hope they learned half as much from the collaboration as we did.

A great many phenomenally bright and experienced people also helped to make this book better. They didn't have the time to spare, but they spared it anyway. They read the manuscript in detail. They offered stories. They helped sand the rough edges off our ideas. They offered insights into how to make our ideas more practical and useful. So, we'd like to heartily thank: Bill Abbott, George Anders, Dan Ariely, Aamer Baig, Les Ball, Vince Barabba, Gordon Bell, Mel Bergstein, Paul Blase, Dan Bricklin, Caroline Calkins, Marie Carr, Charlie Carroll, Kim Carroll, Tim Carroll, George Churchill, Doug Collom, Morgan Davis, Paul Demuro, Bill Dentino, Craig Forman, Jon

Friedman, John Erik Garr, Bob Gilbert, Jack Greenberg, Kevin Grieve, Bernie Hengesbaugh, Pegeen Hopkins, Beth Jenkins, Alan Kay, Andy Kessler, Lisa Laing, Rick Leander, Janet Long, Andy Lippman, Don Listwin, Mark Maltais, Roger McNamee, John G. Morgan, Dean Nicolacakis, Frank Orzell, Tony Paoni, Rachel Parker, Karen Patton, Toby Redshaw, Anand S. Rao, Wes Richards, Dan Roesch, Tim Rohner, Kevin Salwen, Scott Shaull, Alan Siegel, John Sviokla, Jennifer Thatcher, Barbara Ullman, Chris Veit, Tom Waite, Tom Weakland, Eric Wilson, Darin Yug, and Marvin Zonis.

We also acknowledge the fine folks at Reuters, Thomson Financial, and Bankruptcy.com, who provided the raw financial data that fed our analysis.

Special thanks go to our agent, Kris "Tough Love" Dahl, at ICM. She worked us through a couple of iterations of our initial proposal, turning a vague idea into the book you have in front of you. Thanks, too, to Adrian Zackheim, our editor at Portfolio, and to his assistant, Courtney Young. Courtney's insight and enthusiasm helped keep us going in those dark days when we had seemingly been at the book forever but weren't yet in sight of the finish line. Thanks, as well, to the rest of the group at Portfolio and Penguin, especially Allison McLean and Will Weisser. They have helped us get out the word about what we hope will turn out to be an important book.

Finally, thanks to our wives and children, who put up with us during this lengthy project, much more than we deserved.

Research Notes

Our research looks at the data that others have ignored. Most business research studies successful companies and tries to generalize from their traits, tactics, or strategies. But a serious question always lingers: What about companies that tried to do the same thing as the winners did, but failed?

To glean the lessons from those that have failed, we examined a broad cross section of the most significant business failures between 1981 and 2006. We defined failure as writing off significant investments, shuttering unprofitable lines of business, or filing for bankruptcy.

Working with leading information vendors, including Reuters, Thomson Financial, and Bankruptcy.com, we built a comprehensive database of more than 2,500 such failures suffered by publicly traded companies in the United States. We picked U.S. public companies because reporting requirements ensured uniformity and access to data while, at the same time, yielding a large enough universe from which to generalize the results. We picked the twenty-five-year period because it was long enough to span multiple economic cycles but recent enough to be relevant to today's business environment and management practices.

We also did a literature search to look for failures that didn't show up in the vendors' databases—for instance, companies that sold themselves before having to account for a major problem.

Then, aided by a team of researchers from Diamond Management & Technology Consultants, we spent more than a year poring over the data. We first applied several financial filters that narrowed the list to the 750 most meaningful. We narrowed bankruptcies to companies with $500 million or more in assets in the last quarter prior to bankruptcy. We narrowed write-offs and discontinued operations to those greater than $100 million, not including write-offs for in-process research and development. (Accounting rules during the years covered by our data required the immediate expensing of all recognized in-process research and development assets following a business combination. These write-offs were a mixed bag; the charges sometimes represented dead-end projects while at other times they were one-time charges against otherwise worthy, continuing projects. Given that it was difficult to distinguish between the two, we chose to ignore the category of write-offs.)

We then did a root-cause analysis, reviewing financial filings, business and popular press reports, and assessments from industry analysts to understand these failures. Using this analysis, we identified repeating patterns, where failures across multiple industries were variations on a theme. We homed in on failures that seemed to be because of strategic failures, rather than environmental factors beyond management control or mishandled implementation. Out of the 750 cases, we found 355 where strategies led directly to major failures. These cases are shown in tables at the end of this section, organized by failure type.

Next, we drilled further into 80 of these strategic failures, selected to give a representative sample across a broad set of industries and failure patterns. In this further analysis, we turned to a wider set of references, including personal interviews, court documents, local newspaper coverage, and business-school cases. The personal interviews included principals involved in the failure, as well as journalists and analysts who covered the events at the time.

From this analysis we drew the lessons about the common problems, the red flags that might alert management to impending failures, and the tough questions that might avert those failures.

Strategic Failures—Bankruptcies

Except in cases where they are used as a strategic device, such as to protect oneself against civil liabilities, bankruptcies are the clearest indicator of failure. The tables that follow show the cases that passed our initial financial screen of greater than $500 million in assets and our preliminary analysis that linked the failure to a particular strategic decision. Assets and revenues shown are from the last quarterly filing before the company's bankruptcy filing.

STRATEGIC FAILURES—BANKRUPTCIES

Company Name	Filing Year	Assets ($ Million)	Revenues ($ Million)
360networks, Inc.	2001	6,300	511
Adelphia Communications Corp.	2002	21,499	2,909
Al Copeland Enterprises, Inc.	1991	584	460
Allegheny International, Inc.	1988	859	938
Allegiance Telecom, Inc.	2003	1,441	771
Alliance Entertainment Corp.	1997	613	691
Allied Stores Corp.	1990	3,502	2,562
Alterra Healthcare Corp.	2003	1,038	509
AMERCO	2003	3,773	2,059
America West Airlines, Inc.	1991	1,165	1,316
American Banknote Corp. (1999)	1999	504	336
American Business Financial Services, Inc.	2005	1,043	97
American Classic Voyages, Inc.	2001	753	22
American Continental Corp.	1989	5,095	718
American Pad & Paper Co. (2000)	2000	518	662
AmeriServe Food Distribution, Inc.	2000	1,887	7,421
Ames Department Stores, Inc. (1990)	1990	1,602	3,109
Ames Department Stores, Inc. (2001)	2001	2,058	4,000
Anacomp, Inc. (1996)	1996	659	593
Anchor Glass Container Corp. (1996)	1996	1,208	957
APS Holding Corp.	1998	598	859
Arch Wireless, Inc.	2001	2,310	851
Aurora Foods, Inc.	2003	1,251	772
Best Products Co., Inc. (1991)	1991	1,438	2
Best Products Co., Inc. (1996)	1996	717	1,495
Boston Chicken, Inc.	1998	2,005	462
Bradlees, Inc. (1995)	1995	885	1,917
Bramalea, Inc.	1994	4,014	761
Breed Technologies, Inc.	1999	1,650	1,385
Budget Group, Inc.	2002	4,470	2,161
Burlington Industries, Inc.	2001	1,201	1,620

STRATEGIC FAILURES—BANKRUPTCIES

Company Name	Filing Year	Assets ($ Million)	Revenues ($ Million)
Cajun Electric Power Cooperative, Inc.	1994	2,415	0
Caldor Corp.	1995	1,136	2,749
Calpine Corp.	2005	27,216	9,230
Carter Hawley Hale Stores	1991	2,045	2,858
Charter Medical Corp.	1992	1,347	1,188
CHS Electronics, Inc.	2000	3,572	8,546
Cincinnati Microwave, Inc.	1997	542	79
Circle K Corp.	1990	2,045	3,493
Classic Communications, Inc.	2001	711	182
Color Tile, Inc.	1996	550	674
Comdisco, Inc.	2001	8,754	3,867
Conseco, Inc.	2002	61,392	8,108
Consolidated Freightways Corp.	2002	881	2,238
ContiFinancial Corp.	2000	2,355	253
Continental Information Systems	1989	1,926	548
Cornerstone Propane Partners LP	2004	869	4,206
Covad Communications	2001	1,512	159
Dade Behring Holdings, Inc.	2002	1,142	0
Days Inns of America	1991	596	52
divine, inc.	2003	804	200
DR Holdings, Inc., of DE	1992	1,150	1,382
Drexel Burnham Lambert Group	1990	3,698	0
E-II Holdings, Inc.	1992	2,141	489
Eastern Air Lines, Inc.	1989	4,037	4,447
Edison Brothers Stores, Inc. (1995)	1995	894	336
El Paso Electric Co.	1991	1,809	433
Encompass Services Corp.	2002	2,401	3,825
Enron Corp.	2001	63,392	100,789
Enstar Group, Inc.	1991	5,594	659
Envirodyne Industries	1993	1,086	544
e.spire Communications, Inc.	2001	941	0

STRATEGIC FAILURES—BANKRUPTCIES

Company Name	Filing Year	Assets ($ Million)	Revenues ($ Million)
Exide Technologies, Inc.	2002	2,299	2,432
Farley, Inc.	1991	2,408	1,517
Farmland Industries, Inc.	2002	2,700	12
Favorite Brands International Holding Corp.	1999	807	653
Federated Department Stores	1990	7,913	4,576
First Executive Corp.	1991	15,193	1,296
Firstcorp, Inc.	1990	697	66
FIRSTPLUS Financial Group, Inc.	1999	2,447	591
Flagstar Companies, Inc.	1997	1,687	2,542
Fleming Companies, Inc.	2003	3,655	15,628
FLYi, Inc.	2005	678	500
Focal Communications Corp.	2002	728	0
Footstar, Inc.	2004	866	2,461
Formica Corp.	2002	879	774
FoxMeyer Health Corp.	1996	1,577	5,487
FPA Medical Management, Inc.	1998	831	1,166
Fruit of the Loom, Inc.	1999	2,290	2,170
G. Heileman Brewing Co., Inc. (1991)	1991	1,241	0
G. Heileman Brewing Co., Inc. (1996)	1996	783	778
Gaylord Container Corp.	1992	1,100	718
Genesis Health Ventures, Inc.	2000	2,430	1,866
Genuity, Inc.	2002	2,995	1,221
Gillett Holdings, Inc.	1991	986	769
Global Crossing, Ltd.	2002	30,185	3,789
Global Telesystems, Inc.	2001	2,263	1,024
Globalstar LP (2002)	2002	702	4
Goss Graphic Systems, Inc.	1999	1,016	764
Grand Union Company (The) (1995)	1995	1,394	2,477
Grand Union Company (The) (1998)	1998	1,061	2,267
Grand Union Company (The) (2000)	2000	1,089	2,286
Great American Communications Co.	1993	714	211

STRATEGIC FAILURES—BANKRUPTCIES

Company Name	Filing Year	Assets ($ Million)	Revenues ($ Million)
Greyhound Lines, Inc. (1990)	1990	593	1,040
Grove Worldwide, Inc.	2001	729	851
GST Telecommunications, Inc.	2000	1,113	322
Guilford Mills, Inc.	2002	551	644
Ha-Lo Industries, Inc.	2001	533	612
Harnischfeger Industries, Inc.	1999	2,787	2,042
Harrahs Jazz Co.	1995	665	0
Hechinger Co.	1999	1,577	3,449
Heilig-Meyers Co.	2000	1,458	2,298
Hills Department Stores	1991	1,059	1,750
Hooker (L. J.) Corp., Inc.	1989	910	402
Hvide Marine, Inc.	1999	974	0
ICG Communications, Inc.	2000	2,021	479
ICO Global Communications (Holdings), Ltd.	1999	2,567	0
Imperial Corporation of America	1990	12,263	1,162
Imperial Sugar Co.	2001	1,094	1,821
Insilco Corp.	1991	1,105	762
Integrated Resources, Inc.	1990	7,876	1,716
Interco, Inc.	1991	1,148	1,656
Interstate Bakeries Corp.	2004	1,646	3,526
Iridium LLC	1999	3,739	0
IT Group, Inc. (The)	2002	1,323	1,447
JCC Holding Co.	2001	506	41
Jitney-Jungle Stores of America, Inc.	1999	691	0
Just for Feet, Inc.	1999	689	775
JWP, Inc.	1993	2,281	3,594
Kaiser Steel Corp.	1987	621	0
Key3Media Group, Inc.	2003	1,057	236
Kitty Hawk, Inc.	2000	983	715
Kmart Corp.	2002	14,630	37,028
Koger Properties, Inc.	1991	634	206

STRATEGIC FAILURES—BANKRUPTCIES

Company Name	Filing Year	Assets ($ Million)	Revenues ($ Million)
Laidlaw, Inc. (2001)	2001	4,000	2,956
Lason, Inc.	2001	861	480
Leap Wireless International, Inc.	2003	2,164	618
Levitz Furniture, Inc. (1997)	1997	934	967
Loewen Group International, Inc.	1999	4,674	1,136
Macy (R. H.) & Co., Inc.	1992	4,812	6,762
Magellan Health Services, Inc.	2003	1,004	1,753
MarchFirst, Inc.	2001	504	481
Marvel Entertainment Group, Inc.	1996	1,213	829
Maxicare Health Plans	1989	992	1,839
Maxim Crane Works LLC	2004	789	420
Maxwell Communication Corp.	1991	6,352	1,747
McCrory Parent Corp.	1992	1,032	1,531
McLean Industries Inc.	1986	1,569	0
MedicaLogic/Medscape, Inc.	2002	966	48
Memorex Telex NV (1992)	1992	1,643	714
Memorex Telex NV (1994)	1994	1,139	1,326
Mid-American Waste Systems, Inc.	1997	515	157
Montgomery Ward Holding Corp. (1997)	1997	4,879	6,620
Morrison Knudsen Corp.	1996	628	1,709
Mortgage & Realty Trust (1990)	1990	521	66
Motient Corp.	2002	1,572	100
National Equipment Services, Inc.	2003	863	621
NextWave Personal Communications, Inc.	1998	3,994	1
NH Holding, Inc.	1993	531	430
Northwestern Corp.	2003	2,673	1,992
NRG Energy, Inc.	2003	10,884	2,281
NTELOS, Inc.	2003	800	215
NTL, Inc.	2002	13,026	3,190
Oakwood Homes Corp.	2002	922	1,096
OCA, Inc.	2006	660	375

STRATEGIC FAILURES—BANKRUPTCIES

Company Name	Filing Year	Assets ($ Million)	Revenues ($ Million)
Oglebay Norton Co.	2004	688	401
OpTel, Inc.	1999	627	65
Orange County, California	1994	18,297	1,326
Orion Pictures Corp.	1991	1,059	584
Outboard Marine Corp.	2000	848	1,111
Outsourcing Solutions, Inc.	2003	627	612
Pathmark Stores, Inc.	2000	842	3,698
Payless Cashways, Inc. (1997)	1997	1,293	2,651
Payless Cashways, Inc. (2001)	2001	639	2,948
Penn Traffic Co. (1999)	1999	1,564	3,010
Peregrine Systems, Inc.	2002	2,004	565
Petrie Stores Corp.	1995	1,274	1,025
Philip Services Corp. (1999)	1999	1,148	2,001
Philip Services Corp. (2003)	2003	601	1,118
Physicians Resource Group, Inc.	2000	534	412
Pillowtex Corp. (2000)	2000	1,654	1,552
Pillowtex Corp. (2003)	2003	592	555
Pinnacle Holdings, Inc.	2002	1,034	191
Pliant Corp.	2006	777	969
Polaroid Corp.	2001	2,043	1,856
Polymer Group, Inc.	2002	1,232	816
Prime Motor Inns, Inc.	1990	1,144	257
PSINet, Inc.	2001	2,517	996
RCN Corp.	2004	2,346	485
Refco, Inc.	2005	33,333	1,874
Reliance Acceptance Group, Inc.	1998	553	72
Reliance Group Holdings, Inc.	2001	12,598	179
Republic Health Corp.	1989	555	465
Republic Technologies International LLC	2001	1,415	1,033
Resorts International, Inc. (1989)	1989	1,035	456
Resorts International, Inc. (1994)	1994	576	440

STRATEGIC FAILURES—BANKRUPTCIES

Company Name	Filing Year	Assets ($ Million)	Revenues ($ Million)
Revco D.S., Inc.	1988	1,844	2,409
Rothschild Holdings, Inc.	1989	2,778	122
Safelite Glass Corp.	2000	574	877
Safety-Kleen Corp.	2000	4,367	1,686
Satélites Mexicanos, S.A. de C.V.	2005	951	72
SCI Television, Inc.	1993	1,039	209
Semi-Tech Corp.	1999	2,346	1,060
Service Merchandise Co., Inc.	1999	1,627	3,170
Sharon Steel Corp.	1987	662	1,036
Singer Company NV (The)	1999	1,376	1,264
SLI, Inc.	2002	873	851
Southeast Banking Corp.	1991	13,390	1,617
Southern Pacific Funding Corp.	1998	589	189
Southland Corp. (The)	1990	3,439	8,352
Special Metals Corp.	2002	701	25
SpectraSite Holdings, Inc.	2002	3,202	473
SPI Holdings, Inc.	1992	610	173
Spiegel, Inc.	2003	1,890	2,782
Stage Stores, Inc.	2000	555	1,122
Star Telecommunications, Inc.	2001	807	1,062
Statewide Bancorp, Inc.	1991	1,982	203
Stelco, Inc.	2004	2,442	0
Stockwalk Group, Inc.	2002	984	137
Sun Healthcare Group, Inc.	1999	2,468	3,088
Sunbeam Corp.	2001	3,132	2,398
TDII Co.	1993	526	441
Telewest Communications PLC	2004	6,939	2,316
Texaco, Inc.	1987	35,892	0
Tiphook Finance Corp.	1996	560	151
Tokheim Corp. (2000)	2000	691	694
Touch America Holdings, Inc.	2003	3,059	550

STRATEGIC FAILURES—BANKRUPTCIES

Company Name	Filing Year	Assets ($ Million)	Revenues ($ Million)
Tower Automotive, Inc.	2005	2,846	2,816
Tracor, Inc.	1991	992	741
Trans World Airlines, Inc. (1992)	1992	2,865	1,646
Trans World Airlines, Inc. (1995)	1995	2,495	3,408
Trico Marine Services	2004	749	134
Trump Hotels & Casino Resorts, Inc.	2004	2,031	1,161
Trump Taj Mahal Funding	1991	846	357
UDC Homes, Inc.	1995	583	509
UniCapital Corp.	2000	4,005	863
United Australia/Pacific, Inc.	2002	546	177
United Companies Financial Corp.	1999	1,337	441
United Pan-Europe Communications NV	2002	8,475	1,379
United States Leather, Inc.	1998	2,648	305
U.S. Home Corp.	1991	810	676
U.S. Office Products Co.	2001	1,746	2,499
USG Corp. (1993)	1993	1,659	1,777
Venture Holdings Co. LLC	2003	1,416	1,862
Venture Stores, Inc.	1998	688	1,486
Versatel Telecom International NV	2002	1,829	228
Viasystems Group, Inc.	2002	988	1,207
Viatel, Inc.	2001	2,124	333
Wang Laboratories, Inc.	1992	1,418	2,092
Warnaco Group, Inc.	2001	2,762	2,114
Washington Bancorporation	1990	2,802	232
Webvan Group, Inc.	2001	1,290	178
West Point Acquisition	1992	1,493	0
Winn Enterprises	1986	510	0
Winn-Dixie Stores, Inc.	2005	2,619	10,633
Woodward & Lothrop, Inc.	1994	608	855
World Access, Inc.	2001	1,630	306
Zale Corp.	1992	1,789	1,335

Strategic Failures—Write-offs

Write-offs for failed strategies are notoriously hard to isolate. Multiple items are typically combined in what is known, in accounting parlance, as a "big bath charge." Some also refer to it as "taking out the trash." In addition, write-offs associated with a particular failure are typically taken over multiple years. Thus, a pure financial analysis is insufficient for identifying individual failures. Instead, we aggregated all write-offs by a particular company over the research period and further investigated the ones that totaled more than $100 million. The table below lists the companies and the write-offs that led us to identify particular strategic failures.

STRATEGIC FAILURES—WRITE-OFFS

Company Name	Amount ($ Million)
ADC Telecommunications	860
Albertsons, Inc.	385
Alltel Corp.	137
American Standard Companies, Inc.	258
American Tower Corp.	271
Aquila, Inc.	1,751
Barnes & Noble, Inc.	132
BEA Systems, Inc.	136
BearingPoint, Inc.	397
Borders Group, Inc.	166
Broadcom Corp.	2,905
Brown-Forman Corp.	130
Cablevision Systems Corp.	263
CBS Corp.	27,482
Cendant Corp.	960
Champion Enterprises, Inc.	321
Chesapeake Energy Corp.	1,001
Ciena Corp.	3,061
Citizens Communications	1,117
CNET Networks, Inc.	1,976
Conseco, Inc.	1,794

STRATEGIC FAILURES—WRITE-OFFS

Company Name	Amount ($ Million)
Corning, Inc.	507
Crescent Real Estate Equities Co.	387
DaVita, Inc.	144
Dillard's, Inc.	428
DIRECTV Group, Inc.	1,693
Dynegy, Inc.	1,949
Emdeon Corp.	3,816
Emulex Corp.	586
EOG Resources, Inc.	846
E. W. Scripps Co. (The)	125
Express Scripts, Inc.	165
Federated Department Stores	126
FirstEnergy Corp.	112
Fortune Brands, Inc.	1,702
Gemstar-TV Guide International, Inc.	2,953
General Motors Corp.	742
Great Atlantic & Pacific Tea Co. (The)	127
HCA, Inc.	1,667
Humana, Inc.	643
Huntsman Corp.	522
IAC/InterActiveCorp	353
IDT Corp.	563
IKON Office Solutions, Inc.	103
Intel Corp.	715
International Rectifier Corp.	400
Interpublic Group of Companies, Inc.	1,546
J. C. Penney Company, Inc.	633
JDS Uniphase Corp.	57,386
Kroger Co. (The)	1,777
Leap Wireless International, Inc.	250
Lockheed Martin Corp.	1,156
Masco Corp.	928

STRATEGIC FAILURES—WRITE-OFFS

Company Name	Amount ($ Million)
Motorola, Inc.	1,910
Northern Border Partners LP	219
Openwave Systems, Inc.	607
PMC-Sierra, Inc.	276
Progress Energy, Inc.	618
QUALCOMM, Inc.	598
Questar Corp.	254
Qwest Communications International, Inc.	24,465
Redback Networks, Inc.	2,701
Safeco Corp.	1,261
Safeway, Inc.	2,017
Sanmina-SCI Corp.	3,440
SCANA Corp.	433
Sherwin-Williams Co.	374
Solectron Corp.	4,120
Sonus Networks, Inc.	409
Staples, Inc.	216
Sun Microsystems, Inc.	2,180
Tech Data Corp.	329
Tenet Healthcare Corp.	2,850
Time Warner, Inc.	43,248
Time Warner Telecom, Inc.	222
Transocean, Inc.	3,006
Tribune Co.	287
Tyco International, Ltd.	7,553
Union Pacific Corp.	547
United Rentals, Inc.	684
UnumProvident Corp.	856
VeriSign, Inc.	153
Washington Group International, Inc.	1,223
Wendy's International	260
Wyeth	401

STRATEGIC FAILURES—WRITE-OFFS	
Company Name	Amount ($ Million)
Xilinx, Inc.	655
Zale Corp.	140

Strategic Failures–Discontinued Operations

Discontinued operations do not necessarily denote either a strategic or an execution failure. Sometimes operations are discontinued because of valid strategic shifts; other times they might even denote success, such as when an otherwise sustainable operation is sold. Even in the case of failure, it is sometimes hard to distinguish between strategic and execution failures. This is because the unit might have been in business for some time, making it more difficult to isolate cause and effect related to the failure. In general, we tended to be conservative in designating a discontinued operation as a strategic failure. The table below lists the companies and the write-offs that led us to identify particular strategic failures.

STRATEGIC FAILURES—DISCONTINUED OPERATIONS	
Company Name	Amount ($ Million)
ADC Telecommunications	204
American Standard Companies, Inc.	256
American Tower Corp.	392
Avon Products, Inc.	795
Conexant Systems, Inc.	2,541
Conseco, Inc.	469
Consolidated Edison, Inc.	155
Dominion Resources, Inc.	652
Duke Energy Corp.	734
Federated Department Stores	635
FPL Group, Inc.	809
International Business Machines Corp.	277
Masco Corp.	527

STRATEGIC FAILURES—DISCONTINUED OPERATIONS

Company Name	Amount ($ Million)
NiSource, Inc.	289
PPL Corp.	102
Schering-Plough Corp.	161
Solectron Corp.	312
Textron, Inc.	211
Westar Energy, Inc.	356
Xerox Corp.	347

Notes

1. Illusions of Synergy

1. H. Allen Smith, *The Compleat Practical Joker* (New York: Doubleday, 1953).
2. David Harding and Sam Rovit, *Mastering the Merger: Four Critical Decisions That Make or Break the Deal* (Boston: Harvard Business School Press, 2004).
3. Scott Christofferson, Rob McNish, and Diane Sias, "Where Mergers Go Wrong," *McKinsey on Finance*, 2004.
4. Matthias M. Bekier, Anna J. Bogardus, and Timothy Oldham, "Mastering Revenue Growth in M&A," *McKinsey Quarterly*, 2000.
5. Mark Sirower, *The Synergy Trap* (New York: Free Press, 1997).
6. Caroline Calkins, Chad Smith, and Dr. John J. Sviokla, "Mergers and Acquisitions in the Age of Business Platforms," white paper, Diamond Management & Technology Consultants, 2006.
7. Sirower, *The Synergy Trap*.
8. Gavin Souter, "Unum, Provident Join in $5.4 Billion Merger," *Business Insurance*, November 30, 1998.
9. Bob Libbey, speaking on a conference call as part of Best Practices in Corporate Communications e-conference, March 29, 2000.
10. Ron Panko, "Sharpening the Focus: UnumProvident is in the latter phases of a multiyear reorganization to become the leading disability writer and win the favor of equity and ratings analysts," *Best's Review*, August 2, 2002.
11. Thomas Wailgum, "The Quest for Customer Data Integration," *CIO* magazine, August 1, 2006.
12. Memo from Tom Hey, senior vice president of risk management at Provident, 1994.
13. Joan Hangarter, plaintiff, v. The Paul Revere Life Insurance Company, et. al., defendants, United States District Court, District of Northern California, Case No. C 99-5286 JL.
14. Dean Foust, "Disability Claim Denied!" *BusinessWeek*, December 22, 2003.
15. John H. Langbein, "Trust Law as Regulatory Law: The Unum / Provident Scandal and Judicial Review of Benefit Denials Under ERISA," Yale Law School Research Paper No. 329, June 26, 2006.
16. "State Insurance Commissioners Reach Settlement with Unum Provident," Insure.com, November 19, 2004.
17. Edward D. Murphy, "CEO: UnumProvident Healthier," *Portland Press Herald*, December 13, 2005.

18. "UnumProvident Woes Foreseen Before Merger" *Maine Today Business News,* March 31, 2004.
19. Judy Morris, MD, letter to the Maine Department of Professional and Financial Regulation, Bureau of Insurance, May 25, 1999.
20. Robert Berner, "Federated's Fingerhut Fiasco," *BusinessWeek,* December 18, 2000.

2. Faulty Financial Engineering

1. "The Most Dangerous Words on Wall Street," *Fortune,* September 3, 2007.
2. Warren Buffett, Berkshire Hathaway annual report, 2002.
3. Gretchen Morgenson, "There's No Superhero in the Wings," *New York Times,* November 11, 2007.
4. Ben Finkelstein, *The Politics of Public Fund Investing* (New York: Simon & Schuster, 2006).
5. Alex Berenson, "A Boom Built Upon Sand, Gone Bust," *New York Times,* November 25, 2001.
6. "U.S. RMBS Default History Shows Less Than 1 of Rated Cases Have Defaulted," Standard & Poor's, November 18, 2004.
7. Berenson, "A Boom Built Upon Sand, Gone Bust."
8. Ibid.
9. Ibid.
10. Ibid.
11. Ibid.
12. "Marking to Myth," *Fortune,* September 3, 2007.
13. Berenson, "A Boom Built Upon Sand, Gone Bust."
14. Ibid.
15. Ibid.
16. Shawn Tully, "A Deal Too Far," *Fortune,* November 8, 1999.
17. Ibid.
18. Berenson, "A Boom Built Upon Sand, Gone Bust."
19. Ibid.
20. Jonathan Weill and Cassell Bryan-Low, "Report Bolsters SEC's Proposal for Attorneys," *Wall Street Journal,* September 15, 2003.
21. Larry O'Dell, "Furniture Giant Files for Bankruptcy, Announces Closings, Job Cuts," Associated Press, August 16, 2000.
22. Indraneel Sur, "Heilig-Meyers to Close All of Its California Stores," *Los Angeles Times,* August 17, 2000.
23. O'Dell, "Furniture Giant Files for Bankruptcy."
24. Robert F. Bruner and Kenneth M. Eades, "The Crash of the Revco Leveraged Buyout," *Financial Management,* Spring 1992.
25. Ibid.
26. Ibid.
27. Charles W. Mulford and Eugene Comiskey, *The Financial Numbers Game: Detecting Creative Accounting Practices* (New York: John Wiley & Sons, 2002).
28. Elizabeth MacDonald, "Show Me the Money," Forbes.com, June 4, 2007.
29. Elizabeth MacDonald, "How to Really Hate Your Auditor," Forbes.com, May 5, 2003.
30. Ibid.
31. Ibid.
32. Nick Ravo, "Leonard S. Shoen, 83, Founder of U-Haul, the Trailer Company," *New York Times,* October 7, 1999.
33. Mulford and Comiskey, *The Financial Numbers Game.*
34. Eric Young, "The Highs and Lows of Being a CEO," *Chief Executive,* August 1, 2001.

35. William C. Symonds, "Behind Tyco's Accounting Alchemy," *BusinessWeek*, February 25, 2002.
36. Warren Buffett, Berkshire Hathaway annual report for 1989, chairman's letter.

3. Deflated Rollups

1. Edward O. Welles, "Roll Your Own," *Inc.*, February 2001.
2. Guy Dixon, "We Bought the Wrong Company. It Took Us Two Years to Admit It," *Scotland on Sunday*, September 11, 2005.
3. Bernard Condon, "Jon Ledecky Predicts . . . ," Forbes.com, October 5, 1998.
4. *The Loewen Group Incorporated and Raymond L. Loewen vs. the United States of America*, Joint Reply of Claimants the Loewen Group Incorporated and Raymond L. Loewen to the Counter-Memorial of the United States, filed June 8, 2001, with the International Centre for Settlement of Investment Disputes.
5. Erik Larson, "Fight to the Death," *Time*, December 9, 1996.
6. Opinion by the International Centre for Settlement of Investment Disputes in The Proceeding Between the Loewen Group Incorporated and Raymond L. Loewen (Claimants) and United States of America (Respondent), June 26, 2003.
7. Stuart Gilson, *Creating Value Through Corporate Restructuring* (New York: John Wiley & Sons, 2001).
8. Loewen Group company history, Answers.com.
9. Montana Jones, "Canadian Corporate Predator," online article posted in September 2003, http://community-2.webtv.net/solis-boo/CorporatePredator; viewed December 1, 2007.
10. Ibid.
11. Loewen Group company history, Answers.com.
12. Jones, "Canadian Corporate Predator."
13. Gilson, *Creating Value Through Corporate Restructuring.*
14. Ian Giddy, "The Restructuring of the Loewen Group," case study, New York University.
15. Bolaji Ojo, "Remaking a Champion," *Electronics Supply & Manufacturing*, May 1, 2006.
16. Paul F. Kocourek, Steven Y. Chung, and Matthew G. McKenna, "Strategic Rollups: Overhauling the Multi-Merger Machine," *Strategy & Business*, second quarter 2000.

4. Staying the (Misguided) Course

1. Gary Hamel and Liisa Valikangas, "The Quest for Resilience," *Harvard Business Review*, September 2003.
2. Geoffrey Smith, "Can George Fisher Fix Kodak?" *BusinessWeek*, October 20, 1997.
3. Claudia H. Deutsch, "Chief Says Kodak Is Pointed in the Right Direction," *New York Times*, December 25, 1999.
4. Ibid.
5. Bruce Upbin, "Kodak's Digital Moment," *Forbes*, August 21, 2000.
6. Ibid.
7. "Eastman Kodak Co. (Interview with Daniel A. Carp, President and CEO)," *Photo Marketing*, March 1, 2003.
8. Ibid.
9. Nielsen SoundScan Report, January 4, 2008.
10. Patricia Callahan and Ann Zimmerman, "Wal-Mart, After Remaking Discount Retailing, Now Nation's Largest Grocery Chain," *Wall Street Journal*, May 27, 2003.
11. Staci D. Kramer, "Content's King," *Cableworld*, April 29, 2002.
12. Mary Benner, "Securities Analysts and Incumbent Response to Radical Technology Change: The Case of Digital Technology in Photography," Wharton School research paper, February 25, 2007.

13. Jennifer Reingold, "MobileMedia: Anatomy of a Bankruptcy," *BusinessWeek*, May 17, 1997.
14. Ibid.
15. Leslie Brokaw, "Flexible Fliers," *Inc.*, December 1995.
16. Pillowtex Company history, Answers.com.
17. http://www.heritage.org/Research/InternetandTechnology/images/bg1361cht3.gif, viewed May 1, 2008.
18. Michael Porter, *On Competition* (Boston: Harvard Business School Press, 1998).

5. Misjudged Adjacencies

1. Chris Zook, *Beyond the Core* (Boston: Harvard Business School Press, 2004).
2. George S. Day, "Which Way Should You Grow," *Harvard Business Review*, July–August, 2004.
3. Zook, *Beyond the Core.*
4. Ibid.
5. Thomas W. Gerdel, "Oglebay Norton on a New Course," *Cleveland Plain Dealer*, December 29, 1996.
6. Ibid.
7. M. R. Kropko, "Chief Executive Works Without Salary," Associated Press, September 6, 1998.
8. Frank Lewis, "The Wreck of the Oglebay Norton," *Cleveland Scene*, September 22, 2004.
9. Ibid.
10. Ibid.
11. Ibid.
12. Bill Brubaker, "FLYi Says Older Carriers Played Tough," *Washington Post*, November 9, 2005.
13. Bill Brubaker, "FLYi is Latest Airline in Bankruptcy Protection," *Washington Post*, November 8, 2005.
14. Howard Rudnitsky, "World's Largest Up and Comer," *Forbes*, May 18, 1987.
15. Anthony Bianco and Pamela L. Moore, "Xerox: The Downfall," *BusinessWeek*, March 5, 2001.
16. Julie Johnsson, "Dealmakers Sue Ex-Employer Comdisco," Crain Communications Incorporated, June 9, 2003.
17. Ibid.
18. Paul Bagnell, "Laidlaw's Rough Ride," *Financial Post*, September 25, 1999.
19. Timothy Pritchard, "Treacherous Stretch for a Busing Leader," *New York Times*, October 29, 2000.
20. Larry Light, "Halt! You May Owe the IRS $500 Million," *BusinessWeek*, September 14, 1998.
21. John Crudele, "FPL Group in Deal for Colonial Penn," *New York Times*, October 26, 1985.
22. Lee A. Daniels, "Utilities Are Branching Out," *New York Times*, February 19, 1987.
23. Ibid.
24. Constantinos C. Markides, *All the Right Moves* (Boston: Harvard Business School Press, 2000).

6. Fumbling Technology

1. Howard Wolinsky, "Why Motorola Will Sell Iridium," *Chicago Sun-Times*, August 13, 1999.

2. Robert W. Galvin, "Real Leaders Create Industries," *Research-Technology Management*, November/December, 1995.
3. Ibid.
4. "Make Room for Motorola," *Mobile Phone News*, November 21, 1991.
5. "Beam Me Up, Scottie," *Economist*, March 28, 1992.
6. Ronald E. Yates, "Motorola Phone Satellite Project Picking Up Static," Chicago Tribune, August 10, 1992.
7. Yates, "Motorola Phone Satellite Project Picking Up Static."
8. Brian S. Moskal, "Iridium Inc.," *Industry Week*, December 19, 1994.
9. Adam Lashinsky, "Dial Iridium to Anywhere," *Crain's Chicago Business*, December 11, 1995.
10. Roger O. Crockett, "Why Motorola Should Hang Up on Iridium," *BusinessWeek*, August 30, 1999.
11. *Statutory Committee of Unsecured Creditors v. Motorola, Inc.*, Case No. 99-45005 (JMP), United States Bankruptcy Court, Southern District of New York, 2007.
12. Ibid.
13. Sydney Finkelstein and Shade H. Sanford, "Learning from Corporate Mistakes: The Rise and Fall of Iridium," *Organizational Dynamics*, November 2000.
14. John Van, "Hang-ups for Iridium Phone Firm," *Chicago Tribune*, April 1, 1999.
15. Andrew Zajac, "Iridium: Pie in the Sky?" *Chicago Tribune*, June 14, 1998.
16. Nancy Gohring, "Iridium Tests Its Wings," Telephony Online, November 2, 1998.
17. Finkelstein and Sanford, "Learning from Corporate Mistakes."
18. Peter W. Barnes, "Zapmail May Become Passe," *New York Times*, August 24, 1984.
19. Clay Shirky, "Customer-Owned Networks: ZapMail and the Telecommunications Industry," NEC@shirky.com, 2003.
20. Howard Anderson, "Iridium's Demise: A Case of Misreading the Market," *Computer-World*, October 4, 2000.
21. Western Union memo, 1876.
22. Wikipedia entry for Thomas Watson, Sr.
23. Smart Computing Encyclopedia entry for Kenneth H. Olsen.
24. Paul Carroll, *Big Blues: The Unmaking of IBM* (New York: Crown, 1993).
25. Ibid.
26. Joelle Tessler, "An Inside View of Webvan," *San Jose Mercury News*, December 16, 2001.
27. Jorge Rufat-Latre, "What Killed Webvan was Bricks, not Clicks," *Chicago Tribune*, July 18, 2001.
28. Ariane Sains and Stanley Reed, "Electrolux Redesigns Itself," *BusinessWeek*, November 27, 2006.

7. Consolidation Blues

1. Graeme Deans, "Mastering Industry Consolidation: Strategies for Winning the Merger Endgame," *Ivey Business Journal*, July/August 2003.
2. Gary Hamel, *Leading the Revolution* (Boston: Harvard Business School Press, 2002).
3. "Herbert Gilman of Ames Dead at 65," *Discount Store News*, August 6, 1990.
4. Peter Hisey, "Herb Gilman: The Concept Is So Simple," *Discount Store News*, May 23, 1988.
5. Ibid.
6. Ibid.
7. Peter Hisey, "Emphasis on Higher Margins Helps Ames Climb Into Black," *Discount Store News*, April 18, 1994.
8. Ames Department Stores 10-K filed with the Securities and Exchange Commission, January 28, 1996.
9. Tony Lisanti, "Dr. Pistner's Vision Takes Shape at Ames," *Discount Store News*, June 17, 1991.

10. "800-lb. Gorilla Puts Chain in Chapter 11," *Discount Store News,* April 2000.
11. Gerri Wills, "Taking Ames at Wal-Mart," *SmartMoney,* September 29, 1997.
12. Steven N. Kaplan, *Mergers and Productivity* (Chicago: University of Chicago Press, 2000).
13. "Down to Earth: For Piedmont Airlines, Its 1989 'Merger of Equals' with USAir Was More Like a Funeral Than a Wedding," *Business North Carolina,* August 1, 2006.
14. Saul Hansell, "Seagate: Missed the iPod but Selling to Lots of Snoops," *New York Times,* September 10, 2007.

8. Why Bad Strategies Happen to Good People

1. Richard J. Heuer Jr., *Psychology of Intelligence Analysis* (Government Printing Office, 1999).
2. Nassim Nicholas Taleb, *The Black Swan: The Impact of the Highly Improbable* (New York: Random House, 2007).
3. Phil Rosenzweig, *The Halo Effect . . . and the Eight Other Business Delusions That Deceive Managers* (New York: Free Press, 2007).
4. Heuer, *Psychology of Intelligence Analysis.*
5. Interview with Alan Kay, March 8, 2008.
6. Nassim Nicholas Taleb, *Fooled by Randomness: The Hidden Role of Chance in Life and in the Markets* (New York: Random House, 2004).
7. Ibid.
8. Peter L. Bernstein, *Against the Gods: The Remarkable Story of Risk* (New York: John Wiley & Sons, 1996).
9. Interview with Jim Barksdale, March 7, 1996.
10. Heuer, *Psychology of Intelligence Analysis.*
11. Ibid.
12. Ibid.
13. Sydney Finkelstein, *Why Smart Executives Fail: And What You Can Learn from Their Mistakes* (New York: Penguin Books, 2003).
14. Ian I. Mitroff, *The Subjective Side of Science* (Salinas, CA: Intersystems Publications, 1983).
15. James W. Kalat, *Introduction to Psychology* (Belmont, CA: Thomson Wadsworth, 2005).
16. Wikipedia entry for the Milgram experiment.
17. Rich Karlgaard, "Peter Drucker on Leadership," Forbes.com, November 19, 2004.
18. Taleb, *The Black Swan.*
19. Ibid.
20. Ibid.
21. Charles Perrow, *Normal Accidents: Living with High-Risk Technologies* (Princeton, NJ: Princeton University Press, 1999).
22. Chris Argyris, "Teaching Smart People How to Learn," *Harvard Business Review,* May–June 1991.
23. Charles R. Schwenk, *The Essence of Strategic Decision Making* (Lanham, MD: Lexington Books, 1988).
24. Jeffrey Pfeffer and Robert I. Sutton, *Hard Facts, Dangerous Half-Truths, and Total Nonsense: Profiting from Evidence-Based Management* (Boston: Harvard Business School Press, 2006).

9. Why Bad Strategies Happen to Good Companies

1. Flora Guidry, Andrew Leone, and Steven Rock, "Earnings-Based Bonus Plans and Earnings Management by Business-Unit Managers," *Journal of Accounting and Economics,* Volume 26, 1999.

2. Interview with Marvin Zonis, February 26, 2008.
3. Schwenk, *The Essence of Strategic Decision Making.*
4. Interview with Marvin Zonis.
5. Finkelstein, *Why Smart Executives Fail.*
6. Ibid.
7. James Surowiecki, *The Wisdom of Crowds: Why the Many are Smarter Than the Few and How Collective Wisdom Shapes Business, Economics, Societies, and Nations* (New York: Doubleday, 2004).
8. Carroll, *Big Blues.*
9. Dietrich Dorner, *The Logic of Failure: Recognizing and Avoiding Error in Complex Situations* (New York: Basic Books, 1997).
10. Wikipedia entry for Ford Pinto.
11. "The Gift of Prophecy," *Economist*, March 1, 2003.
12. "Study Finds Nearly 200,000 Deaths Annually from Hospital Errors," consumeraffairs.com, August 12, 2004.
13. Perrow, *Normal Accidents.*

10. The Devil's Advocate

1. http://www.brainyquote.com/quotes/quote/a/alfredpsl194029.html.
2. Finkelstein, *Why Smart Executives Fail.*
3. Edward de Bono, *Six Thinking Hats* (New York: Penguin Books, 1990).
4. Interview with David Pottruck, March 3, 2008.
5. Carroll, *Big Blues.*
6. Berkshire Hathaway annual report, chairman's letter, 1989.
7. Alex Rovira and Fernando Trias de Bes, "Do Entrepreneurs Need Good Luck?" About .com, viewed April 18, 2008.
8. Ibid.
9. Jay W. Hopman, "Using Forecasting Markets to Manage Demand Risk," *Intel Technology Journal*, May 16, 2007.
10. Otto Friedrich, "Day of Infamy," *Time*, December 2, 1991.
11. William Stearns Davis, "Herodotus on the Customs of the Persians," parstimes.com, viewed April 18, 2008.
12. Geoffrey Cullinan, Jean-Marc Le Roux, and Rolf-Magnus Weddigen, "When to Walk Away from a Deal," *Harvard Business Review*, April 2004.
13. Bruce Nolop, "Rules to Acquire By," *Harvard Business Review*, September 2007.

11. The Safety Net

1. Clayton Christensen, Stephen P. Kaufman, and Willy C. Shih, "Innovation Killers: How Financial Tools Destroy Your Capacity to Do New Things," *Harvard Business Review*, January 2008.
2. Nolop, "Rules to Acquire By."
3. Rita Gunther McGrath and Ian C. MacMillan, "Discovery-Driven Planning," *Harvard Business Review*, July–August 1995.

Epilogue

1. Arthur Schlesinger Jr., "Are We Trapped in Another Vietnam?" *Independent*, November 2, 2001.

Recommended Reading

Ackoff, Russell L. *Ackoff's Best: His Classic Writings on Management.* New York: Wiley, 1999.

Ariely, Dan. *Predictably Irrational: The Hidden Forces That Shape Our Decisions.* New York: HarperCollins, 2008.

Barabba, Vincent P. *Surviving Transformation: Lessons from GM's Surprising Turnaround.* New York: Oxford University Press, 2004.

Barnett, William P., and Elizabeth G. Pontikes. "The Red Queen, Success Bias, and Organizational Inertia." Stanford GSB Research Paper No. 1936, June 2006.

Beer, Michael, and Russell A. Eisenstat. "How to Have an Honest Conversation About Your Business Strategy." *Harvard Business Review,* February 2004.

Bell, C. Gordon. *High-Tech Ventures: The Guide for Entrepreneurial Success.* New York: Perseus, 1991.

Bower, Joseph L., and Clayton M. Christensen. "Disruptive Technologies: Catching the Wave." *Harvard Business Review,* January 1995.

Brooks, Frederick P. *The Mythical Man-Month: Essays on Software Engineering.* 2nd ed. Reading, MA: Addison-Wesley, 1995.

Brown, Donald E. *Human Universals.* New York: McGraw-Hill, 1991.

Bruner, Robert F. "The Crash of the Revco Leverage Buyout: The Hypothesis of Inadequate Capital." *Financial Management,* Spring 1992.

Buffett, Warren E. *The Essays of Warren Buffett: Lessons for Corporate America.* New York: The Cunningham Group, 2001.

Calkins, Caroline, Chad Smith, and John J. Sviokla. "Mergers and Acquisitions in the Age of Business Platforms." Diamond Management and Technology Consultants working paper, 2007.

Campbell, Andrew, and Robert Park. *The Growth Gamble: When Leaders Should Bet Big on New Business and How They Can Avoid Expensive Failures.* Boston: Nicholas Brealey Publishing, 2005.

———. "Stop Kissing Frogs." *Harvard Business Review,* July–August 2004.

Carroll, Paul. *Big Blues: The Unmaking of IBM.* New York: Crown, 1994.

Chen, Zenglo, Robert B. Lawson, Lawrence R. Gordon, and Barbara McIntosh. "Groupthink: Deciding with the Leader and the Devil." *Psychological Record,* Volume 46, 1996.

Christensen, Clayton M., Stephen P. Kaufman, and Willy C. Shih. "Innovation Killers: How Financial Tools Destroy Your Capacity to Do New Things." *Harvard Business Review,* January 2008.

Christensen, Clayton M., and Michael E. Raynor. *The Innovator's Solution: Creating and Sustaining Successful Growth.* Boston: Harvard Business School Press, 2003.

Cohen, Eliot A., and John Gooch. *Military Misfortunes: The Anatomy of Failure in War.* New York: Free Press, 2005.

Collins, Jim. *Good to Great: Why Some Companies Make the Leap . . . and Others Don't.* New York: Harper Business, 2001.

Crown, Judith, and Glenn Coleman. *No Hands: The Rise and Fall of the Schwinn Bicycle Company, an American Institution.* New York: Henry Holt, 1996.

Cullinan, Geoffrey, Jean-Marc Le Roux, and Rolf-Magnus Weddigen. "When to Walk Away from a Deal." *Harvard Business Review,* April 2004.

Day, George S. "Closing the Growth Gap: Balancing Big I and Small i Innovation." Wharton School working paper, 2006.

———. "Which Way Should You Grow?" *Harvard Business Review,* August 2004.

Deans, Graeme. "Mastering Industry Consolidation: Strategies for Winning the Merger Endgame." *Ivey Business Journal,* July–August 2003.

de Bono, Edward. *Six Thinking Hats: An Essential Approach to Business Management.* Boston: Little, Brown, 1985.

Dorner, Dietrich. *The Logic of Failure: Recognizing and Avoiding Error in Complex Situations.* New York: Perseus, 1997.

Downes, Larry, and Chunka Mui. *Unleashing the Killer App: Digital Strategies for Market Dominance.* Boston: Harvard Business School Press, 1998.

Drucker, Peter F. "What Executives Should Remember." *Harvard Business Review,* February 2006.

———. *The Essential Drucker: In One Volume the Best of Sixty Years of Peter Drucker's Essential Writings on Management.* New York: Harper Business, 2001.

Finkelstein, Sydney. *Why Smart Executives Fail: And What You Can Learn from Their Mistakes.* New York: Portfolio, 2004.

Gallwey, W. Timothy. *The Inner Game of Work.* New York: Random House, 2000.

Gold, Michael, and Andrew Campbell. "Desperately Seeking Synergy." *Harvard Business Review,* September–October 1998.

Hamel, Gary, and Liisa Valikangas. "The Quest for Resilience." *Harvard Business Review,* September 2003.

Janis, Irving L. *Groupthink: Psychological Studies of Policy Decisions and Fiascoes.* Boston: Houghton Mifflin, 1982.

Kanter, Rosabeth Moss. "Innovation: Classic Traps." *Harvard Business Review,* November 2006.

Kleiner, Art, and George Roth. "How to Make Experience Your Company's Best Teacher." *Harvard Business Review,* September 1997.

Lieberman, Marvin B., and Shigeru Asaba. "Why Do Firms Imitate Each Other?" UCLA working paper, 2002.

McGrath, Rita Gunther, and Ian C. MacMillan. "Discovery-Driven Planning." *Harvard Business Review,* July 1995.

Mittelstaedt, Robert E. *Will Your Next Mistake Be Fatal?: Avoiding the Chain of Mistakes That Can Destroy Your Organization.* Upper Saddle River, NJ: Wharton School Publishing, 2004.

Murrell, Audrey J., Alice C. Stewart, and Brent T. Engel. "Consensus Versus Devil's Advocacy: The Influence of Decision Process and Task Structure on Strategic Decision Making." *Journal of Business Communications,* Volume 30, Number 4, September 1993.

Negroponte, Nicholas. *Being Digital.* New York: Alfred A. Knopf, 1995.

Neustadt, Richard E., and Ernest R. May. *Thinking in Time: The Uses of History for Decision-Makers.* New York: Free Press, 1988.

Perrow, Charles. *Normal Accidents: Living with High-Risk Technologies.* Princeton, NJ: Princeton University Press, 1999.

Pfeffer, Jeffrey. *What Were They Thinking?: Unconventional Wisdom About Management.* Boston: Harvard Business School Press, 2007.

Pfeffer, Jeffrey, and Robert I. Sutton. *Hard Facts, Dangerous Half-Truths and Total Nonsense: Profiting from Evidence-Based Management.* Boston: Harvard Business School Press, 2006.

Russo, J. Edward, and Paul J. H. Schoemaker. *Decision Traps: The Ten Barriers to Brilliant Decision-Making and How to Overcome Them.* New York: Currency, 1989.

Schwenk, Charles R. *The Essence of Strategic Decision Making.* Lexington, MA: Lexington Books, 1988.

Statutory Committee of Unsecured Creditors v. Motorola, Inc. Case No. 99-45005 (JMP), United States Bankruptcy Court, Southern District of New York, 2007.

Sull, Donald N. *Why Good Companies Go Bad and How Great Managers Remake Them.* Boston: Harvard Business School Press, 2005.

Watkins, Michael D., and Max H. Bazerman. "Predictable Surprises: The Disasters You Should Have Seen Coming." *Harvard Business Review,* March 2003.

Weber, Roberto A., and Colin F. Camerer. "Cultural Conflict and Merger Failure: An Experimental Approach." *Management Science,* Volume 49, Number 4, April 2003.

Zook, Chris. *Beyond the Core: Expand Your Market Without Abandoning Your Roots.* Boston: Harvard Business School Press, 2004.

Parsons, [illegible] Press, 1999.

Pfeffer, Jeffrey. *What Were They Thinking? Unconventional Wisdom About Management*. Boston: Harvard Business School Press, 2007.

Pfeffer, Jeffrey, and Robert I. Sutton. *Hard Facts, Dangerous Half-Truths, and Total Nonsense: Profiting from Evidence-Based Management*. Boston: Harvard Business School Press, 2006.

Russo, J. Edward, and Paul J. H. Schoemaker. *Decision Traps: The Ten Barriers to Brilliant Decision-Making and How to Overcome Them*. New York: Doubleday, 1989.

Schwenk, Charles R. *The Essence of Strategic Decision Making*. Lexington, MA: Lexington Books, 1988.

Sentencing Transcript of Bernard Ebbers, [illegible] United States District Court, Southern District of New York, 2005.

Sull, Donald N. *Why Good Companies Go Bad and How Great Managers Remake Them*. Boston: Harvard Business School Press, 2005.

Watkins, Michael D., and Max H. Bazerman. "Predictable Surprises: The Disasters You Should Have Seen Coming." *Harvard Business Review*, March 2003.

Weber, Roberto A., and Colin F. Camerer. "Cultural Conflict and Merger Failure: An Experimental Approach." *Management Science*, Volume 49, Number 4, April 2003.

Zook, Chris. *Beyond the Core: Expand Your Market Without Abandoning Your Roots*. Boston: Harvard Business School Press, 2004.

Index